Mindful Pleasures
Essays on Thomas Pynchon

Mindful

Essays on

Little, Brown and Company

Boston   Toronto

Pleasures
Thomas Pynchon

edited by
George Levine and David Leverenz

PS
3566
Y55
Z72

FIRST EDITION

T 11/76

Acknowledgments of permission to reprint copyrighted material appear on page ix.

.

Library of Congress Cataloging in Publication Data

Main entry under title:

Mindful pleasures.

    Bibliography: p.
    1. Pynchon, Thomas—Criticism and interpretation—
Addresses, essays, lectures. I. Levine, George Lewis.
II. Leverenz, David.
PS3566.Y55Z72   813'.5'4   76-21279
ISBN 0-316-52230-9
ISBN 0-316-52231-7 pbk.

*Published simultaneously in Canada
by Little, Brown & Company (Canada) Limited*

PRINTED IN THE UNITED STATES OF AMERICA

To Anne Rutledge, to Marge, and to . . .

perhaps too much kirsch in the fondue

Contents

Acknowledgments   ix

Introduction: Mindful Pleasures   3

Section I: Pynchon in General   13

The Importance of Thomas Pynchon
   by Richard Poirier   15
Pre-Apocalyptic Atavism: Thomas Pynchon's
   Early Fiction
   by Catharine R. Stimpson   31
Caries and Cabals
   by Tony Tanner   49
Pentecost, Promiscuity, and Pynchon's *V*.: From the
   Scaffold to the Impulsive
   by W. T. Lhamon, Jr.   69
Maxwell's Demon, Entropy, Information: *The Crying
   of Lot 49*
   by Anne Mangel   87
Pynchon's Poetry
   by William Vesterman   101

Risking the Moment: Anarchy and Possibility in
    Pynchon's Fiction
    by George Levine   113

Section II: *Gravity's Rainbow*   137

Pynchon's Paranoid History
    by Scott Sanders   139
Gravity's Encyclopedia
    by Edward Mendelson   161
Brünnhilde and the Chemists: Women in
    Gravity's Rainbow
    by Marjorie Kaufman   197
On Trying to Read *Gravity's Rainbow*
    by David Leverenz   229

Appendix: The Quest for Pynchon
    by Mathew Winston   251

Bibliography
    compiled by Bruce Herzberg   265

Notes on Contributors   271

Acknowledgments

The authors are grateful to the following publishers, institutions, and individuals for permission to quote from previously copyrighted materials:

TriQuarterly, for "Maxwell's Demon, Entropy, Information: The Crying of Lot 49" by Anne Mangel, from the Winter 1971 issue (No. 20). Copyright © 1971 by Northwestern University Press.

Harper & Row Publishers, Inc., and Jonathan Cape Ltd., for "Caries and Cabals" from *City of Words* by Tony Tanner. Copyright © 1971 by Tony Tanner.

The Essex Institute, Salem, Massachusetts, for excerpts from the Pynchon-Hawthorne correspondence as published in the *Essex Institute Historical Collections*, 100. Copyright © 1964 by the Essex Institute.

Mathew Winston, for his essay "The Quest for Pynchon." Copyright © 1975 by Mathew Winston.

Richard Poirier, for his essay "The Importance of Thomas Pynchon." Copyright © 1975 by Richard Poirier.

W. T. Lhamon, Jr., for his essay "Pentecost, Promiscuity, and Pynchon's *V*: From the Scaffold to the Impulsive." Copyright © 1975 by W. T. Lhamon.

William Vesterman, for his essay "Pynchon's Poetry." Copyright © 1975 by William Vesterman.

Scott Sanders, for his essay "Pynchon's Paranoid History." Copyright © 1975 by Scott Sanders.

W. H. Freeman and Company, for the diagram on page 89 from "Maxwell's Demon" by W. Ehrenberg published in *Scientific American*, November, 1967. Copyright © 1967 by Scientific American, Inc. All rights reserved.

Portions of this book originally appeared in the magazine *Twentieth Century Literature*.

Mindful Pleasures
Essays on Thomas Pynchon

Introduction: Mindful Pleasures

The essays collected here contradict each other so often that they seem to be in rather than about Thomas Pynchon's novels. In the current explosive multiplication of Pynchon studies — a sure entropic consequence of his already disordered achievements — these go only a little way toward producing a settled reading. And personally, we prefer the present moment of uneasiness, uncertainty, and noise in the reading of his fictions to what must follow: "a routinization of charisma," as *Gravity's Rainbow* quotes Max Weber, a consolidation, a consensus, a canonization that will, against his will, put Pynchon among Them, powerlessly elected out of the preterite he at least half loves and among whom he wants to remain.

The very idea of a collection of essays about Pynchon violates the terms on which he presents himself to us. *V.* mocks the synthetic minds that insist on making shapes out of the meaningless variety and colorfulness of experience, what the original title of *Gravity's Rainbow* called "Mindless Pleasures." A critic of Pynchon needs to consider whether he isn't Ned Pointsman to Pynchon's Roger Mexico, whether he is not mistaking the occurrence of "caries" for "cabals," and thus wasting yet more of the vital energies that might keep us from being turned into mere objects. Pynchon wants no part of the critic's enterprise. One of the conditions of his staying with his present publishers, we have learned, is that they not publish books about his work. So as editors of this volume, we know there's not much we can do to please him. Wherever you are, Thomas Pynchon, we apologize.

But whether he likes it or not, there is no escaping his achievement, and there is no point in pretending to ignore it. The act of writing itself makes Pynchon a public figure. And the better he writes, the more intense will be the pressure to co-opt him and to destroy the conditions that make the writing possible. Even as he drops his false clues and plays with his astonishing knowledge of what appears to be everything, he invites, just as he defensively rejects, the sorts of studies undertaken here. As Richard Poirier suggests in his essay written for this volume, one has to know an awful lot to learn what it is that Pynchon feels — not only about Zap comics and horror movies, but about physics, mathematics, Puritan theology, and a library of literature that he uses or parodies or both. The essays here by Edward Mendelson, Anne Mangel, and Scott Sanders explore aspects of that knowledge, though they use it in ways that tend to contradict each other. So, finally, Pynchon must understand — we're inclined to think that it's an important part of what the books are up to — that his readers have to be put through all the potentially dessicating critical games in order to experience how inadequate are our present ways of knowing.

From the very beginning of Pynchon's public career, critics have found it difficult to resist his work, and the history of his reputation among the critics may suggest the sense in Pynchon's refusal to pay attention. The seductiveness of the praise and the hostility of the criticism might have worked equally well to compromise the special integrity of his talent. At the start, the praise was most dangerous. Indeed, with the exception of *The Crying of Lot 49*, almost every one of his works came in for immediate critical awards. His short story "Entropy" was selected for inclusion in *The Best American Short Stories: 1961*. "Under the Rose," a story reworked as Chapter 3 of *V.*, was an O. Henry prize story for 1962. And then, when *V.* appeared, even *News-*

week felt the need to "hail" it. "This splendid first novel," the review went, "is simply a picture of life."

And yet Pynchon's success story disguises two important elements in the progress of his reputation. First, the *Newsweek* sort of popularity, though likely to be tempting to any first novelist, was spurious, as the quotation from the review suggests. Second, the success and special nature of Pynchon's art has always evoked from a significant minority (speaking usually for the right-of-center of American literary culture) considerable hostility. Pynchon has often been dismissed as merely clever, or as sophomorically obscene, mechanically cold, incapable of creating real characters. One distinguished academic once asked an editor of this volume how he could take seriously so academic a novelist as Pynchon.

Happily, there is little evidence that Pynchon has listened much to what his critics advised. He continues, perhaps uniquely, to give his critics nothing to write about but his fiction. And when *V.* appeared there was almost a quality of desperation in reviews that seemed to scramble for information about him, or at least for traditions in which to place him.

By and large, reviews of *V.* mixed enthusiasm and deference with puzzlement and uneasiness. Of course, there was the *Commentary* review by Irving Feldman, who saw the whole novel as silly collegiate showing off in a tradition of beatnikism that *Commentary* never liked and will, apparently, never forgive. Yet serious critics did see that Pynchon was a writer likely to matter. Stanley Edgar Hyman, in a *New Leader* review, felt obliged to make the inevitable comparison with *Catch-22*, and to put Pynchon in the tradition of black humor. As had Richard Poirier in *The New York Review of Books*, Hyman detected a direct influence of Nathanael West and Djuna Barnes. But, as Hyman says, Pynchon's imagination is wilder than that of any of these other writers, and pushes him to a wider and richer vision.

Poirier's review, seen in the light of his more elaborate and then increasingly laudatory ones of the later novels, seems very cautious. But the caution is mixed with a certainty that with *V.* Pynchon "earns the right to be called one of the best [novelists]

we have now." The reservations have to do with Pynchon's mixture of modes (a mixture that has in fact grown more daring
since *V.*), with the way Pynchon's brilliant and sardonic comic
treatment of characters seems at odds with the seriousness with
which he apparently wants us to take them. In particular, Poirier
objects to the "sloganeering," as he calls it, of McClintic Sphere
in his now famous line, "Keep cool, but care."

For a first novel, *V.* attracted a surprising number of very impressive or very well known critics: aside from Poirier and Hyman, there were, for example, George Plimpton, Ihab Hassan, and
Christopher Ricks. Plimpton, in *The New York Times Book
Review*, called Pynchon "a young writer of staggering promise."
Ricks wrote as though in the presence of a great talent, but
cautiously attributed his difficulties with the novel to a language
barrier. Still, Ricks admitted, Pynchon "knows an enormous lot."
Hassan's review was — characteristically for *V.* — disappoint-
ingly conservative and balanced. The book is "too mannered
and . . . too dull," the comedy too gory, but, Hassan added,
Pynchon's knowledge of the "particular nihilism that ravages our
time is compelling." Surprisingly, one of the most intelligently
sympathetic reviews appeared in *The New Yorker*. There,
Whitney Balliett noted the obvious comparison with the beats,
but argued that Pynchon's novel was superior to their work because it was free of sentimentality and self-pity. Disoriented by
the comedy, Balliett saw the major difficulty of *V.* to be that it
is a "comic novel whose author doesn't take it seriously enough."

When *The Crying of Lot 49* appeared three years later, *V.* had
not yet died as any promising first novel might have been expected to do. But there is a curious dearth of serious reviews of
the second novel despite, or perhaps because of, its compactness,
coherence, and ostensible simplicity. (As Robert Sklar says in his
excellent 1967 essay in *The Nation*, *Lot 49* is a simple novel that
grows increasingly complex with each rereading.) This time
Commentary didn't even bother with a review, although at about
the time a review might have been appropriate, June 1966, it
published an essay by Robert Alter attacking "apocalyptic" fiction and including among those cold, cynical, and faithless fictions *V.* itself. Presumably, *Lot 49*, another apocalyptic fiction, is

taken care of that way. In *The New Republic*, Remington Rose published an astonishingly unintelligent and savage review, calling the book a "well-executed, mildly nasty, pretentious collage." And even Roger Shattuck, in *The New York Review of Books*, read *Lot 49* as a falling off from *V.* — "the tide has gone out," he wrote.

The only important review that attempted to take the book as seriously as it has since been taken was Richard Poirier's. It stands out against the strange neglect of the book among the better critics. Clearly respectful of Pynchon, it reiterates many of the objections Poirier voiced in his earlier review of *V.*, but it is especially valuable in its detailed discussion of the quality of Pynchon's prose. Of course, there was some praise in other reviews. Granville Hicks, obviously much puzzled, saw enough to treat the book respectfully in his column in *The Saturday Review*. And *Newsweek*, as if to prove it was right in 1963, devoted a lavish review to this "brilliant young (27) novelist."

In the long run, however, the "ayes" had it, for the negative reviews could not diminish *Lot 49*'s success. The book was becoming one of those convenient short rich texts that might be used in freshman and sophomore classes. Robert Sklar's 1967 essay is one of the finest early examples of detailed critical re-evaluation of *Lot 49*. By 1973, Pynchon was largely "in" in academia, and his massive new book came forth with an extraordinary panoply of front page red carpets and intellectual champagne. Ironically, the reviews of *Gravity's Rainbow* tend to imply that everyone — not only *Newsweek* on the one hand, Poirier on the other — had known for years that Pynchon is one of the best contemporary American novelists. The book seems to have been reviewed by everybody. The 1973 *Book Review Digest* lists twenty-eight reviews, while the 1966 volume lists only twenty-one reviews of *Lot 49*. There were, of course, many later reviews of *Gravity's Rainbow*, including those in *Commentary*, *Harper's*, and *Partisan Review*.

By and large the reviews deferred to the book even when they showed little sign of coming to terms with it. So intensely curious was the response that *Gravity's Rainbow* actually appeared on the best-seller list. Interesting and favorable reviews appeared in

The New York Times Book Review (by Richard Locke), *The New York Review of Books* (by Michael Wood), and *The New Republic*, where W. T. Lhamon's remarkable essay almost made up for the silliness of that journal's review of *Lot 49* seven years before. In *The Yale Review*, Edward Mendelson praised *Gravity's Rainbow* as one of the truly great American novels. And Richard Poirier's long essay in the *Saturday Review/Arts* makes an excellent introduction to the novel, without the slightest hint of the kind of reservations about Pynchon's fiction that Poirier had expressed in his earlier reviews.

But the *Commentary* position remained stable, if not static. David Thorburn's "A Dissent on Pynchon" is, in fact, a long step in the direction of showing that even *Commentary* will have to come around eventually. Thorburn's dissent is intelligent and sympathetic to Pynchon's talents while remaining highly critical of Pynchon's actual achievements. He identifies, fairly enough, a Pynchon cult (of which this book may be an ugly manifestation), and he mocks reviews, again not altogether unfairly, for revering *Gravity's Rainbow* simply because of its massive size. But he acknowledges the "integrity"of Pynchon's vision and the quality of his prose which, Thorburn says, justifies the comparisons with Dickens and Joyce that have been made. That's a long way for the anti-apocalyptic *Commentary* to go. "But," says Thorburn, "intentions are not achievements" and *Gravity's Rainbow* is a deeply confused book, full of "mordant comic desperation."

Gravity's Rainbow is now more than three years old and is hovering dangerously on the edge of becoming — surely to Pynchon's horror — a classic. The critical labyrinths are becoming more labyrinthine and the battle lines are being drawn with — again wonderfully — no help from Pynchon at all. It may be that what seems to many of us at this moment one of the most remarkable fictional achievements of the century will, from the perspective of a few years, appear to be only a symptom of the peculiar cultural diseases of the 1960s and 1970s. We do not think this will happen. But to many other readers, of course, the book is simply "unreadable," as one of the Pulitzer Prize judges is supposed to have said in voting to overturn the unanimous recommendation of its literature subcommittee. The literary elect have taken Pynchon "in," but in ways perhaps inevitable the people whom Pynchon most cares about are apt to have the most difficulty with his work. Such confusions of communication are central to his world.

Of the essays gathered in this volume, some play the critical games Pynchon pushes us to, some do not. We don't pretend that this book as a whole is anywhere near definitive about Pynchon's achievement, and we are sensitive enough to Pynchon's vision to be pleased by the indefiniteness. His forte, after all, is to seduce us into grail-hunting activities which he then parodies. As Frank Kermode has said, we look to fictions to "make sense" of things, and the possibility that Pynchon is trying to destroy *that* convention, too, may be rather too much for most of us. But there are a lot of ways to "make sense," and one of those ways is by rejecting the traditional ways or by transforming them. In any case, Pynchon invites excess in his critics. Since he risks a lot, they must, too. Frequently, we end up looking silly. Like Dorothy's scarecrow, the first response of many readers has to be, "If I only had a brain," and there has been a significant strain of Pynchon criticism that cries, "If he only had a heart." Often, all we can be sure of is — as his epigraph to the Zone has it — that we're not in Kansas anymore.

We hope, however, that the essays don't look silly. We can't speak for the writers, but we offer their work in this volume, first, as tentative gestures in the direction of a richer experience of Pynchon's fiction; second, as small incursions into the knowledge we need to experience the fiction fully; and third, as gestures of respect to an unwelcoming Pynchon himself.

We have tried to practice restraint, to honor Pynchon not merely through praise but through consideration of his weaknesses as a writer. Some of the essays in this volume — Sanders's, Leverenz's, and Vesterman's in particular — are severely critical of aspects of Pynchon's art. All that the various writers of this volume share in their attitude toward Pynchon is that he is a writer who has to be reckoned with, one whose imagination, for better or worse, both registers intensely the cultural history of these moments and attempts to push us out of where we are.

We originally intended to arrange the book so as to provide a sense of the development of Pynchon's reputation through reviews and already published essays. The second half of the volume was to have been devoted to original essays written for it. That plan proved impracticable both because fair representation of earlier work would have consumed all the space needed for original essays, and because such an arrangement would have entailed much waste and overlap. Limitations of space have forced us to eliminate many valuable essays old and new. The selection that remains will be felt to be arbitrary; but we are at least confident of the value of those arbitrarily chosen. (Some of the original essays were also published in the May 1975 "Pynchon Issue" of *Twentieth Century Literature*, which we edited, and one in the October issue.)

As editors, we struggled for a long time over the question of whether we should in any way try to discuss Pynchon's biography. Mathew Winston's short biography, which we have included as an appendix, seems to us to avoid any encroachment on Pynchon's privacy while providing an incisive summary of publicly available material. Pynchon's famous reclusiveness is frustrating, to say the least. It takes an effort of will, understanding, and even humility to realize that this frustration is another version of what the books put us through: a confrontation with our own urge to snoop, to be informed, to label and "fix." His books detail the massively evil consequences of that mind set, and we admire Pynchon's personal refusal to allow his life to be turned into public machinery. Nevertheless, what is already public *is* public. Gathering it together carefully and respectfully can remind us of what is entailed both by scholarship and by the attempt to sustain even the smallest fragment of integrity and privacy in this culture of instant, overpowering communications.

Finally, as we look back over these essays, we are concerned that Pynchon has been a little too successful in trapping us in his games. The temptation, clearly, has been irresistible to take his allusions, his dropped clues, his metaphors, and run, right into the ordering patterns that welcome us into the Firm. We see V's, or double S's, or WASTE baskets and make criticism. We "do" the themes and the symbols and, if we're lucky, we catch at the peripheries of our own prose some suggestion of the intensities and the fun of his. Of these essays only William Vesterman's concerns itself exclusively with playing with Pynchon's playfulness. Most of the others, sometimes almost in spite of themselves, move to thematic readings, reflecting a very natural discomfort with the puzzlements that are so much a part of the experience of reading Pynchon. Yet we undertook this volume on Pynchon, as I think most of the contributors undertook writing about him, because the experience of the prose is giddying, exciting, terrifying, and very beautiful.

As our own contributions to the volume indicate, even the two of us disagree about Pynchon. For one of us (Levine), the question is whether we can risk the variety and surprises of the prose without routinizing them, without building the sort of structures upon them that their very existence seems to belie. Can we risk a Slothropian scattering into antiparanoia, and a loss — in two senses — of our discipline? The other (Leverenz) questions whether structure-making has to be attended with all that guilt. Pynchon's deliberately centrifugal endings take us in *Gravity's Rainbow* to a primitive Christian anarchist's vision of preterite possibilities that seems not only socially wrong but novelistically imposed, a sermon pretending to be stones.

But disagreements aside, the collaboration has enriched both of us, with the mindless pleasure of friendship, the mindful one of mutual respect. And in the course of struggling toward discoveries about Pynchon we discovered through the U.S. mails an extraordinary network of extraordinary, generous, and talented people, many of whom are represented in this volume. We are grateful to them, as we are to Thomas Pynchon, whose novels, we venture, have made each of us a little more alive.

June 30, 1975

GEORGE LEVINE
DAVID LEVERENZ

Livingston College
Rutgers University

Section I

Pynchon in General

... Pudding, the proof of:

The Importance of Thomas Pynchon

Richard Poirier

One of the many distinctions between American literature and English literature, especially in the nineteenth century, is that most of the American writers whom we would call great were not, while most actively producing their best work, what we would also call popular. I'm thinking of Hawthorne, Melville, James, Eliot, Stevens. There has usually been a time lag between critical and general acclaim. Not that criticism has, by itself, kept up to the mark. There is the conspicuous case of Melville, who wasn't taken seriously until 1921, and even Faulkner had the misfortune of being popular not with his best but with his second-best novels, like *Sanctuary*. His popularity, coming before literary critics could take credit for creating it, put them in no mood to be generous when they at first got round to him. The same condition, with certain variations, has been true of Robert Frost. Serious criticism is still in Frost's case exceptionally begrudging and self-protective. Even now he is looked into as if he aspired to be Yeats or Eliot, not as someone who proposes an extraordinary alternative to them and to the dominant so-called modernist line of the twentieth century.

Among the remarkable facts about Thomas Pynchon is that if we are to believe the best-seller list, the selections of the Book-of-the-Month Club, the reviews, and the committee for the National

Book Awards, then presumably we are to believe that *Gravity's Rainbow* is a popular book and, at the same time, that it ranks with *Ulysses* and *Moby-Dick* in accomplishment and possibly exceeds them in complexity. Something peculiar is happening here. A writer is received simultaneously into the first rank of the history of our literature and also as a popular novelist. Only Mark Twain has been given such praise before, unless Hemingway and Fitzgerald are counted, though not by me, as of the first order.

If what I've said is true of Pynchon's reputation, and even if it only seems to be true on the evidence of what the media and a lot of people want to believe, then we have to ask some questions about the culture in which we find ourselves, a culture which Pynchon himself seems to include within his imagination at once more abundantly and more playfully than anyone now writing. In his inclusiveness he is a kind of cultural encyclopedia. He is also, after Hawthorne, the American writer with the deepest kind of skepticism about the advantages of being "included" by the culture America has inherited and shaped. For the present he is probably less than grateful for the way the culture has decided to include him. He may regard his being "taken in" as a kind of conspiracy, a kind of plot. Not a plot against gullible readers, since they, after all, can be encouraged to own, even to like his books, without reading them, without ever encountering the dizzying and resistant complexities of his style. Rather, he might think of these developments as a plot against himself, and he might wonder what is going to happen to a writer who is hailed both as a genius and a romp, even when he knows that the mass of good amateur readers — the kind who belong to the Book-of-the-Month Club — not only don't but can't much like him. Who are They, to use one of his favorite words, who are the mysterious donors apparently with the power to create and therefore the power to perpetuate his fame? Just because his constituency is so hard to identify, its power over him must be hard to resist; he can't negotiate directly with the They who concocted and therefore control his audience, and They can force him into strange compromises, such as his reluctant acceptance of the National Book Award simply because to have turned it down,

which he most likely would have done had it been given to him
singly, would under the circumstances have been an insult to the
co-beneficiary, Mr. Isaac Bashevis Singer.

Well, who *is* Pynchon's audience? First of all, a certain kind of
educated young reader who was probably trained to read hard
books during the early to mid-sixties and who is also sympathetically responsive to the cultural manifestations of the late sixties —
in rock, adult comic books, drug and black styles, filmmaking;
second, a number of academics, older than the first group but
who nonetheless went through some of the same sequences of
interest and development; third, a growing number of quite
learned academic readers who enjoy puzzles, especially costumed
ones, who relish intellectual play, and who admire Pynchon's
Johnsonian capacities to "work up" a subject (like the Fashoda
incident or life in London during the blitz) wholly remote from
his own personal experiences — Pynchon as the essential classicist;
fourth, the various readers who come from these three groups,
but who are also in the book business, with its hunger for a great
writer, any "great writer" except Norman Mailer or the good
grey champion Saul Bellow; and fifth, a lot of people who take
their cue from these various groups and who are enthusiastic
about a phenomenon without the capacity to understand it, intellectually turned on groupies who see in Pynchon's obscurities
and his personal elusiveness — his refusal to come out of hiding
in any way — a sign of radical contempt. He's a radical to whom
the establishment has simply had to defer — or so it seems.

What is left out of this grouping is of course the central mass
of educated general readers. And a good clue to their reactions,
so far as Pynchon is concerned, can be found in what might be
called the Anglo-Americans. This is a literary nation of educated
general readers who can always flee from the petty tyrannies of
a new interest to the thrones of literary and cultural conservatism:
to the likes of *Saturday Review/World* and the journal of bully-
boy arriviste gentility, *Commentary* magazine. Tepid, conde-
scending, unwilling or unable to submit to the intense pressure of
Pynchon's work, they admire (when they manage to admire him
at all) only what is separably cute or charming or what is com-

pact or economical, like *The Crying of Lot 49*, though even that, not to mention *V.*, is unavailable now, for example, in Great Britain. "Of course what I like is *The Crying of Lot 49*," is the thing to say, equivalent to saying of Henry James that "Of course, what I like is his novel *Confidence*," or of Faulkner (in French) that "What I like is your Faulkner's *Pylon*." It's an old European trick with our stuff, unfortunately imported to this country, with its large core of American Anglophilic readers. When it comes to *The Crying of Lot 49*, the verdict is assisted by the fact that it is the only one of Pynchon's three novels whose size and scope make it usable in class.

I too consider *The Crying of Lot 49* an astonishing accomplishment and the most dramatically powerful of Pynchon's works because of its focus on a single figure. But what is at issue here is something else — the *nature* of Pynchon's reputation. And generally the Anglophilic response of the good reader, of the amateur book lover to Pynchon is, measured against what is offered by his whole achievement, ironic evidence that though Pynchon may be treated with the condescension historically visited on other great American writers by the literary establishment contemporaneous with them, he somehow appears to have escaped the consequences of this. That is, despite the dereliction of a large central core of readers and of the upper brow journals where they find reassurance, he has, again, simultaneously achieved public acclaim and enormous private respect.

I admit to a certain unfairness in these characterizations of the amateur reader, an unfairness of which I would suppose other protective admirers of Pynchon might also be guilty. Amateur readers may be unable to respond to the relentless vitality of Pynchon's writing, but professional academic readers can positively smother it. And perhaps it is better, like an amateur, to be simply oblivious to what is being offered in his books than, like a professional, to set about anxiously to pacify Pynchon's vitality by schemes, structuralist or otherwise. But to believe this, as I've tried to suggest, is to overlook the curious historical change in what it means to be an amateur reader. The trouble with amateur readers now is that they are *too* literary rather than not literary enough. They are too anxious, most simply, that the life imitated by a new novel should resemble only what old novels have taught us to recognize as life. They are not amateur in the positive sense of being open and alive; they are not able to take advantage of their freedom from those premeditations, those utilitarian impulses which necessarily corrupt most professional readers and most of us who are teachers of literature. We're in a situation where neither the amateur nor the professional reader seems capable of reading Pynchon for the fun of it, for the relish of local pleasures, for the savoring of how the sentences sound as they turn into one another, carrying with them, and creating as they go, endlessly reverberating echoes from the vast ranges of contemporary life and culture. The ideal reader of Pynchon probably would be more amateur than professional, but amateur in a positive sense — capable of unscheduled responses even while being generally learned and inquisitive. For that reason, what's happening to Pynchon, as he is moved increasingly into position for a guidebook study, is a cause not for celebration but for misgiving. This is a crucial and instructive problem which tells us a good deal about a larger cultural impasse. Pynchon really has, so far as I can see, no wholly safe constituency except one — the academy — and unless academic writers and teachers are extremely careful they will do to him the damage already done to Joyce and Eliot.

Put simply, the damage consists of looking at the writing as something to be figured out by a process of translation, a process which omits the weirdness and pleasure of the reading experience as it goes along, the kind of experience which, say, we expect from Dickens without being worried about it. The damage consists of treating each of the formal or stylistic or allusive elements in a work as a clue to meaning, a point of possible stabilization. This is an especially inappropriate way to treat Pynchon because each of these elements is in itself highly mobile and dramatic. Each is a clue not to meaning so much as to chaos of meaning, an evidence of the impossibility of stabilization. We are confronted with what, in another context, I call a literature of waste. This is not to say that literature *is* waste but that in certain works there are demonstrations that the inherited ways of classifying experience are no longer a help but a hindrance. All of the formulas by which experience gets shaped or organized around us are themselves a part of the chaos of experience with which one has to deal. The rage to order, Pynchon seems to say, is merely a symptom of accelerating disorder.

Pynchon goes beyond his predecessors because he projects this notion of waste past literature and onto all available systems of classification. Joyce, for example, followed by Barth and Borges and doubtless others, was a great innovator in that he pushed literary parody to the point of literary self-parody, showing how the available conventions, styles, forms of literature were insufficient as a breakwater of order and elegance against the tide of life — to paraphrase Stephen Dedalus. Pynchon extends this perception from literature not only to science, to pop culture, to the traditions of analysis, but even to the orderings of the unconscious, to dreams themselves. In his works dreams are treated as so many planted messages, encoded by what he calls the "bureaucracy of the other side." It is as if human life in all of its *recorded* manifestations is bent toward rigidification, reification, and death. Echoing Norman O. Brown, Pynchon seems to say not only that history is itself a form of repression, but so, too, is the human impulse to make or to write history.

If this is any proper reading of Pynchon then it should constitute a warning to any one of us who wishes to order or regularize his work by whatever plot, myth, symmetry or arrangement. And yet we persist in doing so, because, finally, it is nearly impossible to feel about our cultural (even, sometimes, about our biological) inheritance the way he does. We don't know *enough* to feel as he wants us to feel. I don't mean that it is impossible to appreciate his radical perspectives, since we can do that even if we don't agree with him. I mean that we can't with Pynchon — any more than with Joyce or with the Eliot of the lovably pretentious notes to *The Waste Land* — possibly claim to be as conversant as he wants us to be with the various forms of contemporary culture. He may be as theatrically enlivening and entertaining as Dickens, but a reader needs to know relatively little to appreciate Dickens. Really to read Pynchon properly you would have to be astonishingly learned not only about literature but about a vast number of other subjects belonging to the disciplines and to popular culture, learned to the point where learning is almost a sensuous pleasure, something to play around with, to feel totally relaxed about, so that you can take in stride every dizzying transition from one allusive mode to another.

This means that we are in a true dilemma if we love Pynchon or any writer who resembles him. We don't want to stop the game, we don't want to get out of the rhythm, but what are we to do if we simply don't know enough to play the game, to move with the rhythm? We can't, above all, pretend that such a writer is a regular fellow, the way Anthony Burgess does with Joyce. Burgess's *Re Joyce* is both quite a bad book and an amusing object lesson. With totally false casualness, Burgess has to lay before us an immense amount of requisite learning in the effort to prove that Joyce can be read by Everyman. Burgess makes an obvious, glaring but nonetheless persistent error: he confuses Joyce's material (much of which is indeed quite ordinary and common) with what Joyce does to it (which is totally uncommon, unordinary, and elitist). Another way of answering Burgess, or anyone who says that a writer like Joyce or Pynchon is just a "good read," is to say that nobody in Joyce, and very few in Pynchon, could read the novels that have been written about them. This is particularly true of Pynchon, who loves the anonymous if he loves anyone, loves the lost ones — and writes in a way that would lose them completely. These discriminations would not even need to be made, of course, were it not for the stubborn liberal dream of literary teachers, especially in the last five years, that literature is written for the people who are in it. It makes as much sense to think that blacks should care about literature because they find black experience in it as to say that shepherds should care about pastoral poetry because there are shepherds in it. It is precisely this arrogant overvaluation of literature that the truly great works have often tried to dispel. As much in Shakespeare as in anything written now there is often some sensed resentment about the way literature is itself exploiting life for literary purposes, and Pynchon offers perhaps the most exhaustive and brilliant repudiation of this exploitation in our language.

To know just how masterfully and how feelingly Pynchon reveals the destructive powers of all systematic enterprise, however, one has first to know things about which all of us are in some measure ignorant. Not many of us know about Zap comics as well as about double integrals. Of course we are all relatively ignorant whenever we sit down to read, and notably so when we are reading works by writers who in any way resemble Pynchon, like John Barth or Borges or Burroughs, like Melville or Joyce. But with these our ignorance is usually of a different kind. We can correct it by reading more closely for internal evidence or by reading other novels or classical literature with maybe an excursion into history or film. But we are always pretty much within the realms of fiction, and even where fictional characters are modeled, as in Joyce, on real people it matters little, if at all, that we know about these real people. At most we need to know only a bit about the literary or classical myths with which their fictional counterparts are implicated.

In Pynchon we find ourselves in a curious fictional world which is often directly referring us back to the real one. This is of course always true of novels to some degree. But in Pynchon the factuality seems willingly to participate in the fiction; it disguises itself as fiction to placate us and the characters. Fact is consciously manipulated by "They" in order to create the comforting illusion that it *is* fiction, an illusion contrived to deceive Oedipa or Slothrop into *not* believing in the reality of what is happening to them. Crazy names like Pierce Inverarity turn out, when we do a little investigation, to be a compound of a quite famous, real-life stamp collector named Pierce, and of the fact that if you should go to Mr. Pierce for the kind of flawed and peculiar stamps so important in *The Crying of Lot 49* you would ask him for an "inverse rarity." What sound like crazy schemes turn out to have been actual experiments, such as Maxwell's Demon, again in *The Crying of Lot 49*, or historically important institutions like Thurn and Taxis. With one very slight exception all of

Pynchon's material in *The Crying of Lot 49* about that postal service is historically verifiable, and even a cursory glance into a dictionary will show that some of the figures in *Gravity's Rainbow* were historical, not only obvious ones like the chemist Liebig or Clerk Maxwell, or Frederick Kekulé, but also Käthe Kollwitz and Admiral Rozhdestvenski. Eventually we get to wonder at almost every point if perhaps we are being given not fiction at all, but history.

This is not simply to say that Pynchon's fictions have historical analogues or that he allegorizes history. Rather, his fictions are often seamlessly woven into the stuff, the very factuality of history. His practices are vastly different from such allegorizations as one gets in Barth's *Giles Goat-Boy*, different from Borges's inventions of fictional conspiracies which are analogous to the historical ones of the Nazi period, and different, too, from the obsessive patternings one finds in Nabokov, which are private, local, and, while including certain aspects of American reality, never derived directly from them. In Pynchon's novels the plots of wholly imagined fiction are inseparable from the plots of known history or science. More than that, he proposes that any effort to sort out these plots must itself depend on an analytical method which, both in its derivations and in its execution, is probably part of some systematic plot against free forms of life.

The perspectives — literary, analytic, pop cultural, philosophical, scientific — from which Pynchon operates are considerably more numerous than those available to any writer to whom he might be compared, and it is therefore especially impressive that Pynchon insists not on keeping these perspectives discrete but upon the functioning, the tributary, the literally grotesque relationship among them. All systems and technologies, in his view, partake of one another. In particular, science directs our perceptions and feelings whether we know it or not, even while, as literary people, we may like to imagine that it is literature that most effectively conditions how we feel. Other writers have of course recorded the effects, and seldom recorded them as benign, of technology and science on human lives, and the techniques of literature have in this century shown some conspicuous indebtedness to the technique of machines, as in William Gaddis, who was a most important influence on Pynchon, and in other influences like Dos Passos, Joyce and Burroughs. But again, Pynchon is doing something different, something more frighteningly inclusive.

Perhaps he is the first writer to realize Wordsworth's prediction in the Preface to the third edition of the *Lyrical Ballads*. Writing in 1801, Wordsworth reveals a sense of the power of poetry and the capacities of the poet to incorporate into himself and into his work all other forms of human enterprise that can only be for us now a sad illumination both of his prophetic genius and of his noble but betrayed optimism. It is as if Pynchon set out to do what Wordsworth instructed the poet to do, but to show that the results were not the transfiguration of science but the transfiguration of man.

> Poetry is the first and last of all knowledge — it is as immortal as the heart of man. If the labours of men of Science should ever create any material revolution, direct or indirect, in our condition, and in the impressions which we habitually receive, the Poet will sleep then no more than at present; he will be ready to follow the steps of the Man of Science, not only in those general indirect effects, but he will be at his side, carrying sensation into the midst of the objects of the Science itself. The remotest discoveries of the Chemist, the Botanist, or Mineralogist, will be as proper subjects of the Poet's art as any upon which it can be employed, if the time should ever come when these things shall be familiar to us, and the relations under which they are contemplated by the followers of these respective Sciences shall be manifestly and palpably material to us as enjoying and suffering beings. If the time should ever come when what is now called Science, thus familiarized to men, shall be ready to put on, as it were, a form of flesh and blood, the Poet will lend his divine spirit to aid the transfiguration, and will welcome the Being thus produced, as a dear and genuine inmate of the household of man.

"Carrying sensation into the midst of the objects of the Science itself" — that alone would be a sufficiently original and remarkable accomplishment. Pynchon has had to go knowingly beyond that, however, because all of us have together gone *un*knowingly beyond it, passed *un*knowingly into a world where the effects of exposure to the implementations of science and technology are so pervasive as to have been invisible and inaudible. We have few ways, for example, of measuring the effect of the media within which we live except by the instrumentalities of the media. Pynchon does not set out to rescue us from this condition, in the manner of Lawrence. He is in fact as partial to technology and to science as he is to Rilke, Zap comics, Glen Gould, Orson Welles or Norman O. Brown. He no longer perpetuates the dream of Wordsworth that poetry or a radical esthetics derived from poetry provides a basis for understanding and resisting any of the other systematic exertions of power over human consciousness. Science, the analytical method, technology — all of these are not merely impositions upon consciousness. They are also a corporate expression of consciousness; they express us all as much as do the lyrical ballads. They express us more than does our late and befuddled resistance to them. Put another way, the visual and audible messages offered on the film called *Citizen Kane* tell us no more (and no less) about modern life than does the movie projector which shows the film or the camera which made it. These machines are a product of the human imagination which, if felt as such and studied as such, refer us to the hidden nature of human feeling and human need. In the instance of the movie projector we are referred specifically to the desire first to frame the human image — with all the slang connotations involved in the word "frame" — and then to accelerate it. The movie projector itself necessarily refers Pynchon back to "this strange connection between the German mind and the rapid flashing of successive stills to counterfeit movement, for at least two centuries — since Leibniz, in the process of inventing calculus, used the same approach to break up the trajectories of cannonballs through the air" (*GR*, 407). It refers back to historically verifiable persons and developments and forward, from the time of *Gravity's Rainbow*, to future ones, to the encapsulated trajectory of men in space.

The Crying of Lot 49 is in many ways a novel about the effort and the consequences of "carrying sensation into the midst of the objects of the Science itself." That is precisely what Oedipa Maas does with the idea of Maxwell's Demon, an idea proposed at the end of James Clerk Maxwell's *Theory of Heat* (1871). Maxwell hypothesized a vessel divided into two portions, A and B, by a division in which there is a small hole. He asks us to conceive of a being, subsequently known as Maxwell's Demon, with faculties that allow it to follow the course of every molecule in the vessel. The being is situated beside a small shutter located in the dividing wall between the two portions of the vessel and he opens and closes this shutter so as to allow only the swifter molecules to pass from A to B and only the slower ones to pass from B to A. According to Maxwell this being "will thus, without expenditure of work, raise the temperature of B and lower that of A, in contradiction to the second law of thermodynamics."

Oedipa comes to picture herself as an equivalent of Maxwell's Demon, only in her case she sorts out a vast array of circulating data all seeming to emerge out of the inheritance from Inverarity. She is one of the executors of his estate, and she would like to transform all of the random information that floods in on her into "stelliferous meaning," just as the Demon operated as an agent of order in a system of random occurrences. She wishes, that is, to increase order and to decrease entropy in the system which is the life around her. By decreasing entropy, which is a measure of the unavailable energy in any system, she will forestall the drift toward death as the ultimate state of the entire system of life. However, by the end of the novel she has managed only to prove a point made by one of the later commentators on Clerk Maxwell, Leon Brillouin, in a paper published by *The Journal of Applied Physics*, entitled "Maxwell's Demon Cannot Operate." Brillouin contends that an intelligent being has to cause an *increase* of entropy before it can effect a reduction by a smaller amount. This increase of entropy more than balances the decrease of entropy the Demon might bring about. In the words of W. Ehrenberg in his essay on Maxwell's Demon in *Scientific American* (November 1967), "Similar calculations appear to be applicable whenever intelligent beings propose to act as sorting demons."

What are critics of Pynchon, like myself, but a species of sorting demon? And yet what are we to do with the random material of his books, what is Oedipa to do with the random and maddening material of her inheritance, if we do not all at some point become sorting demons? It is necessary to *know* about sorting demons before one can even know why one should break the habit. This is a way of saying that it takes a lot of work to know what's going on in Pynchon, even though what's going on finally lies importantly on the other side of such knowing, such "sorting" out. Really to see and hear his concerns, we must at least sense how Pynchon *feels* about his knowledge, we must participate in his Coleridgean anxiety about knowledge, about analysis, about any kind of sorting.

Even Clerk Maxwell and the great chemist Kekulé in *Gravity's Rainbow* are imagined as themselves haunted, visited, obsessed and paranoiac in their exploration, just as much as is the fictional heroine, dear Oedipa Maas. Thus, we learn in *Gravity's Rainbow* that the Demon may not in its inception have been a model meant to demonstrate something in the physical sciences. Though it served for that, it might have been designed primarily as an encoded warning to all of us. Instead of being an example of how plots may be created from randomness, it was meant to tip us off to an on-going plot that got carried into the twentieth century, on to World War II and the present. In *Gravity's Rainbow* someone speculates — it is impossible to know who — that Liebig, a renowned professor of chemistry in the last century at the University of Geissen, was an agent whose task was to put Kekulé in a position where he could receive a dream from "the bureaucracy of the other side," the world of the dead — a dream of the shape of the benzene ring. This shape was to be the foundation of aromatic chemistry, which, along with theories of acceleration, made possible the rocket and the nosecone for its destructive re-entry into our lives. Kekulé had entered the University of Geissen as an architectural student but he was inspired by Liebig to change his field.

So Kekulé brought the mind's eye of an architect over into chemistry. It was a critical switch. Liebig himself seems to have occupied the role of a gate, or sorting-demon such as his younger contemporary Clerk Maxwell once proposed, helping to concentrate energy into one favored room of the Creation at the expense of everything else (later witnesses have suggested that Clerk Maxwell intended his Demon not so much as a convenience in discussing a thermodynamic idea as a parable about the *actual existence* of personnel like Liebig . . . we may gain an indication of how far the repression had grown by that time, in the degree to which Clerk Maxwell felt obliged to code his warnings . . . indeed some theorists, usually the ones who find sinister meaning behind even *Mrs.* Clerk Maxwell's notorious "It is time to go home, James, you are beginning to enjoy yourself," have made the extreme suggestion that the Field Equations themselves contain an ominous forewarning — they cite as evidence the disturbing intimacy of the Equations with the behavior of the double-integrating circuit in the guidance system of the A4 rocket, the same double-summing of current densities that led architect Etzel Ölsch to design for architect Albert Speer an underground factory at Nordhausen with just that symbolic shape . . .). Young ex-architect Kekulé went looking among the molecules of the time for the hidden shapes he knew were there, shapes he did not like to think of as real physical structures, but as "rational formulas," showing the relationships that went on in "metamorphoses," his quaint 19th-century way of saying "chemical reactions." But he could visualize. He *saw* the four bonds of carbon, lying in a tetrahedron — he *showed* how carbon atoms could link up, one to another, into long chains. . . . But he was stumped when he got to benzene. He knew there were six carbon atoms with a hydrogen attached to each one — but he could not see the shape. Not until the dream: until he was made to see it, so that others might be seduced by its physical beauty, and begin to think of it as a blueprint, a basis for new compounds, new arrangements, so that there would be a field of aromatic chemistry to ally itself with secular power, and find new methods of synthesis, so there would be a German dye industry to become the IG. . . . (*GR*, 411–412)

This passage is at once portentously impressive and satirically comic. It emanates from the voice of the novel — as if Pynchon were himself a demon for sorting random sounds that pass through the cultural environment carrying information with them. And as always there is a hint of acute paranoia. In Pynchon, however, as sometimes in Mailer or even Melville, paranoia is often the pre-condition for recognizing the systematic conspiracy of reality. So much so, that to think of oneself with any pejorative sense as a paranoiac constitutes in Pynchon a kind of cop-out, a refusal to see life and reality itself as a plot, to see even dreams as an instrumentality of a bureaucracy intent on creating self-perpetuating systems.

Pynchon is a great novelist of betrayal, and everyone in his books is a betrayer who lets himself or herself be counted, who elects or who has been elected to fit into the scheme of things. But they are the worst betrayers who propose that the schemes are anything more or less than that — an effort to "frame" life in every sense — or who evade the recognition of this by calling it paranoiac. To be included in any plot is to be to that extent excluded from life and freedom. Paradoxically, one is excluded who is chosen, sorted, categorized, schematized, and yet this is the necessary, perpetual activity of life belonging to our very biological and psychic natures.

This is a distinctly American vision, and Pynchon is the epitome of an American writer out of the great classics of the nineteenth century — Hawthorne, Emerson, and Melville especially. The vision is not, as has been argued so often, one of cultural deprivation, but rather of cultural inundation, of being swamped, swept up, counted in before you could count yourself out, pursued by every bookish aspect of life even as you try to get lost in a wilderness, in a randomness where you might hope to find your true self. And it is that at last which is most deeply beautiful about Pynchon and his works. He has survived all the incursions which he documents, and he is, as I hope he will remain, a genius lost and anonymous.

Pre-Apocalyptic Atavism: Thomas Pynchon's Early Fiction

Catharine R. Stimpson

The place of women in apocalyptic literature is problematic. They can be ignored. They can act in the eschatological drama. As they do in *Revelation*, they can serve as polarized symbols of the corrupt and the pure, the Whore of Babylon and the Bride of Christ. The pressure of last things can even crush sexual distinctions. As some paranoids find the categories of female/male trivial in comparison to the grand precision of I/Them or Us/ Them, so the apocalyptic can abandon female/male for Elect/ Preterite. Yet the pre-apocalyptic fiction of Thomas Pynchon, before the splendid *Gravity's Rainbow*, grants a privileged place to women. They are actors and symbols. Their characterization — at once generous and warped, shrewd and regressive — provokes a mixture of contempt for contemporary sexuality and reverence for an atavistic mode.

To restate the orthodox, Pynchon sets the angels of possibility dancing on the pincushion of plot. Applauding the complex, he delights in asking if similar events are coincidences, correspondences, or clues to a conspiracy. *The Crying of Lot 49* mourns the contraction of America from a land of diversity to one of binary choice.[1] Yet, the early fiction, the first pages of the atlas of Pynchon's alternate universe, offers simplicities as plain as a needle's point. Among them is a relentless lament for the West. Its decline from the decadent through the mechanical and inanimate to annihilation compels his imagination.[2] Perhaps all secular systems — "galaxy, engine, human being, culture, whatever"[3] — wear out. They are subject to the growing randomness and terminal uniformity of entropy. The West has urged the process along. Politically, it has bred racist colonial empires. It has planted not seeds of life, but the flag. Pynchon uses and inverts sexual metaphors to picture the civilization he ferociously, inventively deplores. The coast of Deutsch-Südwestafrika is an "ash plain impregnated with a killer sea."[4] The rituals and romances of the West reflect a pervasive belief that any sexuality, be it natural, human, or divine, is intertwined with death. Pynchon has taken up the burden of T. S. Eliot's lines:

> Where is the wisdom we have lost in knowledge?
> Where is the knowledge we have lost in information?
> The cycles of Heaven in twenty centuries
> Bring us farther from GOD and nearer to the Dust.[5]

Another simplicity is Pynchon's sexual conservatism, which pervades the early fiction and which reveals itself in the conventional conviction that women, both in sacred and in secular realms, ought to be lovers and mothers. The womb is a gift to life and defiance of death. Such mediation between man and nature is a source of prestige and power. Like Mailer, Pynchon endorses a sexuality that links itself to reproduction. So doing, it may symbolize fertility itself. Part of his hostility towards homosexuality and such phenomena as sexual cross-dressing derives from the fact that they sever the libido from conception. They are barren in terms of the future of the race.

Healthy male sexuality must, at the least, promise fertility. Raunchy Pig Bodine romps towards legendary status, his raw energy that of a satyr in sailor suit. Pigs, Robert Graves says, were sacred to the Moon-goddess.[6] Among the vilest characters in *V.* is the German Foppl. A savage warrior, then a savage settler in Südwestafrika, he personifies virility run wild towards sterility. Domineering, sadistic, violent, he delights in the rape of the living and dead. Sun to *V.*'s moon, he is the male counterpart to her chillier excesses. Though seen as indirectly as she is, through the accounts of others, he seems to take his joy in brutality. Pynchon, however, is no feminist. In his daisy chain of victimization, a sour adaption of a slang phrase for group sex, women are as apt to hurt men as men women. Both sexes wield the whip.

A healthy female sexuality is a primary agent of biological life. Goddesses offer supernatural aid and mythological support. A theme of *V.* is imagining what a goddess ought to be. Because he often hedges the context in which they appear, I am wary of Pynchon's explicit literary allusions. He warns readers not to confuse texts with life, one text with another, Pynchon with a predecessor. Nevertheless, even seen cautiously, Pynchon seems to use Robert Graves's *White Goddess* to help fashion a fit divinity. He mentions Graves, in one of his problematic passages, which is, on a superficial level, a description of Herbert Stencil. At the same time, Pynchon refers to J. G. Frazer, whose anthropology appears to have provided some of the raw material about Mediterranean culture for *V.*

> He would dream perhaps once a week that it had all been a dream, and that now he'd awakened to discover the pursuit of V. was merely a scholarly quest after all, an adventure of the mind, in the tradition of *The Golden Bough* or *The White Goddess.* (*V.*, 61/50)

For Graves, the White Goddess both generates life and inspires culture. He writes:

> [T]he language of poetic myth anciently current in Mediterranean and Northern Europe was a magical language bound up with popular religious ceremonies in honour of the Moon-goddess, or Muse. . . . [T]his remains the language of true poetry. . . . [T]he Moon-goddess inspired [poetic myths] and . . . demanded that man should pay woman spiritual and sexual homage . . . man's love was properly directed towards women. . . . Moira, Ilithyia and Callone — Death, Birth and Beauty — formed a triad of Goddesses who presided over all acts of generation whatsoever: physical, spiritual or intellectual. (pp. vi–viii)

To Graves, Pynchon adds a notion about goddesses that he derives from Henry Adams. (Both Stencil and Callisto in "Entropy" model themselves on Adams.) At the Great Exposition in Paris in 1900, wary of his subjectivity, Adams concludes:

> The woman had once been supreme; in France she still seemed potent, not merely as a sentiment, but as a force. Why was she unknown in America? . . . The trait was notorious, and often humorous, but any one brought up among Puritans knew sex was sin. In any previous age, sex was strength. Neither art nor beauty was needed. Every one, even among Puritans, knew that neither Diana of the Ephesians nor any of the Oriental goddesses was worshipped for her beauty. She was goddess because of her force; she was the animated dynamo; she was reproduction — the greatest and most mysterious of all energies; all she needed was to be fecund. . . . [S]ymbol or energy, the Virgin had acted as the greatest force the Western world ever felt, and had drawn man's activities to herself more strongly than any other power, natural or supernatural, had ever done. . . .[7]

If the two theologies, as it were, fail to cohere fully, they agree that the European past worshipped physical fertility; that the present may blaspheme.

V. bleakly follows Adams to name the American divinity: the machine. Fat Benny Profane ought to recognize a life-enhancing goddess. His pig eyes are set in "pig-pouches." However, in fantasy, his perfect woman is a robot:

> Someday, please God, there would be an all-electronic woman. Maybe her name would be Violet. Any problems with her, you could look it up in the maintenance manual. Module concept: fingers' weight, heart's temperature, mouth's size out of tolerance? Remove and replace, was all. (*V.*, 385/361)

Benny is usually dumb about women, an intellectual sluggishness that fails to bar him from generalizations about them. As bleakly, *V.* refuses to follow Adams and Graves to name explicitly the European divinity. Instead, the novel names and blames her antithesis, the polymorphous and polymorphously perverse V. If she is fecund, she spawns the forces of antilife. As Moon-goddess, she retains only the power to destroy. She is Moira, without Ilithyia and Callone to balance her.

The symbol "V" obviously has many connotations. It can refer to victory; to the stain on a plate a German barmaid is washing in a beer hall in Egypt; to two vector lines (the writer and the twentieth century?) colliding to place vessels on a white, blank page; to Vheissu, a region that symbolizes gaudy glamour dressing a void; to the dominant chord on the major scale. Picturing female sexuality, it evokes the names of Venus and of the Virgin, each of whom, in her way, manifests it. "V" must also be read in conjunction with the letters "N," a double "V," and "M" and "W," each a triple "V." Think, for example, of "Vegetation Myth." In single, double, or trinitarian form, the letter, the words it initiates, and the meanings of the words embody diametrically opposed values. They illustrate the "flip/flop" McClintic Sphere describes. Malta is the womb of the writer (often sententious) Maijstral; the tomb of the Bad Priest.

To trace Stencil tracing V. is to watch the twentieth-century West trying to grasp its antidivinity. His search inverts older, richer mythologies. He is a male Isis hoping to recover parts of the dismembered Osiris. Stencil is also the battered child of the century seeking its parents. The father is weak. His legacy is some facts, some friends, which the son may use but not redeem. The mother is vicious, an adulteress who has abandoned him at birth. The son is sterile. His "seeds" are dossiers, the compilation of which barely keeps him alive. Possibly mad, certainly neurotic, he is the fearful archivist of the period before the apocalypse.

V. first appears as Victoria Wren in Egypt in 1898. Her name is that of England's queen, an empire's goddess and symbolic mother. She wears an ivory comb, on which five crucified English soldiers are carved. The comb connects her to the Oriental goddess Kali, who both succours and devours. (Many Tibetans saw Queen Victoria as Kali's incarnation.) Victoria, as V. figures do, succours only pain. Her sexual loyalties are dubious, her conspiratorial ploys enigmatic. Accompanying the pretty Victoria is her ugly sister Mildred. Few children appear in Pynchon's early fiction, but when they do, their presence signals the possibility of grace.[8] Lovers of children, like lovers of nature, treasure the animate. Though Mildred is plain, she is good. The two sisters symbolize the terrible split between beauty and humanity. Bongo-Shaftesbury, the wired man, repels the child. She also cherishes a rock, which foreshadows Malta, the rocky womb that will bring forth the spirit of survival and workable myth.

That a Victoria will dominate *V.*, while a Mildred disappears, is a clue to the moral that waits, beastlike, at the heart of the labyrinth of story. Victoria will appear as Veronica the Rat;[9] Vera Meroving; Veronica Manganese; and as the Bad Priest of Malta. As she changes, those features that betray the benign goddess will grow. Her body will become more and more opulently mechanical. At her machinelike worst, she will parody the dynamo Americans worship. Her costume will become more and more masculine, not a sign of freedom, but of decline. Her politics will become increasingly reactionary. Her sadism will become both rawer and more refined. If good women in Pynchon use fingernails to stimulate male lovers and to express the pleasure of orgasm, V. rakes them over male flesh. Sometimes a V. will be openly cruel. In Foppl's home in Africa, her surrogate sister sings her theme song. Hedwig Vogelsang's charming lyric also exemplifies Pynchon's ability to adapt the devices of musical comedy to fiction.

> Love's a lash,
> Kisses gall the tongue, harrow the heart;
> Caresses tease
> Cankered tissue apart. (*V.*, 238/220)

V. delights, not in simple sadistic activity, but in any destructive hurly-burly of the will. Pynchon's characters dabble with the notion, which they ascribe to Machiavelli, that human actions, the aggregate of which is history, are the result of the interplay of two forces: *virtú* and *fortuna*, will and fate. V., vain enough to wish to play goddess of fortune, relishes the exercise of an amoral *virtú* as well. However, V. can be a voyeur. In Florence, during a political riot:

> She saw a rioter . . . being bayoneted again and again. . . . She stood . . . still . . . ; her face betrayed no emotion. It was as if she saw herself embodying a feminine principle, acting as complement to all this bursting, explosive male energy. Inviolate and calm, she watched the spasms of wounded bodies, the fair of violent death, framed and staged, it seemed, for her alone in

that tiny square. From her hair the heads of five crucified also looked on, no more expressive than she. (*V.*, 209/192–193)

Finally, V.'s Catholicism will become more pronounced. "Meroving" echoes the Merovingians, rulers of part of France who were Catholic converts. Pynchon treats Catholicism with some distaste.[10] It harms men because it tempts them towards manipulation. Offering themselves as priests of salvation, they actually seek control. Catholicism harms women because it urges them to conceptualize and to live out a tension between the natural and the supernatural; to fear the natural and to prefer the supernatural; to discharge sexuality, if they must, in a falsely romanticized motherhood. The Church tells women they can be whores or saints or earthly mothers. Pynchon says each woman can be all three. V.'s religiosity has two benefits for her: a "seed-time" for the narcissistic self-dramatization in which she expertly indulges; a chance to sublimate sexuality into role-playing as the Bride of Christ, to transform energy into repressed lasciviousness.

The section about V. in love crystallizes her nastiness. To measure her best is, in a dialectical judgment, to measure her worst. The style reflects Pynchon's ability to write about that which he dislikes, a paradox of the rhetoric of *contemptus mundi*. The site of V.'s passion is Paris during an explosion of cultural modernism, a mark of Pynchon's distrust of the street of his century. V. loves a fifteen-year-old dancer, Mélanie l'Heuremaudit (cursed hour). *Her* last romance has been with her father. Though lesbianism is an entry in Pynchon's edition of *The Decline and Fall of the West*, he finds it less appalling than the context in which it occurs. When Mehemet, a gabby Mediterranean sailor, tells Sidney Stencil about sapphism in a Turkish harem, the tale is meant to be cute.

For V. and Mélanie are narcissists, substituting self for others as objects of love, and fetishists, substituting things for persons as objects of love. Male characters also have fetishes. Mantissa (half-weight, a trivial addition) adores Botticelli's Venus enough to steal it. But female fetishism is more sinister, if only because Pynchon assigns women that normative task of acting out and symbolizing natural fertility.[11] The trinity — V., Mélanie, Mélanie's image — mocks the Moon-goddess trinity — birth, death, and beauty. Mélanie's physical death, a probably suicidal impalement on a sharp pole as she dances, mirrors the Western nexus of sex, art, and fatality. V.'s own death is equally appropriate. She does not wish it. Weakly, she asks a group of children on Malta to help, not to torment her. However, the spargefication she endures at their hands, in her guise as Bad Priest, is a result of forces she has cheered. If Germans were not bombing Malta, there would be no packs of bestial children roaming through its ruins.

The "Epilogue" of *V.* is a last reminder of the penalties that may follow if the goddesses of fecundity are abandoned. In June 1919, Sidney Stencil is leaving Malta. The boat that has brought him is taking him away, another connection between a beginning and an end. A powerful waterspout suddenly appears. It is analogous to the earthquake and tidal wave of 9 July 1956 that killed forty-three persons who had "run . . . afoul of the inanimate" in the Aegean (*V.*, 290/270). It lasts long enough

> to lift the xebec fifty feet, whirling and creaking, Astarte's throat naked to the cloudless weather, and slam it down again into a piece of the Mediterranean whose subsequent surface phenomena — whitecaps, kelp islands, any of a million flatnesses which should catch thereafter part of the brute sun's spectrum — showed nothing at all of what came to lie beneath, that quiet June day. (*V.*, 492/463)

Syntactical ambiguity permits the reference to Astarte, one of the great fertility goddesses, to serve two functions. Throat naked, she personifies the spout. Next, she is the figurehead of the boat. The inanimate, which might once have been animate, shatters the inanimate, which might once have been an icon of the living body of myth. A simpler reading might be that the goddess is permanent enough to exact revenge.

V. also concerns women who inhabit a quotidian world. Pynchon grants their behavior a degree of motivation. They lack the elusiveness of V. that arises from Stencil's faulty perceptions; her function as a symbol; and the inexplicability of remnants of the divine. Pynchon, though he suspects tight schemes of cause and effect, grants that culture influences personality. In "Entropy," for example, Aubade shatters the windows of the hermetic apartment in which she and Callisto live. Trying to hasten their heat-death, she longs for "the hovering, curious dominant of their separate lives . . . [to] revolve into a tonic of darkness and the final absence of all motion" (292). She is both French and "Annamese." The child of colonial mating, Pynchon suggests, will be perverse. Fortunately, *V.* avoids the tiresome satire of middle-class American women, be they housewives or government girls, that mars "Entropy" and other of the early stories.

The women in *V.* are judged according to the degree that they resemble V. The more like her they are, the worse they are. The novel's first scene bluntly introduces Americans who have fallen away from the good traditions of the goddesses. One Beatrice, who is a barmaid in the Sailor's Grave in Norfolk, is the sweetheart of "the destroyer U.S.S. Scaffold." Another Beatrice, who owns the bar, sets up artificial breasts to serve beer to sailors to prove her maternal care. In New York, robust Mafia Winsome, a racist Jacqueline Susann, preaches a theory of Heroic Love that reduces love to lust. She also uses contraceptives, to Pynchon less a legitimate act of self-protection than a morally and psychologically illegitimate separation of sex from love and of sex from reproduction. Her dithering husband thinks:

> If she believed in Heroic Love, which is nothing really but a frequency, then obviously Winsome wasn't on the man end of half of what she was looking for. In five years of marriage all he knew was that both of them were whole selves, hardly fusing at all, with no more emotional osmosis than leakage of seed through the solid membranes of contraceptive or diaphragm that were sure to be there protecting them. (*V.*, 126/113)

Esther Harvitz, despite some self-assertion, succumbs to the ministrations of Schoenmaker, disillusioned plastic surgeon. His great love is over: a feudal, homosexual adoration for a pilot in World War I. When Esther has her nose job, Schoenmaker amputates the physical sign of the goddess.[12] Mehemet has described Mara, the spirit of woman, for us:

In her face is always a slight bow to the nose, a wide spacing of the eyes. . . . No one you'd turn to watch on the street. But she was a teacher of love after all. Only pupils of love need to be beautiful. (*V.*, 462/435)

In contrast, Rachel Owlglass has promise. Her fetishistic desire for her MG is an aspect of collegiate adolescence she will outgrow. Though kind to members of the Whole Sick Crew, she is aloof from its decadence. She opposes Esther's abortion because, she believes, it will stunt Esther's capacity for heterosexuality. Her own heterosexuality is active. She offers Benny, whom she pursues, the chance to experience the comminglings of love. She projects a physical desire stronger than ego. In one of the novel's sloppiest passages, she croons to her crotch: " '. . . when it talks we listen' " (*V.*, 384/360). If not in literal fact, then in act, she also mothers: tucking men into bed; washing their faces. Pynchon's Jewish men want to sit *shivah* for the lost of the world; his Jewish women want to nurture and feed them. What wisdom Rachel has she attributes to the more irrational lessons of prelapsarian biology. She murmurs to a seduced Benny:

". . . [Women] are older than you, we lived inside you once: the fifth rib, closest to the heart. We learned all about it then. After that it had to become our game to nourish a heart you all believe is hollow though we know different. Now you all live inside us, for nine months, and when ever you decide to come back after that." (*V.*, 370/347)

Pynchon offers women another acceptable role: that of Marina, a daughter. She can inspire the tender chivalry of the good father. If Paola teaches Pappy Hod the mysterious plenitude of sex, in a surrogate daughter/father relationship that avoids incest, he reveals to her the virtue of forgiveness. Paola will also bring relics of the European goddess to America: the ivory comb. The name she has taken while pretending to be a black prostitute, Ruby, has already connected her to V. and the sapphire V. stitches into her navel. Yet Paola purifies the comb. She gives it to Pappy, an act of domestic fidelity. She will return to Pappy and live in Norfolk where, like Penelope, she will be faithful and "spin." Only the double meaning of the "yarn" she will create — fabric and fable — hints that the wife may not be wholly tamed.

A curious element of the structure of *V.* is that malign V. carries much of its symbolic weight, but the characters most often on page are male. Sailors on leave; anarchists in exile; foreign service officers planning counterespionage; explorers on expeditions — the good old boys and the old boys dominate the action. Two wistful comments, by Rachel and by Brenda Wigglesworth, offer a partial explanation. Boys are permitted more adventures than girls, more "Diesels and dust, roadhouses, crossroads saloons" (*V.*, 27/18). Pynchon's picaresque reflects that social truth. Brenda anticipates Oedipa Maas: banal enough to drink sloe gins and own seventy-two pairs of Bermuda shorts, she is courageous enough to drive around Europe alone and witty enough to recite and to dismiss a poem that summarizes the action of the novel itself. Pynchon deploys her as literary critic.

However, male characters do more than occupy the bulk of narrative space. Pervasively, they provide point of view, even if points of view within the novel undercut and buffalo each other. So Stencil sees Mondaugen seeing Foppl seeing a black woman. The passage is horrible.

> Later, toward dusk, there was one Herero girl, sixteen or seventeen years old, for the platoon; and Firelily's rider was last. After he'd had her he must have hesitated a moment between sidearm and bayonet. She actually smiled then; pointed to both, and began to shift her hips lazily in the dust. He used both. (*V.*, 264/246)

(When men, usually in a lurid homosexual compact, take on a "feminine role," they impersonate such apparently voluptuous submissiveness.) At times the author himself distances us, through the tactical use of direct address, from a woman character. He writes about Rachel at a party:

> You felt she'd done a thousand secret things to her eyes. They needed no haze of cigarette smoke to look at you out of sexy and fathomless, but carried their own along with them. (*V.*, 52/41)

[41]

Some men are granted moral authority as well. Dahoud and Pig both have the snappy one-liner, "Life is the most precious possession you have" (*V.*, 12/4, 361/338). McClintic Sphere cites a credo for dignified survival. A black jazz musician who plays at the V-Note, his figure points to a custom of white American male writers in the 1950s and early 1960s: the transformation of jazzmen and blacks into savants; the use of national outsiders as cosmic insiders. Within *V.* itself the race the West has sought to exterminate provides the texts of its salvation. In his Triumph, driving in the wind, a persistent symbol of spiritual verve in the novel, McClintic thinks:

> Love with your mouth shut, help without breaking your ass or publicizing it: keep cool, but care. (*V.*, 365–366/342–343)

Readers reading my reading of Pynchon, in the mirror game of criticism, may justly say that *The Crying of Lot 49* reverses such structural features of *V.* An elusive, probably malign man, rich Pierce Inverarity, is a core symbol. A woman claims narrative space and the prerogatives of point of view. Oedipa Maas is a twenty-eight-year-old California housewife. Her most mythic role has been as a solipsistic Princess in the Tower. Though an unlikely candidate, she assumes the traditionally male tasks of executor of a will; interpreter of literature, a "whiz at pursuing strange words in Jacobean texts"; and questor. She sets out with only the fuzziest notion of what her job might be. She inhabits a polluted land, the urbanized California of housing tracts, factories, shopping centers, and suicide strips blithely known as "freeways." Construction has numbed nature as much as American society since World War II has narcotized sense and sensibility. Natural language, the frame of civilization, is running down, the victim of entropy, sloth, and the media. In Vesperhaven House, old Mr. Thoth (the Egyptian god of learning and writing) is nodding out in front of Porky Pig cartoons on TV. Rulers, such as the corporate officials of Yoyodyne, are corrupt. Oedipa must ask the right question, but the lesson of earlier quest narratives and of the drama of Oedipus himself is how hard it is to ask the right question; how hard it is to interpret oracular answers; how dangerous it might be to have the answers.

Nevertheless, the sexual conservatism of *V.*, if softened, infiltrates *The Crying of Lot 49*. Pynchon sexualizes ability to give Oedipa the weapons of "gut fear and female cunning" (*Lot 49*, 21/11). That cunning exposes itself in Oedipa's ability to respond to the sea: the symbol of a teeming, insatiable, omnipotent womb. As she drives to a picnic at a lake Pierce has built, she thinks:

> Somewhere beyond the battening, urged sweep of three-bedroom houses . . . lurked the sea, the unimaginable Pacific, the one to which all surfers, beach pads, sewage disposal schemes, tourist incursions, sunned homosexuality, chartered fishing are irrelevant, the hole left by the moon's tearing-free and monument to her exile; you could not hear or even smell this but it was there, something tidal began to reach feelers in past eyes and eardrums, perhaps to arouse fractions of brain current your most gossamer microelectrode is yet too gross for finding. Oedipa had believed . . . in some principle of the sea as redemption for Southern California. . . . Perhaps it was only that notion, its arid hope, she sensed as this forenoon they made their seaward thrust, which would stop short of any sea. (*Lot 49*, 55–56/36–37)

During her quest, Oedipa discovers the Tristero. An underground mail delivery system, it works in opposition to "legitimate" authority. So doing, it includes both criminal and revolutionary; extreme right and extreme left; Mafia enforcer and saint. As she deciphers codes about the Tristero, she becomes increasingly celibate in body and isolated in spirit, but she also releases a suppressed capacity for maternal tenderness. Psychological motherhood marks her moral growth. In a scene that resembles a slum Pietà, she cradles a dirty old sailor suffering from DTs, as if he were "her own child" (*Lot 49*, 127/93).

She may become a supernatural mother as well. As revelations buffet her, she wonders if she can hold to a central truth. In a grim metaphor, Pynchon asks if we are not all like Prince Myshkin; if we are not epileptics in the confrontation with spectra beyond the known sun. Oedipa meditates:

> I am meant to remember. Each clue that comes is *supposed* to have its own clarity, its fine chances for permanence. But then she wondered if the gemlike "clues" were only some kind of compensation. To make up for her having lost the direct, epileptic Word, the cry that might abolish the night. (*Lot 49*, 118/87)

The capitalization of "Word" is vital: it is a translation, linguistically and conceptually, of the Greek "logos," an animating and renewing principle of reason in the cosmos. Oedipa thinks of it once again. After calling upon God, during the dark night of her soul, she remembers

> drifters she had listened to, Americans speaking their language carefully, scholarly, as if they were in exile from somewhere else invisible yet congruent with the cheered land she lived in. . . . And the voices before and after the dead man's that had phoned at random during the darkest, slowest hours, searching ceaseless among the dial's ten million possibilities for that magical Other who would reveal herself out of the roar of relays, monotone litanies of insult, filth, fantasy, love whose brute repetition must someday call into being the trigger for the unnamable act, the recognition, the Word. (*Lot 49*, 180/135–136)

The Tristero may be carrying not simply letters, i.e., written communications, but Letters, pieces of the Word.

Pynchon may be going on to give "the Word" special meaning. Some theoreticians of Logos — the Stoics, the Jewish philosopher Philo, the early Christian apologist Justin Martyr — thought of the divine principle as germinating, seminal, the "*spermatikos logos.*" Justin writes of "the seed of reason . . . implanted in every race of man." He mentions the "spermatic word."[13] The Tristero may be delivering it. Pynchon, exploiting the puns natural language is heir to, literalizing a sexual metaphor, may want us to think of mail as male. If so, as Oedipa succumbs to the languid, sinister attraction of the Tristero, she represents the female body being pierced and receiving some sacred seed. Towards the end of her quest:

> The toothaches got worse, she dreamed of disembodied voices from whose malignance there was no appeal, the soft dusk of mirrors out of which something was about to walk, and empty rooms that waited for her. Your gynecologist has no test for what she was pregnant with. (*Lot 49*, 175/131)

One of the novel's ambiguities is whether she is carrying the child of life or of death. The former will add to and renew this world. The meritorious chance of our redemption may prevail. Bearing it will give Oedipa a salutary public significance. The numbers 49, apparently arbitrary, may prove symbolic: 4 the number of spring, 9 of lunar wisdom. If she is bearing the child of death, it will either add to her isolation or generate disease. Her pregnancy, as it were, will either be meaningless or of morbid public significance. The odds are on this possibility. If Oedipus must marry his mother and father his own siblings, parentless Oedipa must leave her husband and mother sterility.

Oedipa never reaches the Pacific. Only one character does: Randolph Driblette, the director of a Jacobean tragedy. He drowns himself. The closest she comes to the symbol of female fertility is to stand near the shore on old railroad tracks, ties, and cinderbed. She simplifies her choices to one: does the Tristero exist or not? Making sense of her clues, has she discovered or manufactured a reality? If Oedipa has invented the Tristero, then Pynchon's early feminine metaphor for it, a malign and pitiless stripper, is another image for her hidden self. She commits herself to the Tristero and goes to the auction at which some possibly relevant information about it will be sold. The atmosphere is grim. The room is locked; the men inside have "pale, cruel faces"; the auctioneer is like a "puppet-master," a priest of "some remote culture," a "descending angel." The narrative abandons the questor in the Chapel Perilous.

In *V.*, Benny Profane experiences the loss of vital myth. The affirmation of such absence is one of the longest cries in twentieth-century literature. Sitting in Little Italy in New York, amidst the garish shoddiness of a Catholic saint's day celebration, he tries to tell a girl about his job.

> He told her about the alligators; Angel, who had a fertile imagination too, added detail, color. Together on the stoop they hammered together a myth. Because it wasn't born from fear of thunder, dreams, astonishment at how the crops kept dying after harvest and coming up again every spring, or anything else very permanent, only a temporary interest, a spur-of-the-moment tumescence, it was a myth rickety and transient as the bandstands and the sausage-pepper of Mulberry Street. (*V.*, 142/128)

If the early Pynchon were to offer a vital myth, it would have to be flexible enough to verify urban life; radical enough to regenerate the decaying world; tough enough to withstand the testing acids of irony, burlesque, and parody. It would also respect nature. Spring, taking on the role of Paraclete, would descend with tongue of flame. Ordinary women would be fertile. Goddesses would protect the natural bounty of the womb. Like the moon, women would have a dark side that would haunt the imagination of men and remind them of their fragile mortality. However, the early fiction dramatizes the mortifying betrayal of such roles, which some women will and others resist.

Notes

1. For further comment see Annette Kolodny and Daniel James Peters, "Pynchon's *The Crying of Lot 49*: The Novel as Subversive Experience," *Modern Fiction Studies*, 19, 1 (Spring 1973), 79–87. I will be using both editions of *The Crying of Lot 49* (New York: Bantam Books, 1967, first published by Lippincott in 1966). Page numbers of specific citations will be given parenthetically in my text as Lippincott/Bantam.

2. The description of the three-stage process is adapted from Raymond M. Olderman, *Beyond the Waste Land: The American Novel in the Nineteen-Sixties* (New Haven and London: Yale University Press, 1972, third printing 1973), p. 133.

3. Thomas Pynchon, "Entropy," *Kenyon Review*, 22, 2 (Spring 1960), 282. Page numbers of further citations will be given parenthetically in my text.

4. Thomas Pynchon, *V.* (New York: Bantam Books, 1968), p. 267/248 (novel first published by Lippincott in 1963). Page numbers of other citations will be given parenthetically as Lippincott/Bantam.

5. "Choruses from 'The Rock,'" *The Complete Poems and Plays* (New York: Harcourt, Brace and Company, 1952), p. 96.

6. Robert Graves, *The White Goddess: A Historical Grammar of Poetic Myth* (New York: Vintage Books, amended and enlarged edition, 1959), pp. 233–235. Page numbers of subsequent citations will be given parenthetically.

7. *The Education of Henry Adams: An Autobiography* (Boston: Houghton, Mifflin Company, Sentry edition, 1961), pp. 384, 388–389.

8. "The Secret Integration," *Saturday Evening Post*, 237, 45 (December 19–26, 1964), 36–37, 39, 42–44, 46–49, 51, is about children. Set in the Berkshires, it shows a small gang of boys learning to conform to the corrupt, hostile, unimaginative adult world. The story also introduces

the Slothrop family. "Low-Lands," *New World Writing 16* (Phila-delphia and New York: J. B. Lippincott, 1960), pp. 85–108, tells of the near-fabulous adventures of Dennis Flange. He wishes to be a son (his mother, symbolically, is the sea) and to father a child. After a visit from old pal Pig Bodine, he leaves his superrational wife Cindy and accepts the invitation of a beautiful girl, Nerissa, to live with her. Nerissa's only disadvantages are that she lives underground, beneath a garbage dump, and that she is only three feet six inches tall. One of her attractions for Dennis is the maternal kindliness she shows Hyacinth, her pet rat.

9. Veronica the Rat seems a rodent echo of the goddess Venus Cloacina, "patroness of the sewage system" in Rome. See Graves, *The White Goddess*, pp. 535–536.

10. The protagonist of Pynchon's first story is, like Benny Profane, the child of a Catholic/Jewish mixed marriage. While Benny's father is Catholic, Cleanth Siegal's mother is a member (lapsed) of the Church. See Tom Pynchon (*sic*), "Mortality and Mercy in Vienna," *Epoch*, 9, 4 (Spring 1959), 195–213.

11. Marjorie Kaufman, in her eloquent essay in this collection, argues that Pynchon, insofar as Fausto Maijstral is his voice, construes motherhood as accident, impersonal. Even so, mothers carry life. They simply lose the privilege of personalizing and poeticizing the chore. The scene in which the painting is stolen is a good example of Pynchon's sym-bolic farce. The Gaucho's excursion into art criticism reveals the dis-continuity between the twentieth century and its livelier aesthetic tradition. Pynchon also connects Botticelli's Venus to V., to the latter's detriment. The shell on which the goddess stands is, in Italian, "pettine," which is the word for comb as well.

12. Olderman, *Beyond the Waste Land*, p. 129, claims that the nose opera-tion is "a comic inversion of the usual joke about men and the length of their noses, demonstrating a vaguely unhealthy reversal of role play-ing." A misreading, cut along the masculine bias. The surgery, if Schoenmaker can be trusted, is another example of the flip/flop. "[C]or-rection entails retreat to a diametric opposite." The scene, not one for the squeamish, shows two features of Pynchon's style: (1) the tendency to exhaust one episode, even at the risk of making the large fictional structure narratively asymmetrical; and (2) the competent rendering of the technical.

13. "The Second Apology of Justin," *Justin Martyr and Athenagoras. Ante-Nicene Christian Library*, Vol. 11, ed. Rev. Alexander Roberts and James Donaldson (Edinburgh: T. and T. Clark, 1867), 78, 83. The editors, in a note, call the "spermatic word" the "word (i.e. Christ) disseminated among men" (p. 83).

Caries and Cabals*

Tony Tanner

> Cavities in the teeth occur for good reason, Eigenvalue reflected.
> But even if there are several per tooth, there's no conscious
> organization there against the life of the pulp, no conspiracy.
> Yet we have men like Stencil, who must go about grouping the
> world's random caries into cabals. ($V.$, 153/139)†

Thomas Pynchon made his intentions clear from the outset. The
title of his first important short story is "Entropy" and it contains
specific references to Henry Adams. Whereas some novelists
would prefer to cover the philosophic tracks which gave them
decisive shaping hints for their novels, Pynchon puts those tracks
on the surface of his writing. Indeed his work is about those
tracks and, more largely, the whole human instinct and need to
make tracks. Adams wanted a theory which would act as a "trail"
in "the thickset forests of history" and even if we change that
metaphor of the forest to that of the urban wasteland, thick with
the rubble and dead of our century of total wars, the need for a
trail or a track may still remain. A philosophy, a theory of history,
a law of thermodynamics — any one of these may be a "trail"
and their significance may reside not so much in their verifiable
applicability as in the human compulsion to formulate them. Pynchon sees all this quite clearly, and while his work is certainly

* From Chapter 7, *City of Words: American Fiction 1950–1970* (New York:
Harper and Row, 1971), pp. 153–173.
† References to $V.$ will be given with the page number from the Lippincott
edition (New York, 1963) followed by the page number from the Bantam
edition (New York, 1964). — Eds.

about a world succumbing to entropy, it is also about the subtler human phenomena — the need to see patterns which may easily turn into the tendency to suspect plots.

The situation in "Entropy" is simply and deliberately schematic. There is a downstairs and an upstairs apartment. Downstairs, Meatball Mulligan is holding a lease-breaking party which tends increasingly towards destructive chaos and ensuing torpor. This is a recurrent motif in all Pynchon's work, no doubt exemplifying the entropic process (the party is a relatively closed system of people, no one seems able to leave, and the only terminating point is sleep). The entropic process applies to the decline of information as well: two people discuss communication theory and how noise messes up significant signals. Upstairs, an intellectual called Callisto is trying to warm a freezing bird back to life. In his room he maintains a little hothouse jungle, specifically referred to as a "Rousseau-like fantasy." "Hermetically sealed, it was a tiny enclave of regularity in the city's chaos, alien to the vagaries of the weather, national politics, of any civil disorder." His room is his fantasy, a dream of order in which he has "perfected its ecological balance" ("Entropy," p. 64). . . .

The house, then, is some sort of paradigm for modern consciousness; the lower part immersed in the noise of modern distractions and sensing the failing of significant communication, while the upper part strives to remain at the level of music, yet feels the gathering strain as dream is encroached on by life. Life, in this context, is not only the party downstairs, but the weather. Callisto finds that the temperature has remained at 37 degrees Fahrenheit for a number of days, and he is by nature quick to detect omens of apocalypse. "Henry Adams, three generations before his own, had stared aghast at Power; Callisto found himself in much the same state over Thermodynamics, the inner life of that power" (p. 28). What Pynchon puts before us is the effort of the man in his upstairs sanctuary, with life-destroying weather outside, and sense-destroying noise downstairs, to articulate his theory of what is going on. . . . At one point he starts to dictate to his girl, using — like Adams in *Education* — the third person.

As a young man at Princeton . . . Callisto had learned a
mnemonic device for remembering the Laws of Thermodynamics: you can't win, things are going to get worse before they get
better, who says they're going to get better . . . he found in
entropy or the measure of disorganization for a closed system an
adequate metaphor to apply to certain phenomena in his own
world . . . in American "consumerism" discovered a similar tendency from the least to the most probable, from differentiation to
sameness, from ordered individuality to a kind of chaos. He
found himself, in short, restating Gibbs' prediction in social terms,
and envisioned a heat-death for his culture in which ideas, like
heat-energy, would no longer be transferred, since each point in
it would ultimately have the same quantity of energy; and intellectual motion would, accordingly, cease.

This is a man drawing on various ideas or laws which he has
learned, to project adequate analogies for the cosmic processes in
which man is so helplessly caught up. It is an attempt to make
some intellectual music; a music to harmonize the increasing noise.

The story has in effect two different endings: downstairs
Meatball is feeling the temptation to crawl off to sleep somewhere.
But he resolves to do what he can to keep the party from "de-
teriorating into total chaos." He acts; he starts to tidy up, gets
people calmed down, gets things mended. Upstairs however,
Callisto is "helpless in the past," and the bird he had been trying
to save dies in his hands. His girl realizes that his obsession with
that constant 37 degrees has brought him to a state of paralyzed
terror. Her act is a symbolic one — she smashes the window of
their hermetically sealed retreat with her own bare hands. It is
tantamount to the breaking of the shell round their whole fantasy
life of perfect harmonies and maintained ecological balances.

In that composite image . . . , Pynchon offers us a shorthand
picture of the human alternatives of working inside the noisy
chaos to mitigate it or standing outside, constructing patterns to
account for it. Man is just such a two-storied house of consciousness, and in the configuration of that shattered window and
Callisto's paralysis, Pynchon suggests the potential peril of all
pattern-making, or plot-detecting. . . .

Norbert Wiener said that it is always likely to be a problem
whether we interpret whatever it is that makes for disorganiza-

tion in nature as merely a neutral absence of order (the Augustinian view, he calls this), or as a positively malign force dedicated to the annihilation of order. He adds, "The Augustinian position has always been difficult to maintain. It tends under the slightest perturbation to break down into a covert Manichaeanism." . . . The temptation to regard all signs of entropy in the world as the work of hostile agents is like the demonism in the work of William Burroughs. Both represent attempts to "give destruction a name or face" (to take a phrase from Pynchon's short story "Mortality and Mercy in Vienna"), and both those reactions to the world reveal themselves in the individual as a continuous leaning towards paranoia.

One aspect of paranoia is the tendency to imagine plots around you; this is also the novelist's occupation and there is clearly a relationship between making fictions and imagining conspiracies. The difference is between consciousness in control of its own inventions, and consciousness succumbing to its inventions until they present themselves as perceptions. But the line between these two states of mind is inevitably a narrow one and a great deal of oscillation and overlap is common. Adopting Wiener's terms we can say that for a novelist looking back over the first half of the twentieth century the "Augustinian" vision of a world deprived of order in some parts more than in others could easily shade into the "Manichaean" vision of something demonically at work to annihilate all order, with phenomena such as Hitler and the atom bomb only among its more obvious agents.

Pynchon, I think, understands this very well and, while his novel *V.* contains a variety of plot-makers, he is in no sense committed to the plots they might make. It would be too glib to say that his is an "Augustinian" novel about "Manichaean" people; it would also be misleading, since the novelist is clearly inwardly affected by the Manichaeanism of his characters. . . . But he manages to preserve his distance, particularly by locating the main plotting instinct in one character, Stencil. He is the man who is trying to make the connections and links, and put together the story which might well have been Pynchon's novel. . . . The point is that by taking bits of history from different countries at different times during this century and putting them in the novel with no linear or causal relationship, Pynchon is able to explore the possibility that the plots men see may be their own inventions. The further implication of this — that such things as the concentration camps may be simply meaningless accidents — is responsible for the sudden depths of horror in the book.

The narrative material consists of episodes from history since 1899, and episodes in the lives of various people living in contemporary America called, as a group, the Whole Sick Crew. Just as the historical episodes tend to focus on various sieges, and chaotic violent events preceding or involved in the two world wars, so the episodes connected with modern America tend to focus on wild parties sinking into chaos and exhaustion which seem to reveal morphological similarities with the historical events not otherwise directly related to them. . . .

We may start by noting that while the endlessly ramifying and superimposed plots of the book defy summary, the general theme of the operation of entropy on every level serves to relate the disparate temporal and geographic material the book contains. Every situation reveals some new aspect of decay and decline, some move further into chaos or nearer death. The book is full of dead landscapes of every kind — from the garbage heaps of the modern world to the lunar barrenness of the actual desert. On every side there is evidence of the "assertion of the Inanimate." Renaissance cities seem to lose their glow and become leaden; great buildings progress towards dust; a man's car is disintegrating under tons of garage rubble. Benny Profane's late feeling that "things never should have come this far" is appropriately ominous if you allow the first word sufficient emphasis. For the proliferation of inert things is another way of hastening the entropic process. On all sides the environment is full of hints of exhaustion, extinction, dehumanization; and *V.* is a very American novel in as much as one feels that instead of the characters living *in* their environment, environment lives *through* the characters, who thereby tend to become figures illustrating a process. . . .

One common background is the accelerating release of power which Adams spoke of and foresaw. Man's ingenuity in this respect is kept in view by references to trains, planes, ships, all kinds of mechanical appliances and weapons of war. At the same time all these inventions are often more productive of destruction than anything else. At one point Pynchon simply lists the disasters recorded for a short period of time in an almanac, prefacing it with the generalization that at this time "the world started to run more and more afoul of the inanimate" (*V.*, 290/270). This points to perhaps the most inclusive theme of the book: not that man returns to the inanimate, since that is the oldest of truths, but that twentieth-century man seems to be dedicating himself to the annihilation of all animateness on a quite unprecedented scale, and with quite unanticipated inventiveness. . . .

But Pynchon would scarcely have needed to write so intricate a novel if his only intention was to show a graph of increasing destructiveness manifest in recent history. As he indicates, you can cull that from an almanac. What he shows — and here the juxtaposition of the historical and the personal dimensions is vital — is a growing tendency, discernible on all levels and in the most out-of-the-way pockets of modern history, for people to regard or use other people as objects, and, perhaps even more worryingly, for people to regard themselves as objects. There is in evidence a systematic and assiduously cultivated dehumanization of the human *by* the human. Just as the tourists in the book cut themselves off from the reality of the lands they pass through by burying themselves in Baedeker versions, so do most of the characters avoid confronting the human reality of other people, and of themselves, by all manner of depersonalizing strategies. If one theme of the book is the acceleration of entropy, another is the avoidance of human relationships based on reciprocal recognition of the reality of the partner. . . .

One agent in the book is killed because of a fatal lapse into humanity, an act of recognition. The description of his death points to a threshold which is a crucial one for the figures in the book. "Vision must be the last to go. There must be a nearly imperceptible line between an eye that reflects and an eye that receives" (*V.*, 94/82). Death is the moment when that line is irrevocably crossed, but the book shows innumerable ways in which that line is crossed while the body is still technically alive, thus producing a mobile object which reflects but does not receive. That this is related to the narcissistic habit of turning people into reflectors of one's own fantasies and obsessions is alluded to by a series of references to mirrors, culminating in the episode called "V. in love" which describes a Lesbian affair conducted entirely by mirrors. What unspeakable cruelties are made possible when that line is crossed and both self and others are experienced as inanimate objects, the various unpleasant scenes of sadism and sadomasochism, which recur throughout the book, serve to dramatize. The general falling away from the human which is under way is underlined by the transformations in the lady V. . . . Imagining V. as she might be at the present moment, Stencil envisages a completely plastic figure, triggered into action by miracles of technology. This is in line with the more general tendency towards fetishism and away from humanity detectable throughout.

The way in which people avoid their own reality (or are refused it) is paralleled in the book by the way in which events are experienced as staged episodes in a meaninglessly repetitious masquerade. On the political, as on the personal, level role-playing has preempted the possibility of real experience, leaving only symbols and games. History is as "stencillized" as the people who compose it, and the result is the theatricalization of reality on a massive scale. Thus history becomes a scenario which the participants are unable to rewrite or avoid. Once again, we find a vision of people being trapped inside an unreality which seems to be the result of some nameless conspiratorial fabrication; humans are akin to props in a cruel and dehumanizing play by author or authors unknown. (Of course Pynchon is aware of the additional irony that these characters are also caught up in a play arranged by *him* — the affliction of his characters is the condition of his form.)

In this world there is very little chance of any genuine communication. Language has suffered an inevitable decline in the mouths of these stencillized and objectified figures. Rachel Owlglass, the figure who more than any other seems to harbour a genuine capacity for love, is reduced to speaking to her car in "MG words"; while Benny Profane, who seems to want to love, feels his vocabulary is made up of nothing but wrong words. A foreign girl called Paola is presented as a person who has retained her capacity for direct emotion, and she seems to speak "Nothing but proper nouns. The girl lived proper nouns. Persons, places. No things. Had anyone told her about things?" (*V.*, 51/40). In a world in which the human is rapidly being replaced by things, this quaint linguistic limitation offers the possibility of an enviable immunity from the tendency towards a reification of people which is inherent in the prevailing language. At the same time, this kind of restricted language may be put to a very different purpose, as the Whole Sick Crew reveals. They play at verbalizing endless possible versions of things. They use mainly proper nouns, literary allusions, philosophical abstractions, and they put them together like building-blocks. "This sort of arranging and rearranging was Decadence, but the exhaustion of all possible permutations was death" (*V.*, 298/277). . . .

But if the characters in the book seldom truly talk to each other, they often look at each other. As might be expected, various forms of voyeurism are part of the normal behaviour patterns of a world where any attempt at human inter-subjectivity has been replaced by the disposition to regard people as objects — inside the field of vision but outside the range of sympathy, if indeed any such range exists. Eyes, straining or blank and dead, are emphasized throughout. The sailor whose main joy is to photograph his friends while they are having sexual intercourse is only one of many whose most intense relationships to reality are detached and impotent stares. Another reason why so many characters live in, and by, mirrors, and indeed at one point are said to be living in "mirror time," is that they experience life only as spectacle. Voyeurism is another way of evading true selfhood and denying or avoiding the possibility of love. Most of the characters "retreat" from the threat of love when it presents itself, and even the sympathetic Benny wastes himself in avoiding dependencies, and disengaging himself from any field of gathering emotional force. It might be added that Pynchon finds it difficult to suggest what genuine love would be like in this world. Some characters from older civilizations and cultures seem to have retained an ability to love. But the guarded maxim of the black jazz musician, McClintic Sphere, "Keep cool, but care" (*V.*, 366/342–343), is about as much genuine emotion as the book seems to allow. As such it is unconvincing. . . .

Moreover, in the main, people seek to avoid caring. One girl specifically yearns to become like a rock, and a state of emotional impermeability is sought by many others. Just as the main characters move towards the rock of Malta, so more generally the human race seems to be hastening to return to "rockhood." Indeed in Malta we read that manhood is increasingly defined in terms of rockhood. It is part of the basic ambiguity of Malta as described in this book that while on the one level it is an image of an island of life under siege, attacked by the levelling bombs of the Germans, and constantly eroded by the sea, on another level it is an image of a central point of inanimate rock and death drawing people back to that inert state. The Epilogue describes how the ship carrying Stencil's father was suddenly sucked under by a freak waterspout just off Malta, leaving a dead level sea which gave no sign of what now lies beneath the flat surface — this concludes the book.

One way and another, then, everything is sinking. Mehemet, a sage friend of Stencil's father, points out cheerfully, " 'The only change is towards death. . . . Early and late we are in decay' " (*V.*, 460/433). . . . We are always in decay: the question is, is there a plot in the universal rot? Stencil, son of Stencil, is, like his father, inclined to detect plots. A dentist in the book named Eigenvalue regards Stencil's belief in a plot as being like an amalgam to fill "a breach in the protective enamel." He reflects that teeth do indeed decay, but that is no reason to conceive of some conscious organization conspiring against the life of the pulp. "Yet we have men like Stencil, who must go about grouping the world's random caries into cabals" (*V.*, 153/139). It is precisely Stencil's compulsion to group caries into cabals which makes him one of the central figures in the book, and we should now consider his dominant obsession.

This obsession is the quest for V. V. is an elusive female spy/ anarchist who appears in one of her multiple identities in all these episodes; she once seduced Stencil's father, thus becoming, it seems, Stencil's mother. Her names have varied — Virginia, Victoria, Veronica Manganese, Vera Meroving — and at the end Stencil leaves for Sweden to follow up a remote clue connected with one Mme Viola. Stencil's quest is thus linear through time; but as the book shows — and indeed as Stencil realizes as he turns this way and that, following up peripheral clues — there are innumerable Vs, a point made on the first page of the book which shows a V-shaped cluster of innumerable smaller Vs. . . . So from one point of view Stencil has far too much to go on, since he is bound to find clues everywhere — a fact he recognizes near the end: "V. by this time was a remarkably scattered concept" (*V.*, 389/364). Indeed, as this "concept" expands to include ever more manifestations of V., and as opposites such as love and death, the political right and left, start to converge in this inclusiveness, it points to that ultimate disappearance of differences and loss of distinctions which is the terminal state of the entropic process. If V. can mean everything it means nothing.

On the other hand Stencil really has very little to go on. Most of what he has is inference. "He doesn't know who she is, nor what she is." Near the end the suspicion is strengthened that all it adds up to is "the recurrence of an initial and a few dead objects" (*V.*, 445/419). Stencil himself is aware that although he pursues V. as a libertine pursues spread thighs (the comparison is explicit), his quest may all be "an adventure of the mind, in the tradition of *The Golden Bough* or *The White Goddess*" (*V.*, 61/50). Stencil's father had strange fever dreams of exploring for something in his own brain. Stencil is the copy of his father; the quest is his legacy. The historical melodrama of international interconnections which he puts together may be only the map of his own obsessions. At the same time, the sieges and wars were real enough, with or without mysterious links, and Stencil is representative enough to be called "the century's child" (*V.*, 52/42).

He is also representative of many American heroes in as much as he was powerfully attracted to sleep and inertia, wandering around in a slothful directionlessness, before he came across references to V. in his father's papers. In the suggestiveness of this entirely documentary stimulus, Stencil finds his motive for motion. . . . He suspects that he needs "a mystery, any sense of pursuit to keep active a borderline metabolism" (*V.*, 385/362), but such self-knowledge does not obviate the need to pursue the phantom he has at least half-created. The book recognizes that such fantasies may be necessary to maintaining consciousness and purposive motion; yet it reveals the solipsism that is implicit in them as well, for one of the subjects of Pynchon's book is the inability of people to love anyone outside their own fantasy projections.

Stencil is the key figure — one can hardly speak of characters — in the book. The O.E.D. defines a stencil as "a hole in a card which when washed over with colour leaves a figure"; "stencilling" is defined as "a process by which you can produce patterns and designs." Like the lady V. who shows inexhaustible dexterity in handling her different appearances, Stencil is pluralistic in his projection of himself. He also goes in for disguises, finding some relief from the pain of his dilemma in "impersonation." Like children and like Henry Adams in the *Education* (Pynchon again makes the comparison explicit) Stencil always refers to himself in the third person. . . . He thinks of himself as "quite purely He who looks for V. (and whatever impersonations that might involve)." This definition may mean that he is in fact a vacancy, filled in with the colours of his obsession, not a self, but in truth a stencil. And all his techniques of self-duplication and self-extension may be construed as protective screens for avoiding direct engagement with reality.

Stencil's obsession is with a structure of inferences based on an old dossier, cold clues, scraps and fragments from history's littoral which he has transformed into the strange flowers of his fantasy. . . . Like Callisto in "Entropy," Stencil lives in a hothouse of hermetically sealed fantasy where the past is arrested, as in a museum, immobilized in memory pictures to create an inner climate impervious to the inclemency of outer weather. Paradoxically, those objects which fed Stencil's obsession and gave him an illusory sense of vitality sealed him off as well, turning him into a stencil with a hothouse mind. Like a stencil he will admit no configurations of experience that cannot be shaped into the pattern of his fantasy. Like a hothouse, his identity is a protected enclosure, given definition by the exotic growths artificially fostered within it.

If Stencil is trapped in the hothouse of the past, Benny Profane is astray in the streets of the present. The book opens with him walking down a street and we last see him running down a street in Malta. The street is his natural domain, for he is a rootless wanderer, as unaware of clues and indifferent to patterns as Stencil is obsessed by them. He says expressly that he has learned nothing from his peregrinations up and down the streets of the world, except perhaps to fear them. They fuse into a "single abstracted street" which causes him nightmares without yielding him insights. The only job he can do — and that not well — is street repair work. Devoid of all sense of positive direction he reacts passively to any puff of momentum that happens to touch him; by himself he cannot initiate or construct anything — no projects, no relationships, no dreams. His movement is a long flight from nowhere in particular to nowhere in particular.

Himself rather a faded copy of the traditional *picaro* and *schlemiel* figures combined, he is almost a cartoon reduction of another of the century's children, for if Stencil is he who searches for V., Profane is who experiences the street; "The street of the 20th Century, at whose far end or turning — we hope — is some sense of home or safety. But no guarantees. . . . But a street we must walk" (*V.*, 323/303). . . .

It is in the street that the various destructive energies involved in the history of this century erupt — from riots in Florence or Malta to a gang fight in contemporary New York. Throughout the various street episodes, historical and contemporary, there is the sustained feeling that the walls, buildings and shopfronts are an insubstantial façade, that the street itself and all man-made structures are temporary illusions. ("The city is only the desert in disguise," thinks one character in Cairo. "Nothing was coming. Nothing was already here.") . . .

The fact that it is in the street that revolutionary mobs pursue their demands for change prompts Stencil's father to write in his journal: "we carry on the business of this century with an intolerable double vision. Right and Left; the hothouse and the street. The Right can only live and work hermetically, in the hothouse of the past, while outside the Left prosecute their affairs in the streets by manipulated mob violence. And cannot live but in the dreamscape of the future" (*V.*, 469/440). The implication of this is that all political thinking — and by extension all man's mental projections — is either a dream of the past or a dream of the future. By this account man himself can never properly occupy present time. The street and the hothouse are the dreams by which man avoids confronting that nothingness which is the shapeless truth behind the structured fantasy of human history. As with so many apparent opposites, the street and the hothouse meet and merge in V. She is equally at home in both of them. And almost her last reported words are: " 'How pleasant to watch Nothing' " (*V.*, 487/459).

An important part of the intricate spatial geography of the book is that area which lies under the street — the sewers in which Benny Profane hunts alligators under New York, in which Father Fairing converts and seduces his rats. References to channels and tunnels occur in the description of the strange land of Vheissu and the subway travel in modern New York. Hints at the possible existence of an inherited reservoir of primordial knowledge suggest that a deliberate Jungian dimension has been added. The notion that the unconscious nourishes art, even if the unconscious is comparable to a sort of primeval sewer, and that there is much to be gained by descending into our dreams, is so customary by now that one can see that Pynchon has gone some way to turning it into dark farce — Benny and the alligators. At the same time he seems to want to preserve the notion that somehow it is more "real" under the street than in it. When Benny finally has to end his job we read: "What peace there had been was over. He had to come back to the surface, the dream-street" (*V.*, 151/137).

The far-ranging geography of the book provides a composite

image of the various areas of human consciousness. The street is the zone of the waking, planning consciousness which, unable to endure the meaninglessness of the absolute present, projects plans into the future or finds plans in the past. The hothouse is the realm of memory where the mind is sealed up in the secretions of its reveries over the past. The sewer or under-the-street (also compared to under the sea) is that area of dream, the unconscious, perhaps the ancestral memory, in which one may find a temporary peace or oblivion, and into which the artist must descend, but where fantasy can run so rampant that you may start seeing rats as saints and lovers if you remain down there too long. Indeed all three areas suggest the human compulsion or need to construct fantasies, as though each level of consciousness was another form of dreaming.

The modes of motion which prevail in the street are yo-yoing (in the present) and tourism (in the past). The historical episodes are full of references to people living in a "Baedeker world." Tourists are "the Street's own." . . . When Stencil (supertourist) and Profane (super yo-yo) converge on Malta without quite understanding their motives for doing so, we read: "Malta alone drew them, a clenched fist around a yo-yo string." The illusory purposiveness of Stencil's travels, and the manifest purposelessness of Profane's meanderings, both serve to illuminate the condition of movement bereft of all significance except the elemental one of postponing inanimateness. Both modes of motion, in fact, accelerate entropy, just as they both serve to bring Stencil and Benny Profane to the rock of Malta.

As well as writing about a quester and a drifter, Pynchon writes about all kinds of spies and agents. Their epistemological stance — looking for possible clues to possible plots — is only a projection of that of the novelist himself. Perhaps, indeed, they create the patterns of hostility they set out to trace; perhaps, too, does the novelist. Stencil's ingenious linked detections spread back in time and across space. Is this creative vision which sees a truth beneath the drifting contingencies of life; or is it a paranoid fantasy, an obsession akin to an oblivion? If the latter, then is Benny Profane's uncoordinated empiricism of the eye, which looks out and sees no plots and learns nothing, true vision? We can hardly expect to adjudicate finally between them. . . .

The various agents and plotters in the historical episodes while planning their own cabals are always worried that they may in fact be taking part in a larger cabal of which they have no knowledge. Stencil always finds some form of V. connected with some kind of conspiracy, if not a plotter then the cause of plots. Whatever V. might be, Stencil affirms "that his quarry fitted in with The Big One, the century's master cabal." Stencil's father had found that if people cannot find some sort of explanation for "this abstract entity The Situation" (*V.*, 189/173) they "simply run amok." He is implying that for most people, worse than the idea of a master cabal is the notion of no plots at all. One character writes that life really has only one single lesson to teach: "that there is more accident to it than a man can ever admit to in a lifetime and stay sane" (*V.*, 321/300). . . .

In one of the incidents set in South-West Africa there is a character named Mondaugen who has the job of studying "sferic" signals. At first they come through as mere noise, but then he thinks he detects a regularity of patterning which might be "a kind of code." Out of some instinctive wariness he holds back from trying to break the code, but someone else works out a solution. Extracting certain signals from the overall noise, he demonstrates that they add up to Mondaugen's own name, plus the statement DIE WELT IST ALLES DAS DER FALL IST. This of course is the opening proposition in Wittgenstein's *Tractatus* (a proposition, incidentally, which seems to haunt contemporary American writers). As a coded message it would be the supreme irony, like discovering that the secret is that there is no secret. The assertion that the world is everything that is the case repudiates the very notion of plots, and arguably leaves things and events standing in precisely describable inexplicability. As the book shows, human instinct pulls in the other direction: towards cabalism, or demonism, or projected fantasies, and away from the rarified objective clarities attainable through linguistic analysis. . . .

. . . The notion of painting being a compensatory activity for the general decline of things is taken up overtly when Mehemet tells a rather unlikely tale of coming across a strange sight in the middle of the sea — a man "alone on the sea at nightfall, painting the side of a sinking ship" (*V.*, 460/433). The implication is made explicit. We do cover the blank surfaces of our sinking world, and then live within our paintings; as D. H. Lawrence said, we live in the paintings we put on the underside of our umbrellas. For Lawrence this was a suffocation, a deprivation, and he considered it the artist's job to come along and slash a gap in the protective umbrella and let in reality. But in Pynchon's world there is a more ominous feeling that if you did cut through the painting a something or a nothing more frightening might be revealed. In one of the historical episodes there is a plot to steal Botticelli's "Birth of Venus." The thief is entranced by the "gorgeous surface" of the painting, but as he starts to cut it out of the frame a great horror grows in him and he abandons the project. This horror at stripping away the coloured surface is connected with something that a character named Hugh Godolphin told him about the strange land of Vheissu, and we should now consider that unmapped country.

Hugh Godolphin found Vheissu on one of his surveying trips for the British Army; his description of the journey and the land itself reads like a mixture of Borges and Conrad. There are no maps to Vheissu, but it is the country which is really at the heart of the book. As Godolphin describes it to Victoria, it might seem like any other remote region except for the changing colours which are " 'its raiment, perhaps its skin.' " When Victoria asks what is beneath, he admits that he wondered whether the place had a soul. What this meant for Hugh Godolphin apparently was a determination somehow to return to Vheissu and find " 'what was beneath her skin.' " Making his way to the pole he digs for his answer, and when he does penetrate the surface what he finds is — " 'Nothing. . . . It was Nothing I saw' " (*V.*, 204/188). He continues his account: " 'If Eden was the creation of God, God only knows what evil created Vheissu. The skin which had wrinkled through my nightmares was all there had ever been. Vheissu itself, a gaudy dream. Of what the Antarctic in this world is closest to: a dream of annihilation' " (*V.*, 206/190). That last definition is suitably vague as to whether the whole place is Godolphin's dream, or whether in itself it is a dream of annihilation. . . . It is part of the intention of the book to suggest that the world may now be engaged in making actual a mass dream of annihilation, submitting reality to a nihilistic fantasy.

In Malta, in a final talk with Godolphin, V. reveals her similarity to Vheissu further; for, having expressed her delight at watching Nothing, she goes on to say how much she would like to have a whole wardrobe of different shaped feet in a rainbow range of colours. V. *is* all those constantly changing coloured shapes which make up the dazzling and enchanting surface of Vheissu. She is also the void beneath the decoration, the Nothing at the heart of the dream. We need all those coloured dreams to get us along the street — which may also be a dream. At the start we see Benny walking down East Main Street, underneath a row of lamps "receding in an asymmetric V to the east where it's dark and there are no more bars" (*V.*, 10/2). We last see Benny apparently making a bid to leave the street for the last time, this time in Malta. "Presently, sudden and in silence, all illumination in Valletta, houselight and streetlight, was extinguished. Profane and Brenda continued to run through the abruptly absolute night, momentum alone carrying them towards the edge of Malta, and the Mediterranean beyond" (*V.*, 455/428). V. is whatever lights you *to* the end of the street: she is also the dark annihilation waiting *at* the end of the street.

What Pynchon manages to suggest is that the fantasies we build to help us to live represent, in fact, an infiltration of that death we think we are so eager to postpone. They represent an avoidance of reality, by substituting for it a fetishistic construction. One man in the book has a private planetarium which is a highly complex mechanism of moons and planets, pulleys and chains, and yet which is, after all, "a parody of space." If our constructed fantasies are effectively parodies of reality, then this has certain implications for the self-conscious author of the overall fiction of the book. For a particular literary style is a construction analogous to that private planetarium, a personal way of organizing things in space, and thus to some extent a parody of it. . . .

[65]

In this connection we should note Pynchon's systematic stylistic evocation (often parodic) of previous writers as he deals with different episodes in different times and places. Conrad, Evelyn Waugh and Lawrence Durrell are in evidence in many of the historical and colonial episodes; Melville, Henry Adams, Nathanael West, Djuna Barnes, Faulkner and Dashiell Hammett are among the American writers whose work is in some way detectable; Joyce and Nabokov are clearly present in the way the book is organized; and there is one of Borges's mysterious kingdoms at the heart of the book. This is not to suggest that the book is merely a pastiche, a collage of scrambled sources. Pynchon's point seems to be to remind the reader that there is no one writable "truth" about history and experience, only a series of versions: it always comes to us "stencillized." In such a way he can indicate that he is well aware of the ambiguities of his own position, constructing another fiction and at the same time underlining the fallacies involved in all formal plottings and organizations of space.

In addition I think it is part of Pynchon's intention to demonstrate that the various styles of writers of this century who, in a sense, have imposed their private dreams on us are like those iridescent surfaces with which we adorn the walls of our galleries and cover the countries of our dreams. The attendant implication is that under all this decorative sheen there lies the cold truth of the void. One result of this is, I think, that Pynchon himself has written, no doubt deliberately, what amounts to a "hollow" book. . . .

It is worth pointing out here the connection between problems of narration and problems of identity in the contemporary American novel. In *V.* there is a character called Fausto, a man of letters who indeed writes his own book within the book. It is a sort of apologia, and he says this about his activity: "We can justify any apologia simply by calling life a successive rejection of personalities" (*V.*, 306/286). Where Fausto divides himself up into "successive identities" which he has taken on and then rejected, Pynchon takes on and rejects successive styles in his book. For both, this is a way of seeing past all the fictions which fix the world and the word in particular patterns and styles, and as such it is an activity very common among contemporary American writers. But whether man can live beyond all fictions, whether, even when faced by the pathos and mockery of the dream dump, it would be desirable, let alone possible, to put an end to man's addiction to fantasy, is not explored. Perhaps the advice of Mark Twain's Satan to mankind is the relevant consideration here — " 'Dream other dreams, and better!' "

Pentecost, Promiscuity, and Pynchon's V.: From the Scaffold to the Impulsive

W. T. Lhamon, Jr.

Pynchon's verbal complexities astound and confound, amaze and bewilder, because his mixed modes concern the ultimate formlessness of a world that for a decade now he has urged as much as described. Everything bears, and bears on, everything else in Pynchon's coming world; everything discovers some grosser or more petite example of itself; everything leads simultaneously to hope and despair. All these pressures make linear communication inadequate, chronology a joke, and organization destructive. Even the status of life itself is moot.

Since Pynchon calls to issue not merely a metaphorical quality of life, but life's salt origins and biological coherence, the most frequent entrance into his fiction is through the concept of entropy. Indeed, an early story was named just that — "Entropy" — and he has used the concept pervasively in all his work.[1] Yet R. W. B. Lewis has remarked that *V.* is well within the long apocalyptic tradition of American fiction.[2] How can Pynchon be persuaded of entropy's irreversibility and simultaneously of a second coming? How can he claim a winding down of the world and its winding up to spirit?

He manages these, in fact, by slipping beyond simple apocalyptic themes to a reimagining for these days of Apocalyptic as a literary genre — which he also parodies, as he parodies everything. *V.* and the rest of Pynchon's novels "behave" as if the End were past and most of the world didn't even know it, so needed an exemplary convincing. The persuasion largely consists of approximating tongued speech — the voice of apocalypse — and of an anti-organization that may be named Pentecostal. *V.* represents a mode in which the sacred and the profane are so profoundly mixed that an account which aims to experience the novel's primary subversions must attempt to discuss them together.

Pentecost is like entropy in its frightfulness, in its total opposition to customary ways of being in and thinking about the world, and in its position of both finality and gradualness. Pentecost and entropy, Pentecostal and entropic: the final states are imaginable, but not yet fully here; rather, everything is slipping toward them, but Pentecostal and entropic *moments* are what we presently experience. Pentecost is not, however, the same as entropy, even metaphorically.

Entropy, the second law of thermodynamics, is a scientific term which should strike fear in everyone. Entropy evokes death, a state in which no energy is useful, and all life has guttered out into undifferentiable soup. The inanimate, through entropy, merges with the animate. Pentecost is a religious term which strikes fear and loathing in some, but means ultimate life to those who accept it. The spirit, at Pentecost, merges with the profane. Pentecost is as formless as entropy; but if entropy describes the ultimate collapse into material, Pentecost describes an ultimate ascent into the spiritual. They are the same event, but embedded in vastly different assumptions. There is an interface between apocalypse-as-entropy and a Pentecostal-end-of-the-world, and on either side there are names to call the other; but, stated objectively, Pentecost is a version of the state of entropy which takes what is, and celebrates it. Pentecost is entropy with value added — the value of communication. That is, Pentecostal entropy is a lively death — a death which maintains expressiveness in tongues, though not in any familiar mode.

Dealing most natively with language, Pentecost is therefore a concept perhaps more suited for a novelist than is entropy. It might be for this reason that Pynchon never mentions the word "entropy" in *V.*, though he repeatedly writes of Pentecost and tongues. Still, Pentecostal imagery serves him more widely than for fiction-making. If entropy is the carnivore Pynchon looses on literature and the humanities, Pentecost is the dove he holds up to science and the doom-sayers. And it is also his further rebuke to the standing traditions of literature, for Pentecost is a phenomenon of the preterite: it is the delirium tremens of the downtrodden, and a threat to logical, rational, or analytical structures. As such, the ecstasy of tongues has always been a disputed phenomenon, often still repudiated by the learned, just as it was at its inception. Luke described the first Christian tongues in the Bible:

> And when the day of Pentecost was fully come, [the apostles] were all with one accord in one place. And suddenly there came a sound from heaven as of a rushing mighty wind, and it filled all the house where they were sitting. And there appeared unto them cloven tongues like as of fire, and it sat upon each of them. And they were all filled with the Holy Ghost, and began to speak with other tongues, as the Spirit gave them utterance. And there were dwelling at Jerusalem Jews, devout men, out of every nation under heaven. Now when this was noised abroad, the multitude came together, and were confounded, because that every man heard them speak in his own language. . . . And they were all amazed, and were in doubt, saying one to another, What meaneth this? Others mocking said, These men are full of new wine. (Acts 2:1–6, 12, 13)

Some onlookers were astounded, some confounded, but Peter stood up and said the disciples were not drunk; it was, he pointed out, only 9 A.M. Rather, the Holy Ghost had come among them, as Joel had prophesied. Here was the Lord showing wonders in heaven and signs on earth; whoever called on the Lord would be saved.

Despite Peter's speech, however, to some observers talkers of tongues have always been full of new wine, always *infra dig.* The apostle Paul wrote later to the Corinthians that although no man could claim to speak in tongues better than he, still, to talk the tongues was to speak with God and not to edify a single doubter. Doubters come upon a congregation talking in tongues, he wrote,

would "say that ye are mad" (I Corinthians 14:23). Paul's admonition follows his lyrical but somewhat patronizing advice:
"When I was a child, I spake as a child, I thought as a child: but
when I became a man, I put away childish things" (I Corinthians
13:11). Brilliant organizer that he was, Paul wanted people to
know God by reason; the people were finding Him through
childish, emotional, impulsive in-breathing of the "rushing mighty
wind." Rather than talk tongues, Paul would have Christians
interpret rationally, would have them, that is, edify: "Let all
things be done unto edifying" (I Corinthians 14:26).

Against the egalitarian tone of tongues, Paul's letters raise the
voice of hierarchy: "Let all things be done decently and in order"
(I Corinthians 14:40). Paul stands for the visible and respectable
church with its order, edification, and reason; the tongues, Peter,
and Pentecost represent the direct apprehension of a subversive
world in this one's midst. Paul's hierarchical language supports
linear structure; Peter's tongues suggest patterns of immediacy.
Furthermore, the close association between the Jewish (Shabuoth)
and Christian Pentecosts reveals that tongues are the voice of
common, passed-over, preterite people. Christian Pentecost is the
seventh Sunday, so the forty-ninth day, after Easter; Jewish
Pentecost, exactly reflecting the name's Greek etymology, marked
fifty days from the beginning of Passover.[3] At the Jewish celebration, people brought the early harvest fruits to the Temple; at
the first Christian Pentecost, multitudes converted to the early
church. Paul's routinization of the people's charismatic impulse
came later.

But the routinization came well before the events of _V._ The
novel is framed first and last with episodes emphasizing the need
for radical breaks with edifying discourse and customary modes
of understanding. _V._ begins with the words "Christmas Eve" —
an originating, charismatic moment in Western history. But the
Christmas Eve of 1955, Pynchon proceeds to show, is thoroughly
embedded in the advanced decline of its own tradition: " 'Neon
signs of red and green/ Shine upon the friendly scene, / . . .
Santa's bag is filled with all your dreams come true: / Nickel
beers that sparkle like champagne, / Barmaids who all love to

screw' " (*V.*, 10/1).[4] Nevertheless, from the midst of this standard decline may arise the means for combatting it. The scene goes
on, that is, to tell the story of an engineman named Ploy who has
just changed ships from the destroyer U.S.S. *Scaffold* to the mine-
sweeper *Impulsive*, from a ship which destroys to a ship which
saves. While he was on the *Scaffold*, the Navy had decided to
remove all his teeth — an arbitrary decision which, in the hyped
"logic" of *V.*, means that Poly "saw apocalyse, screamed lengthy
obscenities, . . . roamed ghastly" and tried to "kick officers in
the teeth" (*V.*, 11/3).

Ploy's skirmish is the first in the novel's war between those
who try to edify and those who scream with their tongues, a war
which corresponds to the struggle between that part of the
church buttressed by dogma and that part sustained by impulsive tongues. Ploy's transfer to the Impulsive gives birth to the
novel. And on the last page the impulsive element closes the
novel, this time more somberly: "Draw a line from Malta to
Lampedusa. Call it a radius. Somewhere in that circle, on the
evening of the tenth, a waterspout appeared [and destroyed the
elder Stencil's boat in the] Mediterranean whose subsequent surface phenomena . . . showed nothing at all of what came to lie
beneath, that quiet June day" (*V.*, 492/463). The arbitrary language of the surface ("Call it a radius"), the complacently irrelevant details ("on the evening of the tenth"), and the reliance on
linear mathematics ("Draw a line") finally do not suffice, for
they show nothing of what has come to lie beneath. Below is
another increasingly important world which Stencil ignores at his
peril, and which destroys him just as he is beginning to pay it
attention. Because it has thrust out from under the bureaucrat's
blotter, the impulsive experience requires an accordingly different
syntax to describe and express it. Consequently, Pynchon has
turned to a linguistic mode which has been under the rose all
along: the fecund language of tongues.

Just as the novel's entropic instances do not mean the world is
yet wholly entropic, the bulk of *V.* is para-Pentecostal, slipping
near tongues. Pynchon mentions or employs some twenty languages or argots, including the MG language Rachel speaks to

her car, mock Eskimo, Maltese, and Tuareg. In fact, the novel often seems "a tourist's confusion of tongues" (*V.*, 140/126). Paola knows "scraps of all tongues" (*V.*, 14/6); Profane hopes that the alligator he is stalking will suddenly "receive the gift of tongues" (*V.*, 122/110); old Godolphin hopes the objects in his room will "somehow find tongue and rally round him" (*V.*, 183/167). With all this attention to language, and specifically to the language of the Pentecost, the feeling through the bulk of the novel is of a longing for transcendence, and an imminence of the spirit, but of no chance for it to occur: signs of the spirit swim "over the crowd, like a tongue on Pentecost" (*V.*, 92/79), but they are not yet revealed to the people. Most of *V.* leaves the characters at the surface, in straight and linear discourse; in short, it leaves them profane. And the character by that name, Benny Profane, has a vocabulary "made up of nothing but wrong words" (*V.*, 137/123).

The pressure of tongues against "wrong words" is one of the novel's topics. Straight language, like Christmas, has deteriorated and Benny is left with no adequate speech. He moves in the direction of tongues, however, as he becomes more and more paranoid. Paranoia is another indication in Pynchon's work of an alternative world beyond the customary one, for paranoids read signs of mystery and force that philistines never suspect. Paranoids are on to something, some sub rosa and unedifying connectedness that no philistine's grammar can accommodate. In fact, Pynchon's latest novel, *Gravity's Rainbow*, flatly states that the key "that will bring us back" is somewhere "among the wastes of the world" (*GR*, 525). Ultimately, therefore, by forcing insight and grace into waste piles, the elect necessitate their own reversal. Supposedly, bureaucracy and organization mediate between elect and preterite, ruler and ruled, God and man. But Pynchon's bureaucracies buffer professionals from grace.

After their charismatic beginnings, institutions in his fiction have an autonomous momentum that impels them not only past trauma but also past new beginnings, allowing only decadent old age to be their end. For example, the "professionals who'd survived" the Armageddon of World War I "had received no blessing, no gift of tongues" (*V.*, 461/434). And Foppl comes early to see his life and that of his European friends in Southwest Africa as a "Popular Front against deceptively unpolitical and apparently minor enemies, enemies that would be with him to the grave" (*V.*, 274/255). Also, the Baedeker tourist organization has "if not created then at least described to its fullest" a "two-dimensional . . . coordinate system" which is "supranational, like the Catholic Church, and perhaps the most absolute communion we know on earth: for be its members American, German, Italian, whatever, the Tour Eiffel, Pyramids, and Campanile all evoke identical responses from them; their Bible is clearly written and does not admit of private interpretation; they share the same landscapes, suffer the same inconveniences; live by the same pellucid time-scale" (*V.*, 409/384). Therefore, two-dimensional organization inculcates elect discourse by throwing out preterite insight and preterite words — that is, preterite discourse. But the grammars of elect and bureaucratic survival constitute the terms of their peril.

Lending the light touch to this centrally elaborate part of Pynchon's thinking is McClintic Sphere. And he is also the one who suggests the difficult way out. McClintic sings: " 'Gwine cross de Jordan/ Ecclesiastically:/ Flop, flip, once I was hip.' " And then says to Paola-Ruby: " 'what happened after the war? That war, the world flipped. But come '45, and they flopped. Here in Harlem they flopped. Everything got cool — no love, no hate, no worries, no excitement. Every once in a while, though, somebody flips back. Back to where he can love . . .' " (*V.*, 293/273). Clearly, McClintic is going "home," and since he's traveling "Ecclesiastically" he's taking others with him back to the wails and horns and (conceivably) tongues of the battle of Jericho. The problem puzzling him is that it took a war to make love possible, takes death to make life possible.

That problem runs right through Pynchon's fiction: Ploy's kicking officers in the teeth begins this first novel, Inverarity's death yields Oedipa a new life in the second novel, V-2 rockets falling on London give Slothrop the peculiar sort of life he has in the third. And, as we shall see, the bombs raining destruction on Malta give both death and life to Fausto Maijstral and to V. herself. The way out for McClintic is to occupy the interface between flip and flop, hip and cool: "keep cool, but care" (*V*., 366/342–343). However, only three characters in the first three novels are able to follow that credo: Oedipa Maas, Enzian, and possibly Paola. Fausto writes to Paola: "Did the two forces neutralize and leave you on the lonely promontory between two worlds? Can you still look both ways, child? If so you stand at an enviable vantage" (*V*., 331/310). The creed is very difficult to practice because the interface is minute and thus only theoretically inhabitable. In practice, one is either cool with edifying discourse or flipped into tongues.

Partly because the ecstasy of tongues is elusive and nearly impossible to warrant, and partly because the dominant mode of edification is historically just at its breaking point, there is no mass conversion in *V*. In fact, only two characters eventually receive the gift of tongues. And no one is even aware of that until the novel's end: the Epilogue returns the novel to 1919, Malta, a younger V., and Sidney Stencil's "fever dream" about history (*V*., 471/433). When Demivolt interrupts Stencil's dream, the hint is that V. herself is the Paraclete, or Holy Spirit:

> The matter of a Paraclete's coming, the comforter, the dove; the tongues of flame, the gift of tongues: Pentecost. Third Person of the Trinity. None of it was implausible to Stencil. The Father had come and gone. In political terms, the Father was the Prince; the single leader, the dynamic figure whose virtù used to be a determinant of history. This had degenerated to the Son, genius of the liberal love-feast which had produced 1848 and lately the overthrow of the Czars. What next? What Apocalypse?
>
> Especially on Malta, a matriarchal island. Would the Paraclete be also a mother? Comforter, true. But what gift of communication could ever come from a woman. . . .
>
> Enough, lad, he told himself. You're in dangerous waters. Come out, come out.
>
> "Don't turn around now," Demivolt broke in conversationally, "but it's she. At Maijstral's table."
>
> When Stencil did turn around he saw only a vague figure in an evening cape, her face shadowed by an elaborate, probably Parisian bonnet.
>
> "That is Veronica Manganese." (*V*., 472/444)

Veronica Manganese, of course, is V.

Demivolt's comment is characteristic of the demi-revelations in the novel. Here probably both men see only that "she" is the strange Veronica Manganese. Nevertheless, the interjection must have momentarily startled Stencil because the logical antecedents of "she" — going back up the ladder of his mind — are woman, tongues, dove, comforter, and Paraclete. V., then, is as ambiguous as the tongues: are the apostles profanely drunk, or sacredly transfigured? Is Veronica Manganese a conspirator or comforter?

Despite the way it strikes gloomy Stencil, the metaphor of historical passage from the Father's virtù, through the Son's liberalism, to the Paraclete's inarticulate apocalypse is not all negative. A bit later in the chapter a young and gloating Father Fairing will dismiss Stencil's historical construct with the confident tones of an old and gloating apostle Paul: " 'Any tug in the direction of anarchy is anti-Christian. . . . The Church has matured, after all. Like a young person she has passed from promiscuity to authority. You are nearly two millennia out-of-date' " (*V.*, 479–480/451). However, the reverse of his judgment is true. The Church instituted hierarchy, but the coming Paraclete will abolish its authority and return "promiscuity." Promiscuity is the anarchist's dream and bureaucrat's anathema: to be promiscuous is to be pro mix, indiscrete, and fused with the world; it's the condition which the tongues nurture, and from which they flower. From the angle of tongues, promiscuity is positive.

The trend to promiscuity is not merely anti-Christian, but against all control, toward a loosening of all repressive structures, toward more communication. Therefore, Hugh Godolphin tells Vera Meroving, the V. of 1922: " 'our Vheissus are no longer our own, or even confined to a circle of friends; they're public property' " (*V.*, 248/230). The care of history is moving away from professionals to plain people: "politics would become progressively more democratized, more thrown into the hands of amateurs" (*V.*, 489/461). The general move is from secrecy to visibility: Fausto recorded in his journal how the bombardment of Malta exposed to the public gaze even the most sacrosanct room in the English Club — its toilet (*V.*, 333/312). The people became privy even to the privy.

Pynchon's work is also increasingly promiscuous in each successive novel. In *V.* (1963), all revelations are hidden, double, though growing less so as the novel proceeds. In *The Crying of Lot 49* (1966), Oedipa more compactly encounters a greater rush of signals — scrawled on walls and sidewalks, printed on stamps, hidden in obscure plays. She's never sure, but always surer, of a disinherited alternate reality, whose "revelation [may] grow larger than she and assume her to itself" (*Lot 49*, 166/125). In *Gravity's Rainbow* (1973), everything announces, testifies, instructs, and spells itself out: Pensiero reads shivers, Bummer reads reefers, Thanatz reads whip scars, and Slothrop reads mandalas, trout guts, graffiti, paper scraps. The old esoteric reality is lost so far back in the age of the Father and virtù that Pynchon asks, "how can they not speak to Slothrop?" (*GR*, 625) — meaning that literally everything he sees speaks to him, has a tongue, is inspirited as if he were living suddenly in a sacred world. No longer esoteric, Slothrop's world is fully exoteric. It is Pentecostal, promiscuous, indiscrete: tongued. Beginning with the tongues emerging in *V.*, Pynchon's characters know more and more, until everything reveals everything. Therefore, if Sidney Stencil was serious when he asked "what gift of communication could ever come from a woman," the serious retort is: the gift of tongues, the gift of total communication.

As the novels reflect successive stages of history tending toward global Pentecost, the woman V. summarizes the same drift in her lifetime, and in the one book Pynchon devotes to her. V. has six verifiable incarnations, with two in each of her three stages. Representing the Father, she is Victoria Wren first in Cairo, 1898, and second in Florence, 1899. Her name derives from England's imperialist Queen (*V.*, 67/56) and perhaps from Christopher Wren, England's famed architect of St. Paul's, the cathedral named for the apostle of edification. The age of the Father is stabler than its successor, thus Victoria's name is the same in Cairo and Florence, and her character is continuous.

Next representing the age of the Son and His "liberal love-feast," she is thirty-three (*V.*, 408/384), appears in Paris, 1913, and is known simply as V. She causes a riot and participates in a surreal love affair with a young ballerina. Her next appearance is in 1922 as Vera Meroving at Foppl's siege party in Southwest Africa. This incarnation is chronologically inappropriate because she has skipped an appearance in 1919 on Malta. But the temporal lapse constitutes a thematic and formal stroke of genius in that it so handily emphasizes V.'s immunity to normal criteria as well as her reactionary decadence at this point — the siege party is an attempt to recapture the mood of 1904, when von Trotha's troops entrenched orgiastic genocide in the twentieth century. Moreover, chronology is untrustworthy in anything having to do with Malta (where V. will be next), because that island is "alienated from any history in which cause precedes effect" (*V.*, 489/460). The last name, Meroving, evokes the slack Merovingian dynasty which sub-subdivided its ever shifting lands and was characterized by chronic warfare. The first name, Vera, means "faith," but its other connotations qualify that meaning. That is, the wood of the vera tree is used as a substitute for *lignum vitae* — literally, "wood of life." Also, the wood of the vera tree is characteristically yellow (a color which recurs incessantly in *V.*), the same color as the alloys of vanadium, for which "V" is the chemical symbol. The first name, like the last, therefore picks up on the idea of alloys and alliances to suggest adulteration of the pure traditions previously maintained under the earlier elect dispensation. And the name also points not just to adulteration of tradition but to adulteration of life itself, which V. represents in her next two appearances.

In her Pentecostal age, V. appears first as Veronica Manganese in Malta, 1919, where Pynchon (via Demivolt) suggests she is the Paraclete. The legendary Veronica survived Jesus when she lent Him her veil to wipe His face as He carried the cross to Calvary. In addition, Veronica is preterite because she is not listed in official calendars of saints. Also, this name stems from the Greek *Pherenice*, "bringing victory"; thus it faintly bears the genetic strain of Victoria Wren. Unlike Victoria Wren, who is associated with Saint Paul and edification, Veronica Manganese is associated with Saint Peter — advocate of tongues and priest of the first Pentecost — because the legendary veil is preserved in St. Peter's cathedral, Rome. Manganese is a chemically active

[79]

metal which does not occur free in nature, though its compounds are widely found. This description is similar to that of vanadium and implies the increasing inanimateness of V. as she assimilates things beyond her, and as she continues to ally-alloy herself with the world — which is what the ecstasy of tongues is about. Her last incarnation is as the Bad Priest. Father Avalanche summarizes and interprets her creed at this point: " 'Seek mineral symmetry, for here is eternal life: the immortality of rock. Plausible. But apostasy' " (*V.*, 340/319). V.'s life has gone from belief in "virtù, individual agency" (*V.*, 199/183), to advocacy of mineral symmetry; from separation to fusion; from apostolic edification to apostate tongues.

The implications of V.'s death are now evident. Her last voice is that of tongues: "drawn-out wails . . . past speech" (*V.*, 344/322). And Fausto reports:

> in those cries — so unlike human or even animal sound that they might have been only the wind blowing past any dead reed — I detected a sincere hatred for all her sins. . . . The interior darkness was lit by flares over Valletta, incendiary bombs in the Dockyard. Often both our voices were drowned in the explosions or the chattering of the ground artillery. (*V.*, 344/322)

The uncertainty here is no accident, nor merely our inability to penetrate what seems to be. Herbert Stencil warned of precisely this dubious grace early on when he was thinking of his father and Porpentine: "if death did come like some last charismatic bestowal, [Stencil would] have no real way of telling" (*V.*, 63/52). Beyond his anticipation, and the wind, fire, and descriptive words ("wails . . . past speech" and unearthly "cries"), two more clues nudge a reading of this passage toward the sacred. First, V. is talking tongues if merely because Valletta's children have just removed her teeth. Second, Pynchon has carefully juxtaposed her wails to the toothsome "chatter" of the artillery, as if to announce that the deadly sound of warfare is what polite edification has become. Still, the clues merely nudge sacredness into the reader's awareness; they don't cancel V.'s profanity. V. is profane: a Bad Priest, an embodiment of inanimateness — with her clock eyeball, sapphire omphalos, metal feet, false teeth. But V. is also sacred: the Paraclete, the communicator, a significant totem in a world otherwise devoid of meaning.

As with most important issues, one side has no corner on truth. Therefore, Pynchon insists not upon binary judgment but on encompassing inclusion. V. is a profoundly profane sinner afraid and also a profoundly transfigured woman wailing tongues "past speech." She's any dead reed and the instrument of the Holy Ghost. The flares are indeed flares, but they are also tongues of fire: they herald both death for Malta and a possible radical transfiguration of the world.

The possible transfiguration roosts in Fausto Maijstral, the only other character to receive the gift of tongues in the novel. Fausto's is a Pentecostal conversion, a hardly linear leap from one state to another, and occurs at the moment of V.'s death. Fausto's journal — evidencing extreme prolixity during his other stages — has "nothing but gibberish" (*V.*, 306/286), "indecipherable entries," and "sketches of an azalea blossom, a carob tree" (*V.*, 345/323) for this time of his life. In this critical third phase of Fausto's life, he is alloyed with the world, taking on "much of the non-humanity of the debris, crushed stone, broken masonry, destroyed churches and auberges of his city" (*V.*, 307/286). And he speaks of his emergence from this stage as a "return from the rock" (*V.*, 345/323). Importantly, however, he now calls inanimate Malta a "womb of rock" (*V.*, 318/298, ff.), although he had earlier seen her air-raid shelters and catacombs as an "oubliette" (*V.*, 319/298); he sees the rock as not killing but engendering life. In fact, Fausto's clearest understanding of his later state of tongues comes shortly before its onset. It frightens him for he understands, even though the experience is ineffable, how foreign to his discrete existence the life of merger with the world truly is:

> The rock hears everything, and brings it to bone, up the fingers and arm, down through the bone-cage and bone-sticks and out again through the bone-webs. . . . The vibration is impossible to talk about. Felt sound. Buzzing. The teeth buzz: Pain, a numb prickling along the jawbone, stifling concussion at the eardrums. Over and over. . . . You never get used to it. You'd think we'd

all have gone mad by now. What keeps me standing erect and away from the walls? And silent. A brute clinging to awareness, nothing else. Pure Maltese. Perhaps it is meant to go on forever. If "forever" still has any meaning.

Stand free, Maijstral. . . . (*V.*, 319–320/299)

This passage suggests the major themes of tongues: the full communication (" 'the rock hears everything' ") coupled with an inability to make what is known articulate (" 'vibration is impossible to talk about' "); the near-frenzy which the biblical spectators of the first Pentecost reported (" 'You'd think we'd all have gone mad' "); the unassimilable foreignness of the experience (" 'You never get used to it' "); the resistance to giving oneself up to it (" 'Stand free' "); and its timelessness (temporality and such concepts as "forever" don't mean anything in the state of tongues).

Entropy and tongues signify either a state of promiscuous equilibrium, or a condition fast approaching that state; enthalpy (entropy's opposite) and edifying discourse reflect discrete systems, or things moving toward discreteness. In the passage above, Fausto is in the late days of what he calls Fausto II. " 'A brute clinging to awareness,' " he is desperately holding on to his ability to remain discrete, to "stand free" from the coming entropic soup — or, more precisely, from the state of promiscuous tongues. It is more precisely the state of tongues because he imagines a kind of concussive communication in the coming state, a communication which is not understandable from his presently discrete vantage. After he witnessed V.'s wail, Fausto entered into the mineral symmetry, jotted so-called gibberish in his journal, and became not discrete from, but wholly *of* his environment. He was somehow in the rock, had "no further need for God" (*V.*, 345/324) — presumably because the Spirit moved through all things, buzzed through him as well as through the rock. That is, Fausto's passage through mineral symmetry is a birth passage, as Ploy's passage into entropic chaos is for this novel, and as V.'s death is for the increasing prominence of tongues in Pynchon's later novels.

Pynchon does continue to use a Pentecostal mode to describe what Sidney Stencil suggested would be a Pentecostal age, and with increasing confidence.[5] Without understanding the confidence Pynchon places in tongues in his later fiction, one can misinterpret Fausto's flop back into a cool personality following his Pentecostal stage. For Fausto does return to normal, with no ability to articulate his experience, but with an awareness of his qualitatively different consciousness. He validates, then, the flip/flop, set/reset, patterns in the novel, of which the edifying/tongues modes of discourse are a central part.

In the process of that validation he emphasizes not so much a personal failure as a bit of obvious cultural history and a bit of less recognized contemporary literary history. Fausto follows the cultural paradigm of the forties and fifties about which McClintic Sphere spoke to Paola-Ruby. In the cool fifties, not McClintic nor anyone else could live a flipped, promiscuous life. Also, Fausto's drop into the rock and frenzied Pentecostal experience, with his subsequent cool emergence into a new stage, is very similar to other fiction of the period — similar, for instance, to the fortunate fall Ellison's Invisible Man makes in the novel by that name. Like Fausto, the Invisible Man moves back into the normal world with only a surreal record of his interregnum. Moreover, Pynchon establishes the inability of Pentecostal momentum to sustain itself when Benny Profane and Herbert Stencil travel to Malta, talk to Fausto, and leave without conversion. Stencil evidently understands, but represses what he learns; Profane never understands, and for him all the lights go out (*V.*, 455/428). Brilliant though his style and perceptions are, Pynchon is a writer who embeds characters in a cultural and literary world. They can test the hypotheses of that world and they can run contrary to it for a while, but the world — like a procrustean bed — is always there. The task for Pynchon after *V.* has been to discover more promising alternate worlds and different embeddings — where, first, major characters can occupy the interface between the two modes, as in *The Crying of Lot 49;* and, second, where characters can positively acknowledge the language of tongues and the experience of Pentecostal life, as in *Gravity's Rainbow.*

Although he is not the first to use the idea of entropy in fiction, Pynchon is famous for his bridge between science and literature because he is the first to use the idea so fruitfully and so relentlessly. Still, the traffic goes both ways on Pynchon's bridge because he also takes tongues to entropy. Indeed, V.'s wails at her death hover over the Occident until *Gravity's Rainbow*. That novel's first line, "A screaming comes across the sky," implies both the scream of technological weaponry bearing death and (as in *V.*) the scream of life: life for the novel, for Slothrop (who had a knack for intercourse at bombsites), and for Pentecostal possibilities not so completely tapped anywhere in fiction until that moment. More than ever, the Pentecostal entropy begun in *V.* is the condition of the promiscuous closing ditty in *Gravity's Rainbow*: " 'Riders sleep by ev'ry road, / All through our crippl'd Zone, / With a face on ev'ry mountainside, / And a Soul in ev'ry stone.' "

This persistent life snuggled in with persistent death, this miracle of the spirit permeating both bureaucracy and entropy; this percolation of living into dying, animate into inanimate, spirit into matter: is it good or bad? In *V.* it is neither. There is not merely a binary choice. Pynchon's world is more and more besieged by Pentecostal promiscuity. And it is simultaneously more skewed by discreteness and scoured by edification as the momentum of enthalpic organization marches on. The world to come is permeating this one; the world to come is waging silent war with this one for hegemony; the world to come will not be this one. There are warring modes of edification and tongues within *V.* They correspond to an ancient struggle coming to a head beyond the novel, between this world and the one to come.

Pynchon's vision is different from modern ideas of apocalypse because his understanding of it is not contemptuous. He predicts — even urges — a second coming that is frightening and selfless, transforming and subversive, irreversible and natural. From one perspective the coming is entropic, but it is also Pentecostal: the apocalypse strikes awe but is not awful. If Yeats's "The Second Coming" typifies a modern attitude toward apocalypse with its "rough beast" slouching toward the holy center of Christianity — there to wreak what horror? — then Modernism has no hint of welcome, no sense of death's attraction, and instead holds only contempt for the "mere anarchy," "blood-dimmed tide," and "passionate intensity" threatening elect order. Post-modernist fiction has found little to sustain either in Yeats's aristocratic predilections or in the more usual modern longing for authentic order and viable tradition. Tradition of almost any sort is anathema to Pynchon by the fact of its inevitable fossilizing in time's eons; and there is no greater lie for him than myth. He prefers beginnings. Therefore, he has relied on pop preterition, as partly witnessed by his use of tongues. A last and perhaps more striking contrast between the two generations follows from the use of *infra dig* modes by Pynchon and his contemporaries. The younger writers have been gladly "Drinking the foul ditch" that Yeats rejected in his poem "On a Political Prisoner." When other modernists celebrated common folk — Faulkner in Yoknapatawpha, Joyce in Dublin —they often did so by paralleling protagonists with sanctified ancient myth. Where modernists injected significances, Pynchon places people solely on their own terms — vulnerable, costumed, but essentially themselves for whatever they are worth, as much damned as graced, as much nothing as something.

If there is no longer an edifying normalcy of belief, if Paul's bequest is incredible now, then what? What's left is "foul ditch" promiscuity: the spirit of impulsive persistence against scaffolding policy, politesse, and polity — the same persistence which has informed Pynchon's fiction from *V.* to *Gravity's Rainbow.* What's left is antiform: impulsive tongues. Pynchon stands in relation to the world as folk always have at beginnings, when their experience is honest and not yet demystified, when it is promising terribly and also terribly promising.

Notes

1. "Entropy" appeared in *The Kenyon Review*, 22 (1960), 277–292. The best analyses of Pynchon's use of entropy are by Tony Tanner and Anne Mangel, whose essays are included in this volume. See also Alan

J. Friedman and Manfred Puetz, "Science as Metaphor: Thomas Pynchon and *Gravity's Rainbow*," *Contemporary Literature*, 15 (Summer 1974), 345–359.

2. "Days of Wrath and Laughter," *Trials of the Word: Essays in American Literature and the Humanistic Tradition* (New Haven: Yale University Press, 1965), pp. 228–234.

3. *The Dartmouth Bible*, ed. Roy B. Chamberlin and Herman Feldman (Boston: Houghton Mifflin, 1961), p. 1032a.

4. I will refer to *V.* as *V.*, giving first the hardback and then paperback page numbers, separated by a slash. Editions used for *V.* are: New York: J. B. Lippincott, 1963, and New York: Bantam, 1964. Although there are a few silent changes in the Bantam reprint — for instance, at the beginning of the Epilogue — there are none in the passages cited in this paper. Reference to *The Crying of Lot 49* will be as *Lot 49*, with the appropriate page numbers separated by a slash. The editions are: New York: J. B. Lippincott, 1966, and New York: Bantam, 1967. I refer to *Gravity's Rainbow* (New York: Viking Press, 1973) as *GR*; the pagination is the same in the hardcover and paperback editions, which were published simultaneously.

5. In this connection, see Edward Mendelson's essay on *The Crying of Lot 49* (see Bibliography). I am working on articles which show, first, that the two later novels further the principle of tongues as antiform, and, second, that *Gravity's Rainbow* drops much of the reticence about people flipping into it.

Maxwell's Demon, Entropy, Information: The Crying of Lot 49[*]

Anne Mangel

One of the most significant aspects of Thomas Pynchon's writing is his ingenious use of scientific-technological concepts as the basis for his fiction.[1] Pynchon's characters seldom reflect a traditional mythological or religious pattern of thought; in their world, the emphasis is rather on such things as thermodynamics and signal-to-noise ratios. Of the many scientific concepts which occur in Pynchon's fiction, three intrude most dramatically: thermodynamics and Maxwell's Demon, entropy, and information theory, all of which are important in *The Crying of Lot 49*.

The novel is an account of Oedipa Maas's exploration into the estate of the deceased Pierce Inverarity, an entrepreneur, who seems, in the end, to own all of America. While investigating Inverarity's assets, she wanders into "Yoyodyne," a government-contracted industry. There Oedipa meets one of the Yoyodyne workers, Stanley Koteks, who introduces her to the idea of Maxwell's Demon with a breezy but essentially correct explanation of the concept.

James Clerk Maxwell, a nineteenth-century physicist, introduced the Demon in 1871 in his book *Theory of Heat*. Pointing out that the second law of thermodynamics shows the impossi-

* From *TriQuarterly*, No. 20 (Winter 1971), 194–208.

bility of producing "any inequality of temperature or of pressure without the expenditure of work," Maxwell goes on:

> Now let us suppose that such a vessel is divided into two portions, A and B, by a division in which there is a small hole, and that a being, who can see the individual molecules, opens and closes this hole, so as to allow only the swifter molecules to pass from A to B, and only the slower ones to pass from B to A. He will thus, without expenditure of work, raise the temperature of B and lower that of A, in contradiction to the second law of thermodynamics.[2]

As the Demon sorts the molecules, he increases the order in the vessel, and decreases the entropy, or amount of disorder in the system (see diagram).

In *The Crying of Lot 49*, Pynchon uses Maxwell's notion of the Demon as a metaphor for Oedipa's experiences. The frequent allusions to Oedipa's sorting masses of information evoke the idea of Maxwell's sorting Demon. As the novel opens, Inverarity's estate presents Oedipa with "the job of sorting it all out." She begins by "shuffling back through a fat deckful of days" (*Lot 49*, 11/2) trying to isolate the one on which Inverarity had last phoned her. The sorting and shuffling which is mentioned at the start of the novel is just the first indication of the separating Oedipa will have to do to create order out of the mass of clues, symbols, and signs which descend upon her.

After Oedipa hears about Maxwell's Demon from Koteks, she tends to view the Demon in terms of the poles of order and randomness. The Demon, as Oedipa sees it, establishes a point of order and connection in a system of random occurrences. As she puts it, the Demon is "the linking feature in a coincidence." Oedipa's understanding of the Demon's function is pointed out when she thinks of the explanation of entropy given to her by John Nefastis, a Berkeley inventor who has built a machine he believes contains a real Maxwell's Demon: "For John Nefastis (to take a recent example) two kinds of entropy, thermodynamic and informational, happened, say by coincidence, to look alike, when you wrote them down as equations. Yet he had made his mere coincidence respectable, with the help of Maxwell's Demon" (109/80). Again, the Demon manages to bind occurrences.

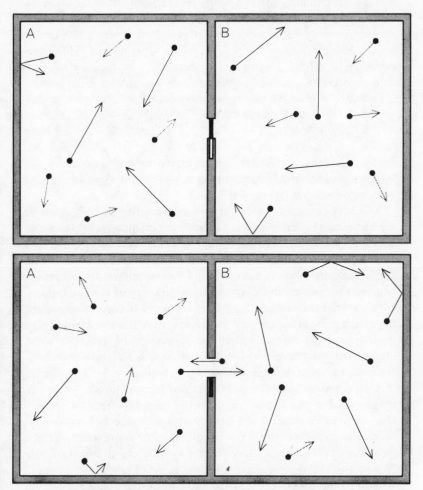

Sorting Demon operates by opening and closing a small hole in a division between two portions of a vessel full of air at a uniform temperature (top). The demon can see the individual molecules, which move at many different velocities. By opening and closing the hole so as to allow only the swifter molecules to pass from A to B and only the slower ones to pass from B to A, the demon could, without expenditure of work, raise the temperature of B and lower that of A (bottom), in contradiction to the second law of thermodynamics.[3]

Copyright © 1967 by Scientific American

Like Maxwell's Demon, Oedipa soon tries to link occurrences, to establish a point of order in what seems to be a random system of information. She vows to be "the dark machine in the centre of the planetarium, to bring the estate into pulsing stelliferous Meaning" (81/58). Her desire to bring order to the mass of confusing interests left by Inverarity leads her to the discovery of "Tristero," a mysterious organization involving a bizarre underground mail system called WASTE. Oedipa sets out to discover the nature and extent of WASTE and Tristero, an obsessive hunt which takes her all over Southern California. Just as the Demon, by sorting the molecules, gains information about them, so Oedipa shuffles through countless people and places, gathering information about the elusive Tristero.

Whatever concrete information Oedipa gains, though, is offset by increasing confusion. The Demon's sorting process can theoretically create a "perpetual motion" machine, and such a machine seems to be operating metaphorically in Oedipa's situation. The clues she gathers yield more clues in an infinite process. Opening out into more and more suggestions, they yield no conclusion. Oedipa gradually senses this. Pondering the information gained from watching *The Courier's Tragedy*, a Jacobean revenge play which contains references to the Tristero, she realizes "these follow-ups were no more disquieting than other revelations which now seemed to come crowding in exponentially, as if the more she collected the more would come to her" (81/58). With her suspicion that the clues are unlimited comes a realization that they will never yield a stelliferous Meaning. She begins to consider whether "the gemlike 'clues' were only some kind of compensation. To make up for her having lost the direct, epileptic Word, the cry that might abolish the night" (118/87).

The parallels between Oedipa and the Demon seem almost too neat. Oedipa painfully discovers that symbols, such as WASTE and its emblem, the muted post horn, do not lead to one stelliferous Meaning. Rather, they point in a thousand different directions and never lead to a solid conclusion. This notion of symbol and metaphor seems to lie at the center of Pynchon's fiction. This idea forms the basis for Pynchon's novel *V.*, where the symbol V. mockingly suggests a chaotic host of irreconcilable things. . . .

Pynchon fashions the Demon metaphor in *The Crying of Lot 49* in a similar way by manipulating it to point in opposite directions. Oedipa does indeed parallel the Demon problem as Maxwell stated it, but paradoxically she also incorporates its opposite, that is, the solution to the Demon dilemma.

The Demon poses a curious problem, partially because it challenges the realm of thermodynamics with a paradox. Since Maxwell introduced the Demon, several scientists have offered solutions to the Demon paradox. Leo Szilard, a physicist, suggested in 1929 that "any action resulting in a decrease in the entropy of a system must be preceded by an operation of acquiring information, which in turn is coupled with the production of an equal or greater amount of entropy."[4] Szilard's idea that the Demon could not actually decrease the net entropy of the system, as Maxwell had supposed, was supported by another physicist, Leon Brillouin, who in 1951 wrote that "an intelligent being, whatever its size, has to cause an increase of entropy before it can effect a reduction by a smaller amount."[5] The innovative idea in Brillouin's solution to the Demon paradox lay in his emphasis on *perception* as increasing the entropy of the system. A summary of Brillouin's argument is as follows:

> Before an intelligent being can use its intelligence, it must perceive its objects, and that requires physical means of perception. Visual perception in particular requires the illumination of the object. Seeing is essentially a nonequilibrium phenomenon. The cylinder in which the demon operates is, optically speaking, a closed black body and, according to the principle enunciated by Gustav Kirchhoff in 1859, the radiation inside a black body is homogeneous and nondirectional because for any wavelength and any temperature the emissivity of any surface equals its coefficient of absorption. Hence, although an observer inside a black body is exposed to quanta of radiation, he can never tell whether a particular photon comes from a molecule or is reflected from a wall. The observer must use a lamp that emits light of a wavelength not well represented in the black-body radiation, and the eventual absorption of this light by the observer or elsewhere increases the entropy of the system.[6]

Brillouin went on further to prove mathematically that the increase in entropy caused by the process of perception was greater than the decrease in entropy which the Demon could produce by sorting the molecules.

Just as the intricacies involved in the Demon's perception of the molecules actually increase the net entropy of the system, so Oedipa's perception of information actually increases the entropy, or disorder, around her. She comes finally to perceive the WASTE symbol and connections with Tristero everywhere and this disorder far outweighs what order she creates through definite information about Tristero. Ultimately, her perception becomes so disordered that she cannot remember when she has seen the post horn and when she hasn't: "Decorating each alienation, each species of withdrawal, as cufflink, decal, aimless doodling, there was somehow always the post horn. She grew so to expect it that perhaps she did not see it quite as often as she later was to remember seeing it" (123–124/91). Perception, here, is working to create disorder. In Oedipa's perception, the post horn replicates infinitely. The entropy increases until finally she is unable to distinguish reality from fantasy-insanity: "Later, possibly, she would have trouble sorting the night into real and dreamed." Here again is the sorting motif, but the increase in disorder is evident. Oedipa's task has shifted from sorting through an estate to distinguishing between reality and fantasy, the attempt to establish order having led to insane disorder.

The self-perpetuating symbols and clues gradually force Oedipa into a closed system of perception. She finally sees nearly everything in terms of post horn and Tristero and she senses that her enclosure in this cycle is the result of some sinister conspiracy: "They knew her pressure points, and the ganglia of her optimism, and one by one, pinch by precision pinch, they were immobilizing her" (124/91–92). Not only is she immobilized by the symbols she perceives; she is also isolated by her progressive loss of contact with all the men she has known. Her last hope is the anonymous member of the "Inamorati Anonymous," an organization of isolates who communicate by phone, and when he hangs up on her, she stands, "her isolation complete."

Though her perception is leading her into a closed system of chaos, Oedipa is still pursuing the distinction between reality and fantasy at the end of the novel, and this at least sets her apart from most of the other characters. The motion involved in a pursuit is in itself important, as it is in *V*. There, Stencil's meandering search for V. at least saves him from inertness. He dislikes thinking about any possible conclusion to his pursuit, preferring to "approach and avoid." The same refusal to resolve confusion and reach any conclusion about the Tristero characterizes Oedipa. Her continual doubt and reevaluation of events differentiates her from the other characters in the novel who do, in fact, end in closed systems of inertness. Oedipa's husband, Mucho, fades into his drug dream; her psychiatrist, Dr. Hilarius, aggravates his relative paranoia into complete paranoia; Driblette, the director of *The Courier's Tragedy*, commits suicide; and the unnamed figure at The Greek Way bar cushions himself in the soothing "Inamorati Anonymous."

The separate closed systems which engulf the characters in the novel suggest a vision of society which is both isolated and headed for disorder and chaos. Pynchon is deliberately applying this scientific metaphor to conditions in society. The relationship is made explicit in Pynchon's short story "Entropy." Callisto, the principal character in this tale . . . explains how he found "in entropy or the measure of disorganization for a closed system an adequate metaphor to apply to certain phenomena in his own world." He goes on to clarify the metaphor:

> He saw, for example, the younger generation responding to Madison Avenue with the same spleen his own had once reserved for Wall Street: and in American "consumerism" discovered a similar tendency from the least to the most probable, from differentiation to sameness, from ordered individuality to a kind of chaos. He found himself, in short, restating Gibbs' prediction in social terms, and envisioned a heat-death for his culture in which ideas, like heat-energy, would no longer be transferred, since each point in it would ultimately have the same quantity of energy; and intellectual motion would, accordingly, cease.

"Entropy" is set in Washington in the '50's and the metaphors in this description come from the '50's — Wall Street, Madison Avenue, consumerism. Consumerism is still at the heart of Inverarity's massive enterprises in *The Crying of Lot 49*, yet other systems of isolation have flourished in the '60's in political undergrounds and freaky California cults. Though the metaphors and closets of isolation have slightly shifted, the point remains the same. Society at the end of *The Crying of Lot 49* is, like the world in "Entropy," in a state of heat-death as its members remain immobilized in isolated chaos.

The concept of entropy is not only related to Maxwell's Demon and to closed systems, but also to information, as Nefastis, the eccentric inventor who believes in the reality of Maxwell's Demon, tries to tell Oedipa. Nefastis points out that "the equation for one, back in the '30's, had looked very like the equation for the other. It was a coincidence" (105/77). The relation between entropy and information is intriguing, and Nefastis's sketchy explanation seems accurate. The equation for entropy in a system, where H is defined as entropy, was given by Boltzmann:

$$H = -\sum_j pj \log pj$$

Physicists in the nineteenth century did apparently see the connection between entropy and information. One information theorist states that Maxwell, Boltzmann, and Gibbs "realized that there was a close relation between entropy and information; but they did not develop a quantitative theory of information."[7] Such a theory was devised in this century by Claude Shannon, whose equation for the average information-per-symbol did turn out to be precisely the same as Boltzmann's for entropy:[8]

$$\text{average information/symbol} = -\sum_j pj \log pj$$

Quantities of information are then related to measures of disorder. The exact relationship between information and entropy is clarified by Hawkins's example using gas molecules:

When the molecules of a gas, for example, are in a collective state of maximum entropy, or disorder, all the alternatives consistent with the given total energy are equally probable, and therefore, by the most efficient method of measurement possible, the precise determination of the exact state of the gas will require the maximum amount of information.[9]

From this explanation, it can be gathered that the more entropy or disorder in the system, the more information will be needed to describe the system.

The relationship between entropy and information leads directly into the complexities of information theory. Some of the concepts in information theory must be mentioned, since Pynchon uses these ideas both in *The Crying of Lot 49* and "Entropy." Pynchon's treatment of information theory is at least partially satirical. His characters frequently take scientific concepts in an absurdly serious manner. . . . Though Pynchon sees the humor in this and often handles his characters' involvement with science in a loosely satirical way, the ideas from science and information theory still form the basis both for his characters' predicaments and also for Pynchon's own style of writing.

One of the things information theory is concerned with is analyzing communication systems and the transmission of information. A communication system is pictured by Shannon as follows: [10]

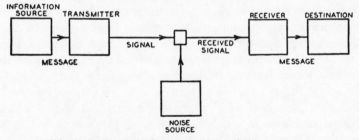

Schematic diagram of general communication system.

The interesting aspects of the system, at least in relation to Pynchon, are the notion of sending information through signals and codes, and also the idea of noise and distortion. The intrusion of noise into the channel may alter the message so that the information which is received differs from the information which was sent originally. The notion of information being altered and lost in the process of transmission is found throughout *The Crying of Lot 49*. Messages are frequently distorted while being transferred, and Oedipa's disc jockey husband, Mucho, must take this into consideration in his broadcasts. After he has interviewed his wife, Oedipa, who is an eyewitness to Dr. Hilarius's burst of insanity at the Hilarius Psychiatric Clinic, he says, "Thank you, Mrs. Edna Mosh." To the bewildered Oedipa, he explains, "It'll come out the right way. I was allowing for the distortion on these rigs, and then when they put it on tape" (139/103–104).

The distortion in meaning as language is transmitted from one source, or person, to another, centers in the novel around words in the Jacobean play Oedipa sees, *The Courier's Tragedy*. Two lines remain in her memory, because of their reference to the Tristero. Oedipa hears the lines as: "No hallowed skein of stars can ward, I trow, / Who's once been set his tryst with Trystero." She begins to pursue the lines with interest, intent on discovering their meaning. As she hunts through various editions of the play, all she finds are a series of transformations. The line "Who's once been set his tryst with Trystero" appears as "Who once has crossed the lusts of Angelo" in the 1687 Quarto edition of the play, and as "This tryst or odious awry, O Niccolò" in the 1670 Whitechapel version. Oedipa finds a further variant on the line when she passes through Golden Gate Park and spots a group of children playing jump-rope while they sing: "Tristoe, Tristoe, one, two, three." The line is repeatedly distorted through transmission until the information in the line is finally negated. Ultimately, the line seems fit only for the children's nonsense game. The distortion of information also occurs to "Thurn and Taxis" which Oedipa also hears in the Jacobean drama. Hoping to find in its meaning a conclusive lead to the meaning of Tristero, she pursues the phrase, only to find another series of aberrations: "Torre and Tassis" and "Turning taxi from across the sea." The pursuit of meaning in language turns into a chimera throughout the novel as information constantly disintegrates through transmission. Ironically, one of the measures of transformation in information theory is termed a "Jacobian."

Throughout *The Crying of Lot 49*, the transmission of information through language paradoxically results in "massive destructions of information." The notion that information may be conveyed through linguistic symbols and codes is repeatedly shattered in the novel. Symbols and codes simply contribute to the chaos and lack of information. "Get in touch with Kirby," the sign about WASTE urges Oedipa; yet Kirby turns out to be nonexistent, "a code name, nobody real." Similarly, the post horn symbol associated at first only with WASTE becomes an all-inclusive sign. It appears not only with WASTE, Oedipa discovers, but along with the etching DEATH on the back of a bus seat, and with an invitation to join the AC-DC, the Alameda County Death Cult. Such symbols continually seduce by suggesting information and meaning, yet they never reveal it. As codes and signals actually work to destroy information, they begin to emerge as something sinister. The nightmare which terrifies Mucho so much is about a sign which unceasingly repeats its initials. As Mucho tells it:

> It was only that sign in the lot, that's what scared me. In the dream I'd be going about a normal day's business and suddenly, with no warning, there'd be the sign. We were a member of the National Automobile Dealers' Association. N.A.D.A. Just this creaking metal sign that said nada, nada, against the blue sky. I used to wake up hollering. (144/107)

Another aspect of information theory which relates to the destruction of information in the novel is probability constraints in language. Different letters and combinations of letters have different probabilities of occurring in a language. The probabilities tend to control what information can actually be conveyed in the language. As one information theorist puts it, "All these frequencies (i.e., probabilities of occurrence) reduce the number of different messages which are possible in an English message of given length."[11] This process is conspicuously at work in *The Crying of Lot 49*, as the probabilities of certain letters and words occurring begin to control the information which is being conveyed. Things tend to move toward a condition of the most probable, and as the novel progresses, almost everything is described in terms of cer-

✗tain symbols, like the post horn, the Tristero, and WASTE. We come back to Callisto's awareness in "Entropy" of a "tendency from the least to the most probable, from differentiation to sameness, from ordered individuality to a kind of chaos," only this time in the context of language. In this sense, the isolated systems which increasingly enclose people are reinforced by the nature of language which itself fails to differentiate and order.

Another area in information theory, related to probability constraints, focuses on redundancy in language. Shannon suggests that "the redundancy of ordinary English, not considering statistical structure over greater distances than about eight letters, is roughly 50%. This means that when we write English half of what we write is determined by the structure of the language and half is chosen freely."[12] Redundancy is used in a very closed, technical sense by Shannon, who defines it as "one minus the relative entropy." Pynchon, however, uses the idea in an extended fashion, adding to it imprecision and irrelevance, as this passage from "Entropy" shows . . . :

> "Tell a girl: 'I love you.' No trouble with two-thirds of that, it's a closed circuit. Just you and she. But that nasty four-letter word in the middle, *that's* the one you have to look out for. Ambiguity. Redundance. Irrelevance, even. Leakage. All this is noise. Noise screws up your signal, makes for disorganization in the circuit."
>
> Meatball shuffled around. "Well, now, Saul," he muttered, "you're sort of, I don't know, expecting a lot from people. I mean, you know. What it is is, most of the things we say, I guess, are mostly noise."
>
> "Ha! Half of what you just said, for example."
>
> "Well, you do it too."
>
> "I know." Saul smiled grimly. "It's a bitch, ain't it."

Here, Pynchon is loosely adopting many of the ideas in information theory — noise, redundancy, disorganization, and entropy. Meatball's watery mutterings are a beautiful illustration of the redundancy and lack of information in language.

The redundancy, irrelevance, ambiguity, and sheer waste involved in language glare from every page of *The Crying of Lot 49*. The one thing Pierce Inverarity transmits, besides his business assets, is an impression of waste in language. His last phone call to Oedipa presents her with "a voice beginning in heavy Slavic tones as second secretary at the Transylvanian Consulate, looking for an escaped bat; modulated to comic-Negro, then on into hostile Pachuco dialect, full of chingas and maricones; then a Gestapo officer asking her in shrieks did she have relatives in Germany and finally his Lamont Cranston voice" (11/2–3). He then assaults Oedipa with the tale of an "old man in the fun house" who was killed by the same gun that killed Professor Quackenbush. "Or something," Oedipa thinks, as if she couldn't really remember the story Inverarity had told and that it didn't matter anyway. . . . The "or something" phrase insidiously negates the tenuous words which are spoken, as if the information is inaccurate or irrelevant. . . . The circuitous tales in the novel might be taken as examples of waste and irrelevance in language, but through them, Pynchon is able to incorporate into his own method and style the notions about language he is trying to convey.

The notions involved in Maxwell's Demon, entropy, and information theory reveal a great deal about what Pynchon is doing. By building his fiction on the concept of entropy, or disorder, and by flaunting the irrelevance, redundancy, disorganization, and waste involved in language, Pynchon radically separates himself from earlier twentieth-century writers, like Yeats, Eliot, and Joyce. Thinking of literature in terms of order, rather than disorder, they saw art as perhaps the last way to impose order on a chaotic world. Yet the complex, symbolic structures they created to encircle chaotic experience often resulted in the kinds of static, closed systems Pynchon is so wary of. Pynchon's use of scientific concepts and disorder in his fiction holds a dual excitement, for not only does it sever him from a previous, more rigid and static kind of writing, but it also links him with contemporary artists working in other media who incorporate scientific ideas and seek randomness in their art.

Notes

1. I wish to thank Professor R. Wasson for his help in rethinking some of the ideas in this paper, for giving the seminar where I discovered Pynchon, and most of all for providing a framework which differentiates Pynchon and other contemporaries from earlier writers of this century. Quotation references will be given for both the Lippincott edition (New York, 1966) and the Bantam edition (New York, 1967).
2. W. Ehrenberg, "Maxwell's Demon," *Scientific American* (November 1967), p. 103.
3. Ehrenberg, p. 104.
4. Ehrenberg, p. 109.
5. *Ibid.*
6. *Ibid.*
7. Stanford Goldman, *Information Theory* (New York, 1953), p. 43.
8. *Ibid.*
9. David Hawkins, *The Language of Nature* (San Francisco and London: W. H. Freeman and Company, 1964), p. 212.
10. Claude E. Shannon and Warren Weaver, *The Mathematical Theory of Communication* (Urbana, Illinois, 1949), p. 5.
11. Goldman, p. 16.
12. Shannon and Weaver, p. 25.

Pynchon's Poetry

William Vesterman

> While nobles are crying in their nights' chains, the squires sing. The terrible politics of the Grail can never touch them. Song is the magic cape. (*Gravity's Rainbow*, 701)[1]

From the first paragraph of his first novel to the last paragraph of his latest one, poems, and particularly songs, make up a characteristic part of Pynchon's work: without them a reader's experience would not be at all the same. Even disallowing translations and quotations, his books average over a line of verse for every printed page. Yet since Pynchon's artistic manner as a whole defines itself more through dislocations of style than through consistencies, any analysis of any "part," however characteristic it might be, risks an emphasis through isolation that the narrator of the passage above avoids.

His voice seems to be making urgent distinctions among the kinds of characters who populate *Gravity's Rainbow* and are concerned with its quest. By extension the distinction applies to *V.* and *The Crying of Lot 49*, to his other characters, his other Grails. But what *is* the distinction? Or, even more simply, what seems to be the narrator's relation to it? It is easier to say what that relation is not. Neither so ignoble as to jeer at terror and suffering, nor so haughty as to disdain security and pleasure, his manner describes and defines hierarchies, but is not at all described or defined by their terms. Neither is it defined by the values and assumptions of "balance" and "reason" implied by my rather Augustan summary of its effect, as the contrast between our styles demonstrates. While he sounds extremely sympathetic toward the nobles in the first sentence, then as if triumphing over them in the next two, the narrator seems on the whole to be outside or beyond or separate from the groups of characters he distinguishes. To me the passage is a characteristic enactment of the ways in which Pynchon achieves a relation to his subjects that is at the same time aloof and sympathetic, inclusive and analytic. The passage also, as I will try to show, describes the compositional principle behind his use of poetry.

Good readers will object that one would have to be tone-deaf to treat the passage as solemnly as I have done, and I agree. Pynchon is fooling around, indulging his fondness for extravagant intonations and lurid, operatic prose. In this case he tries on an exhausted nineteenth-century critical manner which combines anthropological and poetic insights — it tells us *Gravity's Rainbow* is like a Grail Quest. Some insight. And who are the "nobles" and who are the "squires"? Slothrop? Pointsman? Reviewers are fond of calling Pynchon "aristocratic," but no one has yet suggested that his characters can be adequately described in the same dead, not to say un-American, social metaphor. Everyone agrees that Pynchon's "characters," like his style, have only local identities anyway.

The passage makes up a paragraph preceded by the adventures of Dzabajev (Tchitcherine's sidekick disguised as Frank Sinatra); it is followed by a debate between Tchitcherine and Wimpe about opiates of the people (Marxism, Religion) and their "antidotes" (Religion, Marxism). The context therefore partly suggests that songs and/or critical insights about songs are similarly dated sociologically (the debaters end up taking real opiates). The placement of the passage as well as its "local" style work against taking its declaration very seriously.

But that is just the trick that Pynchon's local styles and their contexts at any particular moment always play on serious issues. Conversely, "frivolous" issues (say, Stencil's quest in *V.*) are treated always with the utmost seriousness, once the character is given a name like "Stencil" which, by novelistic tradition, deprecates his importance to the author. Within particular passages, as well as within the larger rhythms of his books, Pynchon's style never allows a reader to take him simply, either as "serious," in the sense of literary solemnity and respectability, or as "frivolous" in the sense of literary fatuity. He seems to strive for an effect described in another connection by Nabokov as "a kind of delicate meeting place between imagination and knowledge, a point, arrived at by diminishing large things and enlarging small ones, that is intrinsically artistic."[2]

The "issue" of the passage I quoted is song and what it can do. And, if I am right in my analysis of Pynchon's general manner, we can be sure song is a very serious issue precisely because of the frivolity with which it is treated. Be that as it may, songs do act like a magic cape in Pynchon's books by concealing not the characters but their author: they protect the author's ability to acknowledge, display and enjoy complexity without being dominated by it. Since readers are baffled along with characters by the mysteries of the books, though the prose narrator keeps addressing us as if we needn't be, Pynchon as an author would seem to pose as having the twentieth century and its troubles completely and easily figured out were it not for the songs. They allow us to feel that the prose narrator stands only partly for Pynchon's sensibility and that Pynchon has other relations to his material. Those relations free him to explore the serious implications of Conditioning, for example, *because* he can be frivolous about them in songs like "Spring in Pavlovia" or " 'Twas a Penis He Thought Was His Own." He can express all the more fully the horror of rockets because the Rocket Limericks acknowledge that no one can be completely horrified by horror all the time, a fact that is itself a source of terrified fascination and wonder.

So much does Pynchon depend on the frivolity associated with his musical comedy songs that when he does use a "serious" poetic form, he has to tone down its style while making the content even more frivolous than it would otherwise need to be. For example, the blank verse of *The Courier's Tragedy* in *The Crying of Lot 49* remains maniacally regular, in spite of the demonstrated range, grace, richness, and confidence of his prosody elsewhere. It is as if even the outrageousness of the play's plot and the proper names (Faggio, Squamuglia, etc.) were not enough to countervail against the "serious" connotations of Blank Verse and Jacobean Drama. In all three novels his prosody is richest where his subject is most serious or intellectually respectable, because richness of prosody means an increase of comedy in a comic song.[3]

Pynchon's use of songs allows his relation to the reader to follow the advice of McClintic Sphere, a well-rounded man who is also a performing artist in *V.* — "keep cool, but care." As Richard Poirier has pointed out, the admonition summarizes the effect of Pynchon's first two books.[4] With themes like Entropy, Conditioning, Technology, and Death Wishes at work in a contemporary novel, the caring part is easy enough. Keeping the authorial presence cool is to a large degree a responsibility of the songs. Like the motives of a college revue (the genre into which most of Pynchon's songs happily fit), the idea is to wear one's learning gracefully, to show by "parody" that one understands intellectual complexity and its pleasures and yet that one also understands just what part of any full life is concerned with them emotionally. I gather that it is largely this undergraduate quality in Pynchon that readers who don't like his books object to, perhaps because it allies itself with those elements in a classroom more dubious about Serious Literature than is convenient for someone trying to explicate difficult books.

V. begins with a paragraph that creates a test or a training ground for its reader. In it Pynchon defies his audience to imagine him as an author by presenting a moving target to avoid a settled definition:

Christmas Eve, 1955, Benny Profane, wearing black levis, suede jacket, sneakers and big cowboy hat, happened to pass through Norfolk, Virginia. Given to sentimental impulses, he thought he'd look in on the Sailor's Grave, his old tin can's tavern on East Main Street. He got there by way of the Arcade, at the East Main end of which sat an old street singer with a guitar and an empty Sterno can for donations. Out in the street a chief yeoman was trying to urinate in the gas tank of a '54 Packard Patrician and five or six seamen apprentice were standing around giving encouragement. The old man was singing, in a fine, firm baritone:

> Every night is Christmas Eve on old East Main,
> Sailors and their sweethearts all agree.
> Neon signs of red and green
> Shine upon the friendly scene,
> Welcoming you in from off the sea.
> Santa's bag is filled with all your dreams come true:
> Nickel beers that sparkle like champagne,
> Barmaids who all love to screw,
> All of them reminding you
> It's Christmas Eve on old East Main.

"Yay chief," yelled a seaman deuce. Profane rounded the corner. With its usual lack of warning, East Main was on him. (*V.*, 9–10/ 1–2)

Although the best part of the passage is clearly the "Yay chief," it only confirms other indications, including the song, of how little it would pay to confuse Pynchon as an author with his apparently ingenuous narrator. The absence of an exclamation point helps to suggest the difficulty of telling how much derision for the chief is mixed up in the applause of the seaman's cheer, just as it is impossible to tell how much of either the author counts on from the audience of *his* performance. To assume the seaman is not at all derisive about the chief's vulgarity reveals certain assumptions about the relation of the vulgar to vulgarity, and identifies the seaman *as* vulgar simply on the basis of his service rank. Making such claims to intrinsic superiority on the basis of extrinsic signs, whether in American society or American novels, frequently results figuratively in getting Pissed On by those we have identified as merely yeoman, as the owner of the Packard Patrician will discover.

The would-be Patrician reader, accustomed to feeling at home with Modern Fictional Techniques and Dirty Talk in Books, is left in an awkward position. If he would respond to the apprentices, yeoman, and Patrician as a Symbol of Class Struggle, the frivolity is there to make him feel that he is off-base, that he hasn't really accounted for the spirit of the passage. If he dismisses those implications as Just a Joke, the patness of the socially labeled hierarchy (emphasized by parallel construction) makes him feel uneasy too. To take the path of least critical resistance and say, "it is a mixture of both" begs the question of proportions that becomes the subject of the passage, since the proportions identify the author. Pynchon is so protective here at the beginning because he has so much to protect throughout his writing. And if I am over-reading, I hope at least to have suggested the provision he makes for being under-read.

The dynamics of the song preview those Pynchon will use in most of the songs to follow; they aid in the unsettlement or protection of the author's identity. The similarities of the mechanism of the humor to that of mock-heroic suggest the term "mock-democratic," a label sufficiently ugly to keep analysis and effect properly distinguished. The technique uses an out-of-date popular style felt to be dead or specious to express a living, contemporaneous content, allowing us to re-enjoy the manner without feeling cheated by the author's asking us to believe in it, to take it seriously, except as ironic implication. In this case the "old street singer" mocks his would-be betters by appropriating a "sophisticated" and dated "popular" tune ("Every Day's a Holiday in Old New York") to express the real popular sentiments of East Main Street. Yet the would-be innocence associated with the tune adds sweetness and helplessness to the sentiments by suggesting that the inhabitants of East Main no more believe in the possibility of their dreams (cheap, good beer and easy screwing — the Good Life) than do New York audiences of the original song, which was made "popular" by the far-from-innocent communications industry. Its imagination of the populace, "fraudulent dreams of teen-age appetites," is what Mucho Maas will later offer with such shame, not as a street singer but as a popular disc jockey with "spots" rather than a Sterno can for donations; while the donations in his case come not from his audience, but from its defrauders. The implications of the style here add salt enough to keep the effect sweet. The reader can respond to the mixture of helplessness and robustness in the sentiments rather than to their vulgarity, since the vulgarity transfers to Tin Pan Alley. Treating real hopes and dreams this way makes Pynchon's first use of "frivolity" in song that of expressing the "serious" issues of loneliness and desire embodied by Profane in spite of his name and his nature. His condition becomes pitiable whether or not he deserves it.

Thus Pynchon introduces at the beginning of his first book his fascination with the preterite, the passed-over, the disinherited, the out-of-it. It is a fascination strong enough to stimulate his imagination through at least fifteen years and three books, and is expressed most generally in characters by The Loser, in theme by Lost Causes and The Inanimate, and in technique, which most concerns me here, by a combination of forms derived in prose from the historical novel and in verse from popular songs — both handled in a mock-democratic way. The frivolity of his songs does what is sometimes left undone even by the playfulness of his prose — they allow him to explore his material without sounding like a second-guesser historically or like a popularizer scientifically. Put another way, his use of verse works to save his fascination from nostalgia and his technique from sentimentality.

Whatever instruction Pynchon's poetic technique involves, it almost always results in delight. I have found that the song most amusing to students, even those indifferent to or annoyed by Pynchon's writing generally, is the "Hymn" sung at the Yoyodyne stockholders' meeting in *The Crying of Lot 49*. They are even willing to sing it in class:

To the tune of Cornell's alma mater, they sang:

HYMN
High above the L. A. freeways,
And the traffic's whine,
Stands the well-known Galactronics
Branch of Yoyodyne.
To the end, we swear undying
Loyalty to you,
Pink pavilions bravely shining,
Palm trees tall and true.

Being led in this by the president of the company, Mr. Clayton ("Bloody") Chiclitz himself. . . . (*Lot 49*, 83/59)

The amusement seems to come from three sources. In addition to feeling that they themselves as singers are getting in a dig at The Military-Industrial Complex by treating it frivolously, my informants feel that the characters in the book, the serious, reverent singers, are laughable because unnatural in expressing for a corporation the human sentiments of loyalty and affection reserved for colleges. Yet the degree of laughter of this sort meaures just how far some institutions, colleges, have become "naturally" the objects of human emotion. The realization can result in more laughter at how natural the process may be that is being derided as unnatural. This is altogether the plot of Pynchon's humor.

In the context of the response to the first song, one's response to the second becomes more unsettling:

. . . and to the tune of "Aura Lee":

> GLEE
> Bendix guides the warheads in,
> Avco builds them nice.
> Douglas, North American,
> Grumman get their slice.
> Martin launches off a pad,
> Lockheed from a sub;
> We can't get the R&D
> On a Piper Cub.
>
> Convair boosts the satellite
> Into orbits round;
> Boeing builds the Minuteman,
> We stay on the ground.
> Yoyodyne, Yoyodyne,
> Contracts flee thee yet.
> DOD has shafted thee,
> Out of spite, I'll bet. (*Lot 49*, 83/60)

Tenderness and longing expressed for a corporation are conceivably funny; those emotions directed to vehicles of death like rockets won't do. Students stop laughing.

Pynchon does not — at least not yet. The first two Rocket Limericks in *Gravity's Rainbow* are the most general:

> There once was a thing called a V-2,
> To pilot which you did not need to —
> You just pushed a button,
> And it would leave nuttin'
> But stiffs and big holes and debris, too.

The tune is known universally among American fraternity boys. But for some reason it is being sung here in German Storm Trooper style: notes clipping off sharp at the end of each line, then a pulse of silence before the attack on the next line.

> [Refrain:] Ja, ja, ja, ja!
> In Prussia they never eat pussy!
> There ain't hardly cats enough,
> There's garbage and that's enough,
> So waltz me around again, Russky!

Drunks are hanging from steel ladders, and draped over cat-walks. Beer fumes crawl in the long cavern, among pieces of olive-drab rocket, some upright, some lying on their sides.

> There was a young fellow named Crockett,
> Who had an affair with a rocket.
> If you saw them out there
> You'd be tempted to stare,
> But if you ain't tried it, don't knock it! (*GR*, 305)

The rest of the limericks are variations on the second as commented on by the first: what was an expression of the emotion of love in the earlier book becomes here a description of the act of love. Various men become "fond of" or have "affairs with" or "sleep with" various parts of the rocket (for instance, the vane servomotor). They make love to the rocket and destroy parts of themselves as the rocket will destroy itself in fulfilling its own inanimate needs and nature. A dirty song for a dirty business, and here the tune and sentiments are in accord. By a kind of emotional algebra, however, the singers are at least redeemed from mindlessness: their derision is intentionally self-directed, unlike that of "popular" dirty songs, though the consciousness adds to the horror in another way.

The motif that began with a hymn to the organization of death, became first a love song and then a dirty song, reappears in the hymn that ends *Gravity's Rainbow.* That hymn marks a change, and though it is pleasant to think of any consciously organized artistic change as a progress, we are faced there, I think, with something else:

> There is time, if you need the comfort, to touch the person next to you, or to reach between your own cold legs . . . or, if song must find you, here's one They never taught anyone to sing, a hymn by William Slothrop, centuries forgotten and out of print, sung to a simple and pleasant air of the period. Follow the bouncing ball:
>
> > There is a Hand to turn the time,
> > Though thy Glass today be run,
> > Till the Light that hath brought the Towers low
> > Find the last poor Pret'rite one . . .
> > Till the Riders sleep by ev'ry road,
> > All through our crippl'd Zone,
> > With a face on ev'ry mountainside,
> > And a Soul in ev'ry stone. . . .
>
> Now everybody — (*GR,* 760)

Like the "Yay chief" of the beginning of *V.,* the "Now everybody — " here might be read as derisive or encouraging depending on how the reader imagines the author and on the meaning both of what precedes it and the silence that follows it. Insofar as we are encouraged, we are invited to put on the magic cape, the comfort of song, which will protect us from the "They," unless the "They" includes the narrator, whose voice has grown progressively more maniacal and sinister toward the end of the book. In that case, perhaps, we are derided for believing in the sentiments and the style.

But what are the sentiments and what is the style? We are offered as a hymn of comfort — of ultimate comfort — a song which begins in regular iambic tetrameter, a form traditionally associated in English poetry with plainness, sincerity, and seriousness ("On the Death of Robert Levet") and is particularly common in hymns ("A Mighty Fortress Is Our God"). The suppression of a syllable in the beginning of the second line ("although" to "though"), however, begins to break the form, which is completely lost in the third line. Our expectations of the meter are unfulfilled, though the meter does not, as it easily could, change to the highly irregular iambic tetrameter strongly associated in English since *Hudibras* with frivolity. The meter becomes merely confused in spite of the specious typographical illusion of careful regularity which is most evident in "crippl'd."

The punctuation and syntax make the meaning follow a similar pattern. We are clear enough in context until line 4, where ellipses keep us from knowing what to do with the puzzlements introduced. Will the light "find" (subjunctive?) the last individual of the preterite class, or will it find that class united as one? The ellipses at the end are similarly disorienting and coy.

My point is that the style creates pseudo-confusions rather than enhancements for the meaning; they seem reflexively added in lieu of an ability to take that meaning in any but a serious way. The meaning of the last song is serious, while its manner is not frivolous but speciously confused. The drama of style and content that protected the identity of the author has ended. The lack of gaiety leads me to suspect that we are reading more than the end of a book, whether it is a complete stop (as I think) or a point of departure.

What we are left with is a hymn to Pynchon's horror. He has called it by many names — the inanimate, waste, entropy, the preterite — but it always involves the surrender of individual human identity to the Other. Here we are offered partly the same comfort of Wordsworth's song "A Slumber Did My Spirit Seal" and Emerson's "Brahma" — "do not be afraid of the not-you; it is or shortly will be yours. You will repossess the universe in death when you *are* it." The twentieth century as seen by Pynchon adds a new "universal truth" — "all this will happen for the race, not at the end of all time, but in our own Δt when the bombs come. Death then will be not for individual human beings, but for the species, making a final democratization for which all the world is now spiritually voting."

Pynchon has never much cared before about the endings of his books, which was not surprising considering his commitment to destabilization. He makes a joke out of his debt to Melville in *V.*, and in *The Crying of Lot 49* he concentrates on teasing any reader who expects that less rather than more mystery would come from one of the fulfillments of its title.[5] I think, however, there is no teasing, no mystery, and no joking here. The show is over. Pynchon cries in his chains. Taking himself with complete seriousness, he dramatizes and reinforces the meaning of his last song by the surrender of the individuality of his style.

Notes

1. All page numbers in parentheses will refer to *V.* (Philadelphia: J. B. Lippincott, 1963); *The Crying of Lot 49* (Philadelphia: J. B. Lippincott, 1966); *Gravity's Rainbow* (New York: Viking, 1973). Page numbers of the Bantam paperbacks for *V.* and *Lot 49* (1964, 1967) follow after a slash. For the Bantam paperback of *Gravity's Rainbow*, references can be found by multiplying the Viking page number by 7/6.
2. *Speak, Memory!: An Autobiography Revisited* (New York: G. P. Putnam's, 1966), p. 167.
3. See for example the logical-positivist love song, "Let P Equal Me" in *V.*, pp. 288–289.
4. *The New York Times Book Review* (May 1, 1966), p. 5.
5. I am indebted to my colleague James Guetti for my view of *V.*

Risking the Moment:
Anarchy and Possibility
in Pynchon's Fiction

George Levine

I

Pynchon's novels disorient. They offer us a world we think we recognize, assimilate it to worlds that seem unreal, imply coherences and significances we can't quite hold on to. Invariably, as the surreal takes on the immediacy of experience, they make us feel the inadequacy of conventional modes of making sense — of analysis, causal explanation, logic. But Pynchon's language is so richly, sometimes so cruelly anchored in the banalities of the colloquial, the obscene, the trivial, the familiar, and it so miraculously spins from these things into high scientific and historical speculation, into melodrama, romance, and apocalyptic intensity, that the experience is not merely — if it is even primarily — intellectual. Yet critics almost invariably respond to the novels with thematic readings that reduce variety to a fairly conventional coherence.

Anticipating such readings, I'm sure, Pynchon made characters like Herbert Stencil and Oedipa Maas pretty good literary critics themselves. Writing about them thematically is like joining them, and that is part of the irony and experience of reading the books, too. A writer so busy implying connections, dropping allusions, thwarting conventional responses invites the sort of criticism Pynchon has been getting; and I don't pretend to stand outside or above it. Furthermore, any attempt to avoid the disorientation of his characters requires that we first join them in their desperate — and sometimes silly — quests.

More important than the possible resolution of the quests is the disorientation and almost visceral disturbance that come of being forced into them. Such disturbance is a condition of growth for the characters and for the readers. Pynchon evokes the terror and anxiety of the disturbance as he describes the feelings of Oedipa, in the last moments of her novel, awaiting silently the crying, the annunciation — of what rough beast?

And there I go, making comfort out of anxiety by invoking a myth and poetic variations on it to "place" Oedipa's experience. The falsification is a serious one, even if the allusion points to something true about the novel. For if the invoked myth of annunciation is one way to talk about Oedipa's situation, it still misses the possibility that nothing is coming, that in fact the book will never yield its secret and threatens to be an elaborate joke, or that whatever is coming is neither divine nor demonic. Even Oedipa's sense of two possibilities — a real conspiracy or a paranoid fantasy — the binary options reminding us of the way Pynchon toys with computer mathematics, flip-flopping, ones and zeroes, misses the possibility of the now excluded middle, the "bad shit" that Oedipa had learned (probably incorrectly) "had to be avoided."[1]

But no myth, no multiplication of intellectual possibilities can quite do justice to the energizing experience of sustaining uncertainty. The full significance of Pynchon's fiction is in its styles, in its language, since the language is called upon to sustain the uncertainty it is structured to deny, to imply what cannot be articulated in language. Pynchon denies resolution into myth by wandering among all the available myths, from those of the Greeks to those of modern science, technology, film, comic books, radio. Verbal and mythic virtuosity is not, in Pynchon, show-off obscuring of what might be made clear, but, in a way, what the books are about; and, like almost everything else in Pynchon's world, virtuosity is both a threat and a possibility.

Pynchon himself understands the connections between his own

kind of virtuosity and the historical decadence with which his books are so much preoccupied. That connection is one of the dominant explicit concerns of *V*. The Whole Sick Crew, sinking into "Catatonic Expressionism," values "technique for the sake of technique . . . parodies on what other people had already done"[2] (*V*., 297/277). And Victoria Wren "felt that skill or any virtú was a desirable and lovely thing purely for its own sake; and it became more effective the further divorced it was from moral intention" (*V*., 198/182–183). The technology of Pynchon's prose parallels the technology of sex and destruction that runs through the three novels. But the recognition of this connection does not entail retreat from virtuosity, or even a conscious attempt to connect skill with moral intention. The prose requires that we make our way beyond the categories of the virtuous to strain the very limits of virtuosity. Eigenvalue, frightened, imagines the End when all the Proper Nouns have been arranged in all their possible combinations, when the last technical manipulation of finite matter has been accomplished: "the exhaustion of all possible permutations and combinations was death" (*V*., 298/277). The Lost Ones of the Hereros are "Sold on Suicide" and attempt to renounce all the things of this world.

But the renunciation can't be complete — never quite. "The trouble with it is," says Pynchon's narrator, "that by Gödel's theorem there is bound to be some item around that one has omitted from the list, and such an item is not easy to think of off the top of one's head, so that what one does most likely is to go back over the whole thing, meantime correcting mistakes and inevitable repetitions, and putting in new items that will surely have occurred to one, and — well, it's easy to see that the 'suicide' of the title might have to be postponed indefinitely!" (*GR*, 320).[3] The materials of the world seem finite, but there are always surprises that will not fit the fictional structures language imposes. There is always "Murphy's Law," crucial, I think, to the unpredictability of Pynchon's prose: *"when everything has been taken care of, when nothing can go wrong, or even surprise us . . . something will"* (*GR*, 275).

The virtuosity of Pynchon's prose is a confrontation with the finite, the determined world. It becomes at times a kind of litany aspiring to the infinite sequence, implying always that there's more where that comes from. And it implies that nothing is predictable in the particular, despite Pointsmanesque conditioning and pervasive paranoia. With such ambitions, the prose must also be self-consciously amoral, as though the ultimate morality is in a truly Whitmanesque embrace of everything, of coprophilia, sadism, masochism, gangbangs and daisy chains, genocide, incest, sodomy, fellatio, transvestitism, torture, physical decay, murder, pie-throwing, decomposition, toilet bowls. But not only these. It is a prose that seems almost desperate in the tricks it will invent to keep from its own finitude, to find some sort of life in the very decadence and de-animation of which it is a symptom. If, as many critics propose, Pynchon not only describes but participates in paranoia, it is not the sort of selective paranoia that sustains itself by screening out the details that don't fit. It survives in the quest for the surprise or the aberration that nobody ever noticed before.

The exhaustiveness of Pynchon's catalogues of waste moves him beyond decadence because he challenges us to resist the entropic reductionism of the systems we have been trained to impose on them. The question the prose proposes for us at every moment is whether we are strong enough to accept the details as they come to us. Pynchon anticipates the risk of such acceptance. To live exclusively in and with the moment is difficult and dangerous not only for readers but for characters within the fiction; characters who do this reject relations to the past or thought of the future, lose the capacity for love. Moreover, they tend to join in the very betrayals and de-animations, within the culture, that have driven them outside into the fragmentary moment. Benny Profane thus summarizes the effect of his experiences in *V.*: "offhand I'd say I haven't learned a goddamn thing" (*V.*, 454/428). Tyrone Slothrop manages to unlearn everything his experience offers him, and betrays Bianca as Benny betrays Fina. His personality, his "temporal bandwidth," dwindles to zero as his memory goes with everything but the merest sliver of the present, and, consequently, even that. If we have to choose between facing each moment as it comes to us or making the present moment part of a pattern between past and future, we haven't, in Pynchon's world or ours, much choice.

But choices imply finality and systems, and if the terror for Pynchon's protagonists resides often in their discovering that they must make a choice, their lives remain full of unsystematic surprises. Experience belies the simplification of binary choices into which our logic and our language bind us. The strength thus required is somehow to honor *both* the moment and the memory, to allow almost any possibility while holding on to or creating a genuinely human self. But this, of course, is much easier to say than to feel. Like Oedipa, we must confront the worst possibilities, be driven to choice, if we are to avoid reduction to Tupperware and the plastic prose of a plastic culture; like her we must relearn the past, reimagine the possibilities of connection. Her husband, Mucho, is driven half mad by his power to see in the detritus of used cars whole lives of misery. Everything comes to him as intensely present and, metonymously, as ever more intensely past and future.

But unless we arrive with Oedipa at the point of taking the risk of that intensity, we are doomed to a kind of yo-yo LSD escape, or to enrollment among the members of the Firm. The effect is the same. If we do take the risk, we are driven by Pynchon's art into reconsidering our fundamental assumptions about the way things connect. The discontinuities, the surprises, the refusals of categories, the fake mythologizing — these all confront us with the possibility that art is most valuable, in a culture where power resides among the organizers, when it rejects the tradition of organic coherence we take as a universal standard. Might not that art be best — at this moment, in this place — that constantly pushes toward the possibility of fragmentation? Might it be that not order but anarchy is the most difficult thing to achieve in this culture? The pressure toward anarchy, in a world structured to resist anarchy at any cost, might release us, ironically, into a more humane order, where the human continuities with stones and mountainsides become visible and possible and not plastic reductions to SHROUD and SHOCK or even Imipolex G; where,

then, paranoia is not a mental disease but a vision, where either/
or is not the option and Oedipa's "mixed shit" isn't shitty.

I'm not trying to reduce Pynchon into an "anarchist," though
there are anarchists in each novel. The point is to recognize the
risk-taking in his art as no mere decadent virtuosity (though it
is partly that). There are thermodynamic surprises everywhere,
shocks of possibility that can rip us out of our literary critical
and human reductionism. The possibilities of an anarchic style
and structure seem to me more centrally the "subject" of Pynchon's fictions than even entropy or charisma or the preterite and
elect of Calvinism or paranoia. Thematic analysis is inescapable
and essential (part of the pain of Pynchon's vision is that he does
not pretend that we can escape system or language), just as anarchy is ultimately impossible in our world. But the moments are
there beyond any patterns into which they may be made to fit.
Pynchon can be so intellectualized that we ignore how deeply,
viscerally painful, indeed nauseating, he can be; we ignore too
what I regard as his most astonishing and overwhelming power,
to imagine love out of the wastes of a world full of people helpless to love. These qualities live in the moments, not the patterns.
For his characters and, I think, for us, the challenge is to penetrate the moments as they come and then find a way to live with
them.

II

There is, obviously, no simple way to characterize Pynchon's
prose, and no selection of passages can begin to account for its
varieties. It is deliberately unstable, parodic, various, encyclopedic, fragmented (what *are* all those ellipses doing in *Gravity's
Rainbow?* why does the narrator, in and later out of Slothrop's
consciousness, stutter on "a-and"?). Though capable of traditional
decorum, it is characteristically indecorous in its refusal to be
locked into a mode. It is perfectly at ease in technical scientific

and mathematical analysis, historical reconstruction and documentation, evocative and ominous descriptions, chitchat about films, metaphorical leaps from one area of discourse to another. But perhaps its most disorienting and testing quality is its almost sullen resistance to judging the various horrors it coldly narrates. It is almost impossible to locate the narrator, who refuses to protect us with his own disgust, or with ironies that don't cancel each other out.

One of the earliest completely uncomfortable moments in Pynchon's fiction is Esther's nose job, in the fourth chapter of *V.* Easy enough to talk about admiringly, the passage is physically discomforting and unpleasant, so much so that it requires, from me at least, an act of will to keep reading through it. Insofar as the revulsion is merely from the precision with which the plastic surgery is described, we can say that we have here only a virtuoso extension of the tradition of naturalistic fiction. But the experience is very different from that of naturalism. It is not merely clinical, but clinical and vulgar, and not merely that but clinical vugarity observed as though it were funny — which it almost becomes. As the two-inch needles are shoved up Esther's nose to administer anesthetics, she discovers pain: "nothing before in her experience had ever hurt quite so much." To be given Esther's pain in such a context is, at least, to be protected by a confirmation of our own sense of a reasonable response to the physical manipulation; it is to make us feel satisfyingly that Esther made a mistake and is learning that she did. But at the same time, she is sexually aroused, in part by Nembutal, in part by the very manipulation that causes the pain. Schoenmaker's assistant, Trench, "Kept chanting, 'Stick it in . . . pull it out . . . stick it in . . . ooh that was good . . . pull it out'" (*V.*, 105/92).

The scene becomes a kind of show, but a show in which we — and Esther — are forced to participate. The brutal playfulness is combined with an efficiency complete and routinized, so that the extremity of the experience is reduced both by the play language ("'That boy,' you expected her to say"), and by the total professional detachment of Schoenmaker and the surgical description. Though we feel the extremity, we are not allowed by the language to come to terms with what we feel: "It was a routine operation; Schoenmaker worked quickly, neither he nor his nurse wasting any motion" (*V.*, 105/93).

Schoenmaker's technical efficiency has its correspondence in the clinical textbook language used to describe it. As we begin to be impressed by the particularity and precision, then to marvel at the virtuosity, we begin to participate in the unnatural act Pynchon is forcing us to watch, to shift our focus from the human significance to the technical virtuosity. The moral enormity of the manipulation of a human being becomes routine, and the loss of normal focus is reinforced by the simile — a non-technical intrusion — in which cutting bone is like cutting hair, and the man in the barber chair is merely a head, though belonging to a body, presumably, that gives high tips (*V.*, 105=106/93). The technical term "undermining," describing the procedure, may have a literary-symbolic resonance, but the voice is neutral, and the moment is wrenched free of the normal social and moral context of action.

For Esther, spectator and object, the experience is sexual and then, madly and convincingly, religious. Her selfhood is lost in her transformation into an object. And the next image is of Schoenmaker looking from the plastic mask to Esther as though she were a rock, for sculpting. "Your hump is now two loose pieces of bone, attached only to the septum," Schoenmaker tells Esther. "We have to cut that through, flush with the other two cuts." And the narrator's voice: "This he did with an angle-bladed pull-knife, cutting down swiftly, completing the phase with some graceful sponge-flourishing" (106/94). "Graceful" is the Pynchonian flourish, the word that forces the scene into virtuosity and releases the human subject into objecthood.

We can, of course, place this morally, and Pynchon gives us the context of the whole book to do it. We can connect Esther's rockhood with Mildred Wren's rock, with the rock of Malta itself, and with the progressive de-animation of V. and the society; we can connect Schoenmaker's surgical skill with the skill involved in the slaughter of the Hereros, with the high technology that threatens Profane and all the characters in the book. But to read this as a document of moral outrage is to read in what Pynchon has, to our discomfort, left out. The prose participates in the brutal virtuosity it describes. It recognizes, in part by allowing Schoenmaker to adopt a mock Nazi accent, how much it all has become a subject for cynical comic distance. Esther, after all, has asked for it. And beyond this, Schoenmaker is genuinely enthusiastic about his work, his skill, his flourishes, regardless of their human uses. Pynchon doesn't rescue us from the consequent disorientation. The narrator, like Schoenmaker, has something of the quality of the little boy showing off.

It is important to see how much Pynchon participates in the horrors he describes, how much he knows he participates, and how much, consequently, he must resist simple moral placing that allows him and us to judge, as though we were separate from what we see. Like Esther, we are separated only in that we are drugged; like Schoenmaker, we cannot help admiring the skill that happens to make victims. By giving us no easy position from which we might judge the experience, Pynchon forces us into it beyond morality. The more we admire the prose that can make us feel the pain, the more it implicates us in it. The writer who makes us feel that something quite horrible has been routinized and socially accepted participates in the technical joys and power lust involved in the activity. Moral judgment becomes irrelevant, and the question is whether the prose, in facing the tyranny of its own skills, can release Pynchon or us from them.

The special difficulties and graces of Pynchon's art are early put to the test in the wonderful third chapter of *V.*, "in which Stencil, a quick-change artist, does eight impersonations." The "impersonations" are of narrators who neither know each other nor care very much about the apparent subject of the narrative. Each narrator is one of the preterite, preoccupied with a private life into which the tourists intrude themselves briefly. Since the narrators' stories seem not to be connected, we, as readers, are seduced into piecing together the tourists' story, which looks very much like an exciting Edwardian spy adventure. We teach ourselves to see the continuity of character behind flaking sunburn, suggestive nicknames, blue eyeglasses, fatness. We might say that we become Stencil, or Stencilized, in our attempt to make order out of various fragments.

We may, at first, believe that once we have pieced together the narrative, we have "made sense" of the fiction; but we must soon recognize that in exercising our deductive skills, working on conventional assumptions of continuity and cause and effect, we have been tricked into acting out our own touristic assumptions about the nature of reality. We must understand that narrative tradition itself entails the exercise of a Schoenmakerian skill in rejecting unwanted material and shaping what is wanted. To "make sense" of the narrative we must exclude most of the evidence. We become tourists, like the characters whose fate most absorbs us, and though the natives tell us the story, we read it as though their lives don't matter. Entropy is high: the expenditure of energy and the rejection of material entailed in the reading creates order at great expense. To read the story right, we must come to terms with disorder.

Aïeul, the waiter, watches Goodfellow and Porpentine disappear from his life:

> . . . I will see neither of you again, that's the least I can wish. He fell asleep at last against the wall, made drowsy by the rain, to dream of one Maryam and tonight, and the Arab quarter . . .
> Low places in the square filled, the usual random sets of crisscrossing concentric circles moved across them. Near eight o'clock, the rain slackened off. (*V*., 66/54–55)

The best we can do if we are to participate in Stencil's preoccupation with V. is reconstruct the story he has obviously already constructed. That is, the fullest exercise of our ingenuity in decoding the narrative from the irrelevancies of the lives of the narrators can only put us where Stencil already is. But Pynchon gives us other options, if we choose to exercise them. We can decide that Maryam, and tonight's meeting with Aïeul, are as important as Porpentine and Goodfellow. We can recognize that the Arab quarter exists beyond the experience of the English characters, beyond the prose that invokes it. We can feel the ominousness of the precise physical details (the low places in the square filled, the raindrops making crisscrossing concentric circles) but take them as the expression of physical necessities rather than as meaning something for the spy adventure. The circles in the puddles can be taken as a figure for the crisscrossing concentric circles of the narrative. But the center, we know, is Stencil, not the natives like Aïeul. Only if we take Stencil's imagination as primary can we accept the circles as figuratively concentric. Otherwise, we must live with randomness.

Randomness, of course, is what neither Stencil nor we can live with. Thus, we read the "irrelevant" details thematically, make them relevant not to the particular passage, but to the themes of the novel as a whole. There is comfort even in recognizing that the theme of tourism is important everywhere in *V.*, ironically, however, that theme justifies our ignoring Aïeul once we understand that he is there as a sign of the way tourists ignore the real life of the country, of the way empire exploits and denies the reality of what is natively there. Suppose we are left, however, with the reality of Aïeul and Maryam, whom we will never see, or with the rain flooding the Place Mohammed Ali. Suppose we refuse to connect the eight different narratives. Suppose they are juxtaposed only in Stencil's imagination. Do we know how to honor what we see but do not know?

Pynchon's prose works to make us see and to know, to know by seeing intensely, excessively. The prose has a passion for the lost and dispossessed, the preterite, as *Gravity's Rainbow* has retaught us to call them. It entails not placing but recognition; nothing is mean enough not to be recorded, everything matters. The traditions of nineteenth-century realism implied that the ordinary was latent with the extraordinary; in the romantic program of the realists, the ordinary is endowed with wonder. Ironically, Pynchon, in rejecting the realist tradition, carries out in his prose the extreme of the realist vision, allowing the ordinary, the base, the obscene to threaten us with significances we do not, perhaps need not, understand.

Pynchon has been criticized for not creating "real" characters and, especially, for creating loveless worlds. But traditional character is an imagination of order and structure that belies the pervasiveness of change, variety, aimlessness, waste. Character, in traditional fiction, is the clearest emblem of the elect — dominating and controlling the action of the world. And Pynchon creates character by imagining it as participating in the energies of the world created around it. He mocks (especially in the names) and uses the notions of character fiction has inherited, but, as Fausto Maijstral insists, even the self is an invention.

Character is an abstraction that allows us to see through the moment, not to experience it. Explanation of actions in terms of motives, psychoanalysis, instincts, gets us off the hook of responsibility to each lived moment. The self is unintelligible as a stable "thing," except when it has *become* a thing; and it must be seen in relationship, or in the failure of relationship. The prose, in any case, gives us the experience of *being* before (if ever) it tries to explain it. Profane, looking into the desolation of the winter seascape "which meant nothing more than the turbulence of the screws or the snow-hiss on the water," needs no analysis. Our capacity to accept such moments depends on our capacity to resist the coherences of narrative or even of rational expectation. We enter Pynchon's moments, as Oedipa does, discovering new and terrifying realities behind the conventions of reality — that is, of selection and election — we have been trained to believe in.

One powerful and characteristic example of such a moment comes in Oedipa's encounter with the ruined old man who had left his wife in Fresno: "When [Oedipa] was three steps from him the hands flew apart and his wrecked face, and the terror of eyes gloried in burst veins, stopped her" (*Lot 49*, 125/92). She imagines him as one of the lost and forgotten, living in a flop house:

> What voices overheard, flinders of luminescent gods glimpsed among the wallpaper's stained foliage, candlestubs lit to rotate in the air over him, prefiguring the cigarette he or a friend must fall asleep someday smoking, thus to end among flaming, secret salts held all those years by the insatiable stuffing of a mattress that could keep vestiges of every nightmare sweat, helpless overflowing bladder, viciously, tearfully consummated wet dream, like the memory bank to a computer of the lost? She was overcome all at once by a need to touch him, as if she could not believe in him, or would not remember him, without it. Ex-

hausted, hardly knowing what she was doing, she came the last three steps and sat, took the man in her arms, actually held him, gazing out of her smudged eyes down the stairs, back into the morning. She felt wetness against her breast and saw that he was crying again. He hardly breathed but tears came as if being pumped. "I can't help," she whispered, rocking him, "I can't help." It was already too many miles from Fresno. (*Lot 49*, 126/93)

Entering such a moment entails believing in the reality that nothing has taught Oedipa, or us, to see. The wreck with his wife in Fresno is recorded only in an insatiable mattress that absorbs the secret salts of the lost. Oedipa is discovering America, feeling the tenuousness of the discovery, the possibilities of despair, and the further possibility that despair is a way to avoid the responsibilities of caring.

Of course, there are more possibilities, but there remains also the inescapable experience of Oedipa and the old man. The language, whatever else it is, can only be an expression of a passionate concern, every precisely imagined detail intimating luminescent gods beyond, sad and lost lives within. It is merely a convention, and a disastrous convention within and outside of fiction, that we can care only for what we know well. The ruined old man makes only a brief appearance in *The Crying of Lot 49*. Oedipa risks caring for him.

By all this I only mean that in Pynchon's work I am far more disposed to trust the moments than any ideas I might invent to account for them. Good critics can and do assume that Pynchon is (a) paranoid or (b) mocking the traditional structures that imply paranoia; that he is (a) asserting the inevitable heat-death of the world and the futility of resisting it, even in its local manifestations, or (b) suggesting that life, in its extraordinary capacity to produce surprises, constantly resists the heat-death, as must we all; that there is nothing to be done, or that there is everything to be done; that he is on the side of the elect, or that he is on the side of the preterite; that he is asserting disorder, or that he is implying some kind of transcendent order; that choices are binary or multiple. I keep thinking that I know what I believe on these matters, and then keep discovering that I don't. Rereading Pynchon I find it surprisingly difficult to account for particular passages in particular places, and yet a condition of their power that they be difficult to account for. My uncomfortable feeling is that not knowing is an important qualification for participating imaginatively in his fictions. Only by surrendering our demands for order can we be released into the terror of the moment, as Oedipa is released, and as she grows.

III

And what does it mean, in Pynchon, to penetrate the moment?

Leni Pökler tries it, as a matter of life and death. Somehow, however, her husband Franz has a "way of removing all the excitement from things with a few words" (*GR*, 159), and for him this is instinctive. The removal of excitement is the removal of risk and is connected with the fact that, as Leni says, Franz is "the cause-and-effect man." Words that embody the imagination, causal explanation, participate in the large fictionalizing of experience that Walter Rathenau, speaking from the other side, calls "secular history," "a diversionary tactic" (*GR*, 167). Secular history in Pynchon is, I think, the faithless construction of defenses that, as they justify by explanation the power of the empowered, participate in the plasticizing of life and death.

To get into the moment and experience it, it is necessary to find a way to withdraw from the secular diversions of language. Leni, of course, has no language to explain herself to Franz, nor, I think, does Pynchon. Both of them try very hard. Leni, like Pynchon, invokes the language of calculus, of "Δt approaching zero," but is rebuked by Franz: "Not the same, Leni" (*GR*, 159). Calculus is used here as a metaphor, and Leni is putting it to uses for which it is not intended. Franz is thus not persuaded, and removes the excitement from things. Pynchon tries to put it back.

Here is how he describes the movement into the moment that Leni requires. Against Franz's need for "security," his language full of the fear of "consequences" that keeps us all from resisting, we have Leni:

> She tried to explain to him about the level you reach, with both feet in, when you lose your fear, you lose it all, you've penetrated the moment, slipping perfectly into its grooves, metal-gray but soft as latex, and now the figures are dancing, each pre-choreographed exactly where it is, the flash of knees under pearl-colored frock as the girl in the babushka stoops to pick up a cobble, the man in the black suitcoat and brown sleeveless sweater grabbed by policemen one on either arm, trying to keep his head up, showing his teeth, the older liberal in the dirty beige overcoat, stepping back to avoid a careening demonstrator, looking back across his lapel how-dare-you or look-out-not-*me*, his eyeglasses filled with the glare of the winter sky. There is the moment, and its possibilities. (*GR*, 158–159)

The central implicit image of the street demonstration is exactly right for the attempt to describe the condition of passing from spectator to actor, from user of words to thrower of stones. The risk is clear for any liberal reading as for the liberal with the glare of the winter sky on his glasses (used, no doubt, for much reading, and reflecting not absorbing experience). The options — active (tossing the cobble), passive (resisting when captured and overwhelmed), or withdrawal (seeing the human demonstrator in the language of "careening" matter) — are imagined with the particularity that always offers more than can be systematized (the flash of knees, the babushka, the black suitcoat and sleeveless sweater, the dirty beige overcoat). The moment, however systematized our reading of it, suggests almost infinite possibilities and particularities, and that any verbal efforts to locate it will pass over far more than can be chosen.

This is one of those passages that resists the easy placing it tempts us to make. One feels the urgency, even the moral power, of Leni's willingness to lose her fear and penetrate the moment. But the moment remains obscure — why here, in the presence of such courage and energy to freedom, is the moment imagined as a kind of long-playing record? You slip "perfectly into its grooves, metal-gray but soft as latex," and the dancing figures are "pre-choreographed." Are we here, in the moment of freedom and risk, when the life of the street penetrates the hothouse of cause-and-effect history and suburban security, back in some paranoid fantasy, unreleased even as we act and choose?

Leni's is an act of faith because the primary restraining fact is the terror of what lies behind the order of secular history. "What if there's violence?" is always Franz's question when Leni tries to induce him to act. But the "if" in Pynchon's world is an absurdity: all of secular history is an act of violence, the transforming of life into waste. The possible act is, simply, acceptance of the moment on its own terms, finding one's own place, two feet in the water, moving, then, with the current and the spinning of the earth itself. But if my language makes it sound easy, Pynchon's does not. Leni hates the "street," which "reaches in, makes itself felt everywhere." "Rest" is impossible.

Part of the difficulty of Pynchon's fiction and of the prose from moment to moment is, I think, that he is constantly engaged in the struggle to make language, a kind of cause-and-effect hothouse constructed to resist the disorder of the street, lead us into the street, into the moment. And when we get there we may find a more terrifying order. But the risk begins in the terrifying break from Franz's kind of order. We have seen the terror in Oedipa Maas's story, and, as in that story, the release contains no assurance but the discovery of the lost. Whatever the reality, Tristero or paranoia, Slothrop's paranoia or the dissolution of antiparanoia, "personal identity" or "impersonal salvation," as Mondaugen sees the possibilities (*GR*, 406) — each version is frightening and morally expensive.

The language describing Leni's attempt to penetrate the moment echoes the language describing the "anarchist miracle" of *The Crying of Lot 49*. In one of those wonderfully screwy Pynchonian inventions that manage to bear heavy weight despite apparent ridiculousness, Oedipa finds herself in the middle of a left-wing convention of deaf-mutes. She is dragged into a dance "by a handsome young man in a Harris tweed coat and waltzed round and round, through the rustling, shuffling hush, under a great unlit chandelier" (*Lot 49*, 131/97). Playing with sound as he plays with words, Pynchon somehow reinforces the absurdity and counters it. All those assonating, dull "u's," the softening "n's," the deliberate quiet sibilance of "rustling" and "shuffling" help make perfect the craziness of the "unlit chandelier," dull and sibilant and literally senseless. Vision without light, sound without noise, movement without direction, and the joke is translated, though remaining darkly funny, into something more than a little frightening:

> Each couple on the floor danced whatever was in the fellow's head: tango, two-step, bossa nova, slop. But how long, Oedipa thought, could it go on before collisions became a serious hindrance? There would have to be collisions. The only alternative was some unthinkable order in music, many rhythms, all keys at once, a choreography in which each couple meshed easy, predestined. Something they all heard with an extra sense atrophied in herself. She followed her partner's lead, limp in the young mute's clasp, waiting for the collisions to begin. But none came. She was danced for half an hour before, by mysterious consensus, everybody took a break, without having felt any touch but the touch of her partner. Jesús Arrabal would have called it an anarchist miracle. Oedipa, with no name for it, was only demoralized. She curtsied and fled. (*Lot 49*, 131–132/97)

All the normal empirical assurances are gone, and yet instead of chaos and disorder there seems to be a higher order.

It remains problematical for me how seriously we are to take the implicit otherworldliness, perhaps religiosity, of Pynchon's world. Oedipa's curtsy is too wonderfully funny, and yet too precisely appropriate to be unambiguous. Neither the deaf-mute's waltz nor Walter Rathenau's discussion from the other side can be taken merely as a joke. Trying to explain why cause-and-effect thinking won't work, Leni says, "not cause. It all goes together. Parallel, not series. Metaphor. Signs and symptoms. Mapping on to different coordinate systems, I don't know" (*GR*, 159). But whether the language is out of geometry, mathematics, literature, none of it is equal to the experienced reality, which takes metaphorical, comic and dramatic shape in Oedipa's dance and curtsy.

Leni's sense of the "pre-choreographed" experience of the moment echoes Oedipa's overwhelming feeling of "a choreography in which each couple meshed easy, predestined." Oedipa, dragged

[129]

into the moment where Leni, as it were, leaped in, is demoralized by this sense of mysterious order. It is as though anarchy does not free Oedipa — she will not allow herself to be freed — from the rigidly determined structure of her life. She is afraid of the freedom, terrified by the possibility that it might work, that by admitting the disorder of the street she will be released from the fake order of the suburban hothouse.

Gravity's Rainbow, however, is built as Leni's world is — parallel, not series, metaphor, signs and symptoms, mapping on to different coordinate systems. Leni dares the possibility of mysterious orders, and the anarchy and cacophony of the narratives and fragments of *Gravity's Rainbow* may well be an anarchist miracle of the kind Arrabal describes. But Oedipa approaches the language of *Gravity's Rainbow* just before she returns to the dance in the hotel. Watching the old man in a fit of delirium tremens, she connects the DT's with Leni's kind of dt, evoked in her attempt to describe penetrating the moment:

> "dt," God help this old tattooed man, meant also a time differential, a vanishingly small instant in which change had to be confronted at last for what it was, where it could no longer disguise itself as something innocuous like an average rate; where velocity dwelled in the projectile though the projectile be frozen in midflight, where death dwelled in the cell though the cell be looked in on at its most quick. She knew that the sailor had seen worlds no other man had seen if only because there was that high magic to low puns, because DT's must give access to dt's of spectra beyond the known sun, music made purely of Antarctic loneliness and fright. (*Lot 49*, 129/95–96)

Moments later she will be dancing with people who seem to hear that music. A book before, Pynchon had evoked that Antarctic loneliness for old Hugh Godolphin. A book later, Pynchon confronts the change "where velocity dwelled in the projectile" though the projectile is frozen over the heads of the audience in the Orpheus theater in L.A. In all these cases there is a connection among the terror of choice, and the possibility of change that will undermine or destroy the world we know, and the terror of a reality other than that we believe in. They all inhere in the vanishingly small instant that we must risk. The dt's, Vheissu, the rocket are all metaphors for the moment — "a thrust at truth and a lie" (*Lot 49*, 129/95).

Pynchon's language risks the lie, sustains the faith (like Arrabal's in another world) of the high magic in low puns. Pynchon also seems to understand, as in Leni's failure to make the moment present to Franz (that, we shall see, is possible only through risk and surrender, not through persuasion), as in Oedipa's recognition that "I can't help," that language may suggest the possibilities it cannot present, may bring us within sight of "the pure light of zero" (*GR*, 159). This is only possible if language does not protect us with the comfort of its structure, if the word can somehow put us in the presence of "whatever it is the word is there, buffering, to protect us from" (*Lot 49*, 129/95).

The anarchists in the three novels work to get beyond words, and beyond the labyrinths words construct. The Gaucho, in *V.*, prefers to use a bomb than to assist in the absurdly elaborate, labyrinthine plans to steal the Botticelli. Arrabal believes in some spontaneous revolution, "automatic as the body itself" (*Lot 49*, 120/88–89). And most explicitly, Squalidozzi (can we take him seriously with such a squalid name?), also Argentinian, espouses spontaneity and immediacy against the Argentinian, Borgesian need for building labyrinths. As he responds instinctively — resisting his own impulse to speculate on Argentina and anarchism — to Slothrop's hunger, Squalidozzi finds for Slothrop sausage and fondue before going on. And only then does he tell Slothrop: "Beneath the city streets, the warrens of rooms and corridors, the fences and the networks of steel track, the Argentine heart, in its perversity and guilt, longs for a return to that first unscribbled serenity . . . that anarchic oneness of pampas and sky . . ." (*GR*, 264). Anarchy is the quest for a pre-verbal directness of experience, for something like Leni's absorption — "both feet in" — in the moment. But, Squalidozzi says, such moments, such "oneness," can only come, now, from "extraordinary times" (*GR*, 265). Squalidozzi sees the war, "this incredible War," as a time when things might be "wiped clean"

(*GR*, 265). In this anarchist vision, close, I think, to the mood of the whole labyrinthine book opposing labyrinths, the war and the rocket become a kind of last chance to penetrate to a new reality, to break through to an unscribbled, a wordless moment.

Anarchy becomes the kind of aesthetic and political program of these novels, a risk whose possibilities Pynchon doesn't know, though he tries them out on different coordinate systems, metaphors, signs. And we come back to the risk of Leni's moment. The narrative of Franz's discovery of the need to enter the moment enacts as miraculously as anything in *Gravity's Rainbow* the wonders, the risks, the achievements of Pynchon's prose and brings us to the edge of silence, the shuffling dance under unlit chandeliers.

Franz's refusal to risk what Leni risks keeps him in the intellectual hothouse of his life. Only his daughter Ilse's presence threatens to break that vacuum "in one strong rush of love" (*GR*, 407). But before Ilse can bring Franz back to the streets he had rejected with Leni, Franz "put as much labyrinth as required between himself and the inconvenience of caring" (*GR*, 428). Intellectual hackwork — minor contributions to the technology of the rocket — is what consumes Franz's time and concern. Engineering skill protects him from knowing what goes on in the prison camp Dora, just behind the walls where he worked. The violation of Pökler's vacuum is the intrusion of that other world, like the world of the wrecked old man Oedipa encounters, into the world of technology and cause and effect. Understanding at last that his daughter has been in Dora, "beaten, perhaps violated," Franz manages at last to risk the loss of his security. Franz's penetration of the moment becomes an act of love, a wordless engagement with the hitherto invisible and silent lost ones, almost unbearable because, as for Oedipa, there is nothing Franz can do except risk and love.

The cleverness, the labyrinthine obscurities, the obscenities are here extended into what I need to call high seriousness, despite all the Pynchonian tricks to short-circuit solemnities. The passage is evidence that all of those tricks are part of Pynchon's intense vision of the high magic of lowness, of what happens when we suddenly learn to see what lies behind the wall, within the threatening moment:

> The odors of shit, death, sweat, sickness, mildew, piss, the breathing of Dora, wrapped him as he crept in staring at the naked corpses being carried out now that America was so close, to be stacked in front of the crematoriums, the men's penises hanging, their toes clustering white and round as pearls . . . each face so perfect, so individual, the lips stretched back into death-grins, a whole silent audience caught at the punch line of the joke . . . and the living, stacked ten to a straw mattress, the weakly crying, coughing, losers. . . . All his vacuums, his labyrinths, had been the other side of this. While he lived, and drew marks on paper, this invisible kingdom had kept on, in the darkness outside . . . all this time. . . . Pökler vomited. He cried some. The walls did not dissolve — no prison wall ever did, not from tears, not at this finding, on every pallet, in every cell, that the faces are ones he knows after all, and holds dear as himself, and cannot, then, let them return to that silence. . . . But what can he ever do about it? How can he ever keep them? Impotence, mirror-rotation of sorrow, works him terribly as runaway heart-beating, and with hardly any chances left him for good rage, or for turning. . . .
>
> Where it was darkest and smelled the worst, Pökler found a woman lying, a random woman. He sat for half an hour holding her bone hand. She was breathing. Before he left, he took off his gold wedding ring and put it on the woman's thin finger, curling her hand to keep it from sliding off. If she lived, the ring would be good for a few meals, or a blanket, or a night indoors, or a ride home. . . . (*GR*, 432–433)

IV

Such a Pynchonian moment is of the sort that Profane and Slothrop approach and retreat from. The wedding with randomness, the vision of the other side is, like the crossing of the Δt into the pure zero, an act of caring, of connection. The danger, of course, is that we will end with the "losers," among the waste. Another danger is the dissolution of self, the entering of the moment so completely that all connections before and after are lost. Unanchored to a past which had been invented and pro- grammed for him, increasingly losing his connection with a future that was only rocket, Slothrop finds no way to make love a part of his life beyond that instant when it happens. He cannot hold both the moment and the memory. Slothrop's orgasm with Bianca comes in the shape of a rocket; like a rocket it explodes, destroys, ends.

Of course, there is caring in Slothrop. He goes over to the preterite without willing it, and he seeks a freedom that Points- man's world cannot allow. But the freedom is only negative, de- fined against the imprisonment of Pavlovian, cause-and-effect science and fiction. Yet before he dissolves into his world, Slothrop has a moment rather like Squalidozzi's "anarchic oneness of pampas and sky." The precariousness of such moments is en- acted in Slothrop's disappearance: the risk and the ambiguities remain. If Slothrop is a failure, as, in his betrayal of Bianca, we see him to be, it is nevertheless wrong to read past the richness and sense of possibility in the language of Slothrop's last moment.

Slothrop, we are told, becomes a "crossroad." He half remem- bers from his youth one of those catalogues of waste, struggling not to pass over anything in the infinite series of the passed over: "rusted beer cans, rubbers yellow with preterite seed, Kleenex wadded to brain shapes hiding preterite snot, preterite tears, news- papers, broken glass, pieces of automobile" (*GR*, 626). Slothrop is not quite remembering the fragments of his past: "instructing him, dunce and drifter, in ways deeper than he can explain, have been faces of children out the train windows, two bars of dance music somewhere, in some other street at night, needles and branches of a pine tree shaken clear and luminous against night clouds . . ." (*GR*, 626). His life has been full of barely appre- hended moments latent with the richness of other worlds. And so, in his last moment, he achieves the anarchist ideal:

> and now, in the Zone, later in the day he became a crossroad, after a heavy rain he doesn't recall, Slothrop sees a very thick rainbow here, a stout rainbow cock driven down out of pubic clouds into Earth, green wet valleyed Earth, and his chest fills

and he stands crying, not a thing in his head, just feeling natural. . . . (*GR*, 626)

It is difficult to mistake this language for the language of failure or of impending doom. Freed to be "simply here, simply alive," as Webley Silvernail, "guest star," wishes despairingly we all might be, Slothrop cannot survive on the terms of Pointsman's or Blicero's world. The moment becomes the enactment of the anarchic visionary ideal that animates much of Pynchon's fictions.

Since it is an ideal it must, in Pynchon's world, dissolve, but if we are willing to risk it, there may be at the center of each preterite moment a stout rainbow cock and a wet valleyed earth. It is commonplace now to talk of Pynchon as our poet of death, but like everything else we might invent to say about him — perhaps more so — it is a falsification. Certainly, he rubs our faces unsparingly in shit, as though we were all General Puddings. That, however, is the price of attempting to articulate the inarticulable, of attempting to make present to us what our language will not let us see, of attempting to disorient us so much that we will risk what each moment, unpenetrated, hides from us. There are, amid the infinite possibilities that Pynchon's virtuosity begins to suggest to us, alternatives to the way we currently imagine our lives. Pynchon's world is prepolitical; it implies that every political program is, at best, one more warren in the labyrinths we build between us and the moments, the caring, we ignore. It is not, however, antipolitical. Like Leni Pökler, we must risk action and loss by penetrating the moment; it would be good if we could do it as Pynchon does, terrified but lovingly, for the risk is the possibility.

Notes

1. References to *The Crying of Lot 49* are to the Lippincott edition (New York, 1966), followed by the Bantam edition (New York, 1967). It is appropriate to indicate here that this essay is more or less consciously

indebted to many of the other essays, and writers of essays, in this book. In particular, some of its initiating ideas derived both from the original essay by Richard Poirier included in this volume, and from talks with him. Some of the focus on material relating to the "delta-t" is influenced by the interesting essay of Lance Ozier, "The Calculus of Transformation: More Mathematical Imagery in *Gravity's Rainbow*," *Twentieth Century Literature*, 21 (May 1975), 193–210. And, though I was not conscious of it at the time, I probably was influenced in my discussion of Leni Pökler by the essay of Marjorie Kaufman. But, as in Pynchon's worlds, connections are too many and too diffuse to be clarified in footnotes. I am grateful to all the writers of *all* the other essays in this volume and the Pynchon number of *Twentieth Century Literature* for ideas borrowed, unreflectingly stolen, or original.

2. All references to *V.* are to the original Lippincott edition (New York, 1963), followed by the Bantam edition (New York, 1964).

3. All references to *Gravity's Rainbow* are to the original Viking edition (New York, 1973). Page numbers for the Bantam edition (New York, 1974) can be found by multiplying the Viking references by 7/6.

4. As yet another addition to the game of decoding Pynchon, I would suggest that Vheissu, usually read "*Wie heisst du?*" might also be thought of as "*vécu*," Sartre's term for "lived experience." There is, I think, a lot of Sartre buried in *V.* aside from Pig Bodine's mocking question about Sartre's view of the nature of identity (130/118). David Leverenz further suggests that Vheissu can be read as "V. is you," in a trilingual French-German-English version. Latin type makes "V is U" even easier to assume.

Section II

Gravity's Rainbow

Bananas!

Pynchon's Paranoid History

Scott Sanders

I

God is the original conspiracy theory: behind floods, deaths in the family, the sprouting of seeds or splatter of rain, behind every heartbeat and thought of man himself, monotheists discerned the single guiding will of a deity. An otherwise chaotic world made sense because it was perceived as a plot, narrated by God, who worked through angels or lightning bolts or by subtle prods on the linings of men's souls. Whether we agree with Feuerbach and Marx that such a mastermind God is no more than a paradigm of our own alienated powers, or with Freud that He is a projection of our superego, or with believers that He simply is, the notion of God still orders the world more elegantly and thoroughly than any other hypothesis.

Among the varieties of Christian monotheism, none is more totalitarian, none lodges more radical claims for God's omnipotence, than Calvinism — and within America, the chief analogue of Calvinist theology, Puritanism. According to Calvin every particle of dust, every act, every thought, every creature is governed by the will of God, and yields clues to the divine plan. Given such a religious cast of mind, the disappearance of God robs the world of all meaning. The physical universe becomes a clutter of debris, lacking all transcendence; life becomes an accident in matter.

A mind that preserves Puritan expectations after the Puritan

God has been discredited will naturally seek another hypothesis that explains life as the product of remote control, that situates the individual within a plot whose furthest reaches he cannot fathom, that renders the creation legible once again. Paranoia offers the ideally suited hypothesis that the world is organized into a conspiracy, governed by shadowy figures whose powers approach omniscience and omnipotence, and whose manipulations of history may be detected in every chance gesture of their servants. It substitutes for the divine plan a demonic one. Viewed in this perspective, paranoia is the last retreat of the Puritan imagination.

Our recent fiction yields so many instances of conspiratorial vision that I am tempted to paraphrase Richard Hofstadter and speak of the paranoid style in American literature. Thomas Pynchon, whose novels confront us with every degree of paranoia from the private to the cosmic, offers the most thoroughgoing example within literature of the mentality Hofstadter has identified in politics, a mentality which assumes "the existence of a vast, insidious, preternaturally effective international conspiratorial network designed to perpetrate acts of the most fiendish character."[1] *The Crying of Lot 49*, *V.*, and *Gravity's Rainbow* all exhibit the habits of language and the view of history which Hofstadter has named the paranoid style:

> The distinguishing thing about the paranoid style is not that its exponents see conspiracies or plots here and there in history, but that they regard a "vast" or "gigantic" conspiracy as *the motive force* in historical events. History *is* a conspiracy, set in motion by demonic forces of almost transcendent power. . . . The paranoid spokesman sees the fate of this conspiracy in apocalyptic terms — he traffics in the birth and death of whole worlds, whole political orders, whole systems of human values.[2]

My purpose in the following pages is to show how this conspiratorial view of history structures Pynchon's fiction, to examine some of its stylistic consequences, and to elaborate the suggestion I have already made that it is rooted in a theology from which God has been withdrawn. Finally, since worldviews survive not simply for reasons of ideological inertia, but because they make sense of a particular experience of society, I shall try to identify, within the advanced industrial system about which Pynchon writes, a social basis for his paranoid worldview.[3]

I shall concentrate upon *Gravity's Rainbow*, which is by far the most complex of the novels; here the mental structures and stylistic patterns evident in *V.* and *The Crying of Lot 49* have been elaborated with Byzantine intricacy. If my analysis succeeds in elucidating the ideological structure of *Gravity's Rainbow*, it will be found to apply all the more transparently to the earlier novels.

II

Tyrone Slothrop, the American whose hapless peregrinations form the bulk of *Gravity's Rainbow*, is beset at every turn by suspicions which he himself describes as paranoid. From infancy onward he has in fact been manipulated by external forces, first by the scientist Laszlo Jamf, subsequently by the Pavlovian Pointsman, and finally, in an anarchic Germany at the close of World War II, by a host of operators ranging from expatriate Africans to Soviet agents to blackmarketeers. Like Benny Profane in *V.*, he is a schlemihl, perpetual victim of others' plots.

Having been the butt of real conspiracies, Slothrop finds it easy, in fact necessary, to project imaginary ones. Thus when he discovers himself alone in a games room, surrounded by betting tables and money rakes, he cannot let the furnishings remain what they are, mere idle objects:

> These are no longer quite outward and visible signs of a game of chance. There is another enterprise here, more real than that, less merciful, and systematically hidden from the likes of Slothrop. Who sits in the taller chairs? Do They have names? . . .
>
> For a minute here, Slothrop . . . is alone with the paraphernalia of an order whose presence among the ordinary debris of waking he has only lately begun to suspect.[4]

[*141*]

A few pages later on the games imagery undergoes paranoid transformation to describe Slothrop's sense of being subject to external control:

> Oh, the hand of a terrible croupier is that touch on the sleeves of his dreams: all in his life of what has looked free or random, is discovered to've been under some Control, all the time, the same as a fixed roulette wheel. . . . (209)

These passages reveal the key features of Slothrop's thought throughout the novel: the perception of reality as either governed by chance, and therefore meaningless, or else governed by some hidden powers at once "more real" than chance and more ruthless; and the belief that this order, which is felt to lurk behind the debris of the world, is not merely secret, not just passively mysterious like a remote deity, but "systematically hidden from the likes of Slothrop."

One of Pynchon's most distinctive and at times maddening stylistic features follows directly from this deliberate veiling of the conspiracy. All of his central figures — Oedipa Maas in *The Crying of Lot 49*, Stencil and Profane in *V.*, Slothrop and Tchitcherine and Pirate Prentice in *Gravity's Rainbow* — are, in a phrase used to describe Tchitcherine, "held at the edge." They are situated as far from the centers of their respective conspiracies, real or imagined, as the Puritan from his God, and consequently must piece together the most obscure hints and petty revelations to make any sense of the plot at all:

> Those like Slothrop, with the greatest interest in discovering the truth, were thrown back on dreams, psychic flashes, omens, cryptographies, drug-epistemologies, all dancing on a ground of terror, contradiction, absurdity. (582)

Pynchon's reader dances on the same ground. Like Oedipa, Stencil and Slothrop, we are forced at every turn to distinguish genuine glimpses of the conspiratorial order from sheer static. We are also "held at the edge"; we rarely know more than the characters themselves, and they do not know much; and the narrator, if he knows more, rarely tells.

Slothrop's paranoia appears in various guises, ranging from his suspicion that the rocket-bombs falling on London have his name written on them to his fantasy that he is the intended victim of a Father Conspiracy. Freudian readers will discover in the latter episode grounds for interpreting his paranoia in Oedipal terms: wishing to kill the father, the child denies this wish, projecting it onto the father himself, so that the father is believed to desire the death of the son, and therefore becomes a fit object for the son's hatred. Thus Slothrop's fantasy of the Father Conspiracy:

> [T]here is a villain here, serious as death. It is this typical American teenager's own *Father*, trying episode after episode to kill his son. And the kid knows it. Imagine that. So far he's managed to escape his father's daily little death-plots — but nobody has said he has to *keep* escaping. (674)

There are two difficulties in the way of regarding the Freudian account as sufficient. The first is that Slothrop actually has been the victim of a father conspiracy: his father volunteered him as an infant subject for psychological experiments conducted by Laszlo Jamf — a trauma from which Slothrop has never fully recovered, and a manipulative enterprise from which he has never escaped. Pointsman, the English Pavlovian, subsequently takes the place of the father, once again subjecting him to experimentation. Having finished with Slothrop, Pointsman sends two doctors to castrate him. Although they fail in their mission, castrating Major Marvy by mistake, they have in fact been sent. Thus Pynchon explains to us that Slothrop fears a father conspiracy because he has been the victim of one; he fears castration because his experimental controllers wish to castrate him. In this instance, Slothrop is not so much paranoid as perceptive.

The other difficulty in the way of a Freudian explanation is that Pynchon connects Slothrop's paranoia, and therefore by implication his Oedipal terrors, to an inherited religious cast of mind. We are frequently informed of Slothrop's Puritan ancestry, which includes one Salem witch and at least one minister, and which entails expectations of discovering transcendent meaning in the details of everyday life. At one point, hearing a sinister note in a casual comment, he wonders if perhaps he's genetically predisposed — all those earlier Slothrops packing Bibles around the blue hilltops as part of their gear, memorizing chapter and verse the structures of Arks, Temples, Visionary Thrones — all the materials and dimensions. Data behind which always, nearer or farther, was the numinous certainty of God. (241–242)

Later, upon entering the Zone of postwar Germany where conspiracies proliferate with anarchic splendor, he searches for hidden meanings in everything:

> Signs will find him here in the Zone, and ancestors will reassert themselves . . . his own WASPs in buckled black, who heard God clamoring to them in every turn of a leaf or cow loose among apple orchards in autumn. (281)

Slothrop still hears the voices clamoring through the data of his world, but no longer knows whence they come; having lost "the numinous certainty of God," he hunts for conspiracies.

Pynchon himself ventures the claim that paranoia is a secular form of the Puritan consciousness, telling us that Slothrop is possessed by "a Puritan reflex of seeking other orders behind the visible, also known as paranoia" (188). In *Gravity's Rainbow* descriptions of the truth accessible through paranoia similarly evoke the religious notion of revelation:

> [P]aranoia . . . is nothing less than the onset, the leading edge, of the discovery that *everything is connected*, everything in the Creation, a secondary illumination — not yet blindingly One, but at least connected, and perhaps a route In for those like Tchitcherine who are held at the edge. (703)

No matter how many connections he suspects or perceives, however, the paranoiac must still posit some governing agency at the Center, to replace the numinous God. At various moments Slothrop imagines the conspiracy to be directed by industrialists, secret agents, the Rocket, the Earth, or simply by an unspecified Them. Pynchon himself, as we shall see, posits Gravity.

Many other characters in *Gravity's Rainbow* are brushed by the dark wings of paranoia. Pirate Prentice, whose specialty is suffering other people's fantasies, regards himself as dwelling within the pervasive influence of "the Firm." At an early point in his surrogate fantasies he imagines a gigantic rampaging Adenoid which impresses upon England its "master plan" — a parody reminding us that the true home of the paranoid style is science fiction. Roger Mexico, statistician for the British psychological warfare team, fancies himself subject to a "Controlling Agency." Pointsman, who is responsible for many another's anxieties, and who is involved in a conspiracy to bring the kingdom of Pavlov to pass on earth, imagines himself along with the other keepers of Pavlov's "Book" to be the victim of a counterplot. Gwenhidwy yarns about London as "the City Paranoiac." Silvernail, caging his Pavlovian rats, imagines himself a rat in a more comprehensive experiment.

Of course many of the paranoias have a potent basis in fact: Greta Erdmann, Tchitcherine, Enzian, Franz Pökler. The reader could extend the list; nearly every character about whom we are told more than a few paragraphs lapses into paranoia, or dwells there full time. Part of the difficulty in reading *Gravity's Rainbow* derives from the fact that we are presented not with a plot of interwoven fates, but with overlapping case histories of private manias, each character locked within his or her own conspiratorial fantasy. Clinical paranoia is zealously self-referential: the paranoid asserts that (1) there is an order to events, a unifying purpose, however sinister, behind the seeming chaos; and (2) this purpose is focused upon the self, the star and victim. Thus the paranoid individual becomes a hero once again, he stands at the center of a plot; but it is an incurably private one, into which others can enter only as threat.

This pattern of conspiratorial visions is reinforced in *Gravity's Rainbow* by the recurrent imagery of external manipulation. We are told of pigs driven to slaughter, lemmings to the sea. We learn of characters like Katje and Greta Erdmann who are trapped on film, subject to the whims of a Projector. We are reminded that each of us might have a radio implanted in his head, whispering every urge upon us from some remote transmitter. We witness mediums turned into puppets by spirits from the Other Side; in fact we are treated to a good deal of psychic business, all of which amounts to the projection of conspiratorial visions onto a spirit world. Elsewhere we are shown dogs trained to salivate on command, rats to run mazes. There are roulette wheels, carnival rides, an entire Masonic lodge full of pinball machines. The latter seem the most appropriate analogue for Slothrop, like the yo-yo for Benny Profane, because the rocket-chaser is bounced from group to group within the Zone, driven by nothing but inertia and the impulse from his last encounter. And of course at the center of the novel is the Rocket itself, the consummate image of the object governed by external controls. In each case the object controlled may run amok — go mad if it is a creature, haywire if it is a machine — but it may not take upon itself responsibility for its own destiny, its own movement.

The single most persistent conspiratorial vision in the novel, one shared by Slothrop, Tchitcherine and Enzian, is of an industrial cartel which has become (to recall a phrase from Hofstadter) "the motive force in historical events." The theme is announced early on at a séance in which the shade of Walter Rathenau — "prophet and architect of the cartelized state" — is guest spirit. Those attending the séance, suspiciously enough, are also "from the corporate Nazi crowd":

> It might almost — if one were paranoid enough — seem to be a collaboration here, between both sides of the Wall, matter and spirit. What *is* it they know that the powerless do not? What terrible structure behind the appearances of diversity and enterprise? (165)

Several among the powerless in the novel are indeed sufficiently paranoid to suspect that the terrible structure lurking within current history is that of an industrial conspiracy. Slothrop, as the novel's virtuoso paranoiac, subjects us to interminable catalogues of liaisons between General Electric, I. G. Farben, Shell, Siemens and a host of other corporations, many of the links passing through the sinister figures of Laszlo Jamf and Lyle Bland, both of whom were involved in the experimentation upon young Slothrop and in the Rocket's development. Pynchon even makes Bland a Mason, thereby reminding us that he is also familiar with the history of paranoid thought in America: "There is a theory going around that the U.S.A. was and still is a gigantic Masonic plot

under the ultimate control of the group known as the Illuminati"
(587).

The vision of a global industrial conspiracy is in fact a classic
instance of the paranoid style described by Hofstadter, according to which the enemy — here the cartel or the Rocket itself — is

> a free, active, demonic agent. He wills, indeed he manufactures,
> the mechanism of history himself, or deflects the normal course
> of history in an evil way. He makes crises, starts runs on banks,
> causes depressions, manufactures disasters, and then enjoys and
> profits from the misery he has produced.[5]

Slothrop goes so far as to attribute the entire course of the
twentieth century to the machinations of the cartel. Enzian pushes
the analysis one step further, imagining that the cartel itself is
only a cover for a deeper conspiracy:

> [T]his War was never political at all, the politics was all theatre,
> all just to keep the people distracted . . . secretly, it was being
> dictated instead by the needs of technology . . . by a conspiracy
> between human beings and techniques, by something that needed
> the energy-burst of war. . . . The real crises were crises of alloca-
> tion and priority, not among firms — it was only staged to look
> that way — but among the different Technologies, Plastics, Elec-
> tronics, Aircraft, and their needs which are understood only by
> the ruling elite. . . .
>   We have to look for power sources here, and distribution net-
> works we were never taught, routes of power our teachers never
> imagined, or were encouraged to avoid . . . we have to find meters
> whose scales are unknown in the world, draw our own sche-
> matics, getting feedback, making connections, reducing the error,
> trying to learn the real function . . . zeroing in on what in-
> calculable plot? Up here, on the surface, coaltars, hydrogenation,
> synthesis were always phony, dummy functions to hide the real,
> *the planetary mission.* . . . (521)

I quote at length because this is the metaphysical moment in Pynchon: the moment at which fears of conspiracy are projected
onto the cosmos itself. Enzian suggests that the cartel is governed by the needs of technology, technology by matter. And
matter, as every reader of Pynchon knows, is governed by the
laws of thermodynamics, which point toward annihilation. The

planetary mission, the incalculable plot —as the Rathenau shade suggests at his séance and as Pynchon insists throughout the novel — is a movement toward death. What I shall call Pynchon's entropic vision is paranoia grown cosmic.

III

From his earliest published stories, one of which was entitled "Entropy," on through his three subsequent novels, Pynchon has described a universe bent on self-destruction. Viewed in the perspective of this cosmic process, human history is no more than a transient episode, a bubble adrift upon the tide of death. The entropic movement within history and in the universe at large is a conspiracy on the part of matter itself, a conspiracy which tears down molecules and the best-laid plans of men, leading toward numb chaos, toward a state of minimal energy, toward zero. In Pynchon's metaphysic, the Zero, the goal toward which all history lurches, takes the place of the Puritan's Last Judgment.

The irreversible process lies at the heart of *Gravity's Rainbow*. All human action in the novel takes place within the context of war, which Roger Mexico thinks of as the "culture of death." According to Pynchon's entropic view of history, war is not an aberration but a spell of candor, when the deepest historical impulses are nakedly revealed:

> The real War is always there. The dying tapers off now and then, but the War is still killing lots and lots of people. Only right now it is killing them in more subtle ways. Often in ways that are too complicated, even for us, at this level, to trace. But the right people are dying, just as they do when armies fight. (645)

Although couched once again in conspiratorial language, and inserted into an American colonel's fantasy, the passage suggests what the entire movement of the novel makes clear: that Pynchon regards war as a synecdoche for history itself, the drift towards death.

Within the war, and later within the Zone, which serves Pynchon as an image of moral and physical anarchy, there are several mistresses of death who, like V., incarnate the impulse towards annihilation. There is Katje Borgesius, for example, destroyer of General Pudding among others; there is Margherita Erdmann, a masochistic victim in her films and a murderer of Jewish children in real life; and finally there is Nora Dodson-Truck, seeker of the Zero, in love with immobility. The Hereros, who were driven out of Southwest Africa by Von Trotha's campaign of genocide, and who are thus one of several links between *V.* and *Gravity's Rainbow*, are described as the very people of the Zero, dwindling toward extinction. In fact one sect among them, the "Revolutionaries of the Zero," the "Empty Ones," set out on a program of racial suicide. And even Enzian, who leads an opposing faction, is said also to desire the entropic "movement toward stillness" (319).

The deathward movement is also figured in human relations, most graphically in the triangle of torture which links Blicero, Gottfried and Katje, and which echoes the inhumanity of the war. Katje thinks of it as a "formal, rationalized version of what, outside, proceeds without form or decent limit day and night, the summary executions, the roustings, beatings, subterfuge, paranoia, shame" (96). There are in *Gravity's Rainbow*, as in the two previous novels, a few interludes of tenderness and compassion between human beings; but these are so fragile and evanescent that they only accentuate by contrast the general drift toward brutality. Like Jessica, whose love Roger Mexico sought to cultivate as a hedge against the culture of death, every character in the novel is ultimately infected by the war.

The dominant image of deathward movement in the novel is the Rocket itself, whose arched flight is figured in the title. It is at once the focus of enormous human energies of construction, and the agent of destruction; its firing portrays the irreversible process, the shift from order to disorder. Pynchon stresses the bitter link between construction and destruction by situating one of his most moving chapters — that involving Franz Pökler's reunions with his surrogate daughter — in the Nordhausen rocket works, which were separated only by a wall from the extermination camp of Dora. Engineering performed astonishing feats on both sides of the wall, perfecting means of murder. "Every true god must be both organizer and destroyer," thinks Weissmann/ Blicero at one point (99) — and the Rocket is such a god.

The entire novel takes place under the Rocket's parabolic arch, Gravity's Rainbow, because the Rocket whose crossing is announced in the opening sentence actually plummets down at the close, annihilating both speaker and reader as it ends the book. We all ride with Gottfried in the final Rocket, rising with him on the promise of delivery, only to be hustled down again along the parabola's far side toward destruction. In one of her messianic transports, Nora Dodson-Truck imagines herself to be "the Force of Gravity": *"I am That against which the Rocket must struggle, to which the prehistoric wastes submit and are transmuted to the very substance of History"* (639). Gravity indeed becomes, in Pynchon's entropic metaphysic, the very substance of history.

Katje sees in the Rocket's "great airless arc . . . a clear allusion to certain secret lusts that drive the planet and herself, and Those who use her" (223). We are meant to read the same allusion in the Rocket's trajectory. We are meant, along with Slothrop and Katje, to see in it a rainbow whose meaning is the inverse of that in Genesis:

> [I]t is a curve each of them feels, unmistakably. It is the parabola. They must have guessed, once or twice — guessed and refused to believe — that everything, always, collectively, had been moving toward that purified shape latent in the sky, that shape of no surprise, no second chances, no return. Yet they do move forever under it, reserved for its own black-and-white bad news certainly as if it were the Rainbow, and they its children. . . . (209)

The rainbow of Genesis is precisely a token of second chances, a promise of renewal. The rainbow of Gravity is the trajectory of matter, from order to disorder, a process remorseless and irreversible. Gravity, in other words, serves Pynchon as a name for the power at the center of his cosmic conspiracy, the entropic lust that drives the planet, the inimical power bent on dragging all the universe, and mankind along with it, toward death. Gravity becomes the paranoid God, wreaking destruction upon an entire cosmos imagined, in Puritan terms, as innately depraved. There are no possibilities for grace in this metaphysic: it is Calvinist theology conceived in the mode of perdition rather than salvation.

IV

There is in Pynchon's world view one possibility worse than being trapped in a conspiracy leading toward death — and that is not being trapped in a conspiracy at all. The only prospect more terrifying than being caught in Gravity's entropic tide, than being the object of a cosmic plot, is standing outside all plots, swimming free of all tides. Once again Slothrop provides us with a classic formulation of this dreaded anomie:

> If there is something comforting — religious, if you want — about paranoia, there is still also anti-paranoia, where nothing is connected to anything, a condition not many of us can bear for long. Well right now Slothrop feels himself sliding onto the anti-paranoid part of his cycle, feels the whole city around him going back roofless, vulnerable, uncentered as he is. . . .
> Either They have put him here for a reason, or he's just here. He isn't sure that he wouldn't, actually, rather have that *reason.* . . . (434)

This binary perception of the possibilities for understanding history is the single most important feature of Pynchon's world view: paranoia or antiparanoia; either everything is connected, or nothing is connected; reality either radiates from a Center, or it is centerless; history is either wholly determined from without, or it is wholly meaningless; the individual is either manipulated, or he is simply adrift. Once again the pattern of theological expectations is evident: either there is some principle as powerful and absolute as God to order the universe, or else the universe is chaos.

In Calvinist theology — and subsequently in Puritanism —

everyone is held to be either elect or preterite. If elect, one's life is filled with meaning, because one is incorporated into God's scheme of salvation. If preterite, one's life is meaningless, not so much damned as simply void, because one is excluded from God's plan. These are exactly the binary possibilities imagined by Pynchon. And he makes the connection explicit by employing the Calvinist terms throughout *Gravity's Rainbow*. Slothrop would rather be the object of someone else's scheme than simply drift in the chaos of history. His ancestor, William Slothrop, whose hymn closes the novel with a last sad glance at the "poor Pret'rite," wrote a treatise *On Preterition*, which was burned in Boston because no Puritan enjoyed contemplating life without grace, "Nobody wanted to hear about all the Preterite, the many God passes over when he chooses a few for salvation" (555). Enzian, on the other hand, sickened by what he perceives to be the deathward movement of the cosmic conspiracy, identifies with those who are passed over: "Who will believe that in his heart he wants to belong to them out there, the vast Humility sleepless, dying, in pain tonight across the Zone? the preterite he loves" (731). He is the one from whom Slothrop learns the preterite mantra, "mba-kayere," meaning "I am passed over."

To be passed over, to drop out of all plots, is to lose one's identity. Isolated from external schemes, character dissolves. Pynchon formulates this view in Mondaugen's Law, which states that character is a function of historical awareness: "The more you dwell in the past and in the future . . . the more solid your persona. But the narrower your sense of Now, the more tenuous you are" (509). Since for the paranoid all history is conspiratorial, to be dropped from conspiracies is to lose all connection with past and future. In *Gravity's Rainbow* Slothrop is the most spectacular instance of Mondaugen's Law in operation. Having shuffled through various disguises, Slothrop loses all sense of who he *is*. Losing track of where he has come from or where he is going, losing, that is, all historical perspective, Slothrop disintegrates. Others suffer similar fates. Katje, Prentice and Mexico are all cast out of their respective plots, are set adrift among the preterite, and begin to dissolve. Within the novel Pynchon always speaks of freedom in this guise: as a freedom *from* conspiracies, and hence as a ticket to death. The binary possibilities remain: subjection to external control, or disintegration.

The dread that there *are* no conspiracies appears to be Pynchon's chief spur to fiction-making. Like the paranoiac, the artist must invent plots where there are none, must detect voices where there is only static, must project meanings out of sheer terror of meaninglessness. Fausto Maijstral in *V.* speaks for poets, but seems to be speaking for all artists, when he says that they "are alone with the task of living in a universe of things which simply are, and cloaking that innate mindlessness with comfortable and pious metaphor" (*V.*, 326/305). Metaphor — the projection of analogies and correspondences — is the key feature of Pynchon's style. The elaborate search for codes and maps, the desperate efforts to "read" every conceivable sort of data, are all expressions of the dread that there are in fact no patterns in the world, no meanings to be read.

For this reason I take the painting which haunts Oedipa in *The Crying of Lot 49* to be a parable of the artist's dilemma. In that painting she sees girls in a tower

> embroidering a kind of tapestry which spilled out the slit windows and into a void, seeking hopelessly to fill the void: for all the other buildings and creatures, all the waves, ships and forests of the earth were contained in this tapestry, and the tapestry was the world. (*Lot 49*, 21/10)

The manic energy of Pynchon's writing suggests such a hopeless attempt to roof the void with words. *Gravity's Rainbow* reads at times like one long stylistic filibuster, a proliferation of symbolically charged passages, all designed to postpone the apocalyptic fall of the Rocket, the reassertion of the inanimate.

V

I have tried to show that the mental structures implicit in Pynchon's fiction reproduce dominant features of Calvinist and Puritan doctrine — a kinship of which he takes note in *Gravity's*

Rainbow. The analogues which have emerged in my argument
might be schematically listed as follows:

Pynchon	*Puritanism*
paranoia	faith
cosmic conspiracy	God's plan
Gravity	God's will
membership in the Firm	election
exclusion from conspiracy	preterition
multiple narrative patterns	typology
remote control	grace
binary vision	theism/atheism
decadence of history	depravity of man
paranoid self-reference	personal salvation
the Zero	Last Judgment

There are other parallels — his characters speak of demonic and
benevolent agents, of dossiers kept by some remote authority —
but those listed are the primary ones, and sufficient to demonstrate
the theological cast of Pynchon's worldview.

There are in the novel a few nostalgic evocations of a past or
future in which God is enthroned and the world is lucid. General
Pudding, for example, yearns for a bygone time in which men
believed in a Chain of Being, and therefore in a Chain of Command. Slothrop imagines a film of history running backwards,
men rising from graves, bullets retreating harmless into guns —
"the Great Irreversible" entropic movement actually reversed.
To Mexico and Jessica Swanlake is ascribed the oldest of Christian
hopes: an Advent service inspires in them a yearning for

> another night that could actually, with love and cockcrows, light
> the path home, banish the Adversary, destroy the boundaries
> between our lands, our bodies, our stories, all false, about who we
> are: for the one night, leaving only the clear way home and the
> memory of the infant you saw. . . . (135)

But like all Pynchon characters, they live in an irredeemably
secular age; and hence, when leaving the evensong, they find no
clear way home, but stumble into night and snow, seeking "the
path you must create by yourself, alone in the dark" (136).

In addition to the obvious reasons why any writer might translate the structures of a religious ideology into a secular one — reasons such as the conservatism of intellectual systems, or nostalgia for an age of belief — what other influences might have urged Pynchon to articulate this world view? The question, it seems to me, is primarily sociological rather than biographical — however much we might eventually learn about his ideas from a study of his life. That is to say, we need to ask: What features of our economic and political system, what shared social experiences, seem to be explained or expressed in his worldview? Within the confines of this essay I can only suggest the directions in which I believe answers are to be found.

By his choice of period and setting Pynchon identifies one crucial historical influence. All of *Gravity's Rainbow* takes place during the latter months and immediate aftermath of World War II, with extensive flashbacks to the thirties and to the earlier years of the war. This was an era in which paranoia was erected into state policy: the Nazi campaign against the Jews, Stalin's purges, the American incarceration of Orientals, the early salvos of the Cold War. It was the era in which means of controlling public opinion and of spying on private lives were brought to an early blossoming: propaganda became a science, and not only in Germany; intelligence agencies proliferated, espionage became commonplace. Rationing, conscription, mobilization of resources — all the devices for regimenting civilian populations during the war accelerated the movement toward our present administered society. Techniques of "human engineering" and "behavior modification" were developed at that time. In short, the era of the war, and particularly the immediate aftermath in the German Zone, offers a heyday for Pynchon's conspiratorial imagination. His entropic vision gains plausibility in the context of thirty million war-dead. Paranoid suspicions become a measure of mental health in a garrison state.

Hofstadter has suggested that the outbreak of paranoid modes of thought usually occurs in times of

> social conflicts that involve ultimate schemes of values and that bring fundamental fears and hatreds, rather than negotiable

interests, into political action. Catastrophe or the fear of catastrophe is most likely to elicit the syndrome of paranoid rhetoric.[6]

The war was precisely such a time. Pynchon's characters wander
about within the moral and political anarchy of the Zone, trying
to build for themselves private tents of belief to shelter them from
the encroaching night. The Displaced Persons who populate the
Zone epitomize the predicament of all Pynchon's characters. They
are precisely the marginal social types among whom, according
to Norman Cohn, apocalyptic and conspiratorial visions of history
have traditionally arisen.[7]

Several of the war's more ominous technical and political
developments have become prominent features of our own society.
The scale of organization, whether of business or government or
labor, has increased, dwarfing the individual; through mass media
and through electronic surveillance devices, the individual has
become increasingly subject to external observation and manipulation; power has become at once more ruthlessly centralized,
through the interlocking of corporations and unions and governments, and more remote, mysterious, secret; automation has tended
to reduce the individual to a functional, replaceable unit in the
work process; the imperatives of a consumption economy have
generated an array of products which bear no relation to human
needs.

Paranoia is the psychological correlative to these modes of social
organization. If one accepts Herbert Marcuse's argument that we
live in a society which is organized along increasingly rational
lines to serve increasingly irrational ends, then one can see how
the individual may suspect himself to be the victim of a vast and
sinister plot. The citizen of advanced industrial society encounters
a world that is intricately and obscurely organized, that operates
from remote centers of power, that is governed by a technocratic
elite of specialists who command esoteric knowledge, and who
control him by devious means; he is surrounded by gargantuan
institutions whose interconnections are often a mystery even to
their officers, and whose combined decisions around the globe
have a profound, perhaps determining, influence on the course of
history itself. In other words, the typical citizen of advanced

industrial society lives inside a paranoid vision that has come to pass. Pynchon is our most accomplished chronicler of the structures of thought and feeling that correspond to the experience of living in the administered society.

VI

To recognize that Pynchon's world view arises as a creative response to our shared social experience is not, of course, to say that it is the only possible response, or the best one. In conclusion I wish to raise four objections against his view of man and history, objections which are political and philosophical in nature, although they have aesthetic implications.

First of all it seems to me that Pynchon's conspiratorial imagination tends to make our social organization appear even more mysterious than it really is, tends to *mystify* the relations of power which in fact govern our society. Since his leading characters all hover at the margins of conspiracies, they are condemned to be either victims of enterprises they cannot understand, or impotent by-standers, ignorant and ignored. What fragments of the plot they do uncover only make them feel more helpless, more isolated.

My second objection is that the paranoid style of understanding the world is inevitably solipsistic. The paranoiac is capable of imagining only plots which center upon himself; and since few of a society's energies are ever in fact polarized upon any given individual, the paranoiac can never understand more than a minute fraction of his world. Because everyone else might be an agent of the conspiracy, no one can be trusted, and the paranoiac must keep his own counsel. Cut off from all forms of community, he can never work to alter the society which is father to his fears. Pynchon raises the possibility that this solipsism may itself be a goal of the conspiracy: "What if They find it convenient to preach an island of life surrounded by a void? Not just the Earth in space, but your own individual life in time? What if it's *in Their interest* to have you believing that?" (697). Stripped of its mystifying overtones, this becomes a crucial question to ask of the administered society. For what are the social consequences of the belief that every man is an island, armed against every other? Men who are afraid of joining together for collective action obviously make tamer citizens than those who are not so afraid. A nation of paranoiacs would be a totalitarian's dream — as witness the universal efforts of dictators to breed fear and mistrust among their subjects.

My third objection is that Pynchon reifies technology. That is, instead of treating it as a body of knowledge which men have developed for satisfying their needs and for dealing with the material world, instead of presenting it as a complex of relations among men, Pynchon has elevated technology into a metaphysical principle standing outside human control. By capitalizing the t., by surrounding the Rocket, its chief token, with an aura of necessity, he has invested Technology with supernatural force. Any sensible man must agree with Pynchon's own observation that our industrial system, if it continue on its present course, will exhaust the earth. But the surest way to bring that catastrophe about is to believe that it is inevitable, that it is dictated by the logic of technology.

My fourth and last objection is that Pynchon has presented a particular social condition — the experience of the anomic, manipulated, paranoid individual within advanced industrial society — as if it were the human condition. He treats the Zone as the World, the Displaced Person as Everyman. He interprets an era of decadence in a particular form of society as proof that we are doomed to fall away from the human, that we are tugged along in a cosmic tide of death. It is this leap from historical observation to metaphysical assertion that I find unacceptable. Pynchon seems to me a brilliant chronicler of our prevailing anxieties, but a faulty philosopher. His fiction is so dominated by an awareness of the pressures that lead to a dissolution of personality and to the disintegration of culture itself that he finds scant space for imagining contrary historical impulses, possibilities for recovery, for renewal, for reunion.

Notes

1. *The Paranoid Style in American Politics and Other Essays* (New York, 1965), p. 14.
2. *Ibid.*, p. 29.
3. For a discussion of the sociological theory which underlies the following analysis, see my article, "Towards a Social Theory of Literature," *Telos*, No. 18 (Winter 1973–74), pp. 107–121.
4. I quote from the Viking Press edition (New York, 1973), p. 202. All future quotations from *Gravity's Rainbow* will be taken from this edition; references will be noted in parentheses. References to *V.* and *The Crying of Lot 49* will note both the Lippincott editions (*V.*, New York, 1963; *Lot 49*, New York, 1966) and the Bantam paperbacks published a year later.
5. Hofstadter, p. 32.
6. Hofstadter, p. 39.
7. Norman Cohn, *The Pursuit of the Millennium*, 2nd ed. (New York, 1961), pp. 314–315.

Gravity's Encyclopedia

Edward Mendelson

I

*In both its range and, one may predict, its cultural position,
Gravity's Rainbow*[1] recalls only a few books in the Western
tradition. To refer to it as a novel is convenient, but to read it
as a novel — as a narrative of individuals and their social and
psychological relations — is to misconstrue it. Although the genre
that now includes *Gravity's Rainbow* is demonstrably the most
important single genre in Western literature of the Renaissance
and after, it has never previously been identified. *Gravity's Rainbow* is an *encyclopedic narrative*, and its companions in this most
exclusive of literary categories are Dante's *Commedia*, Rabelais's
five books of Gargantua and Pantagruel, Cervantes's *Don Quixote*,
Goethe's *Faust*, Melville's *Moby-Dick*, and Joyce's *Ulysses*.

Each major Western national culture, as it becomes fully conscious of itself as a unity, produces an encyclopedic author, but
not all encyclopedists produce a single encyclopedic narrative. In
England the encyclopedic role is divided among the tales of
Chaucer and the plays of Shakespeare. The only unified encyclopedic narratives written in England thus arrive too late to
fulfill a central cultural role, and are self-consciously aware of the
limitations of their belatedness. These encyclopedic latecomers
include most notably the mock-encyclopedia *Tristram Shandy*
which, like the "Tristra-paedia" it contains, collapses under the
weight of data too numerous and disparate for its organizing

mechanisms to bear; and the satiric imaginary encyclopedia *Gulliver's Travels*, which fulfills all the formal requirements of an encyclopedia but, through its displacement from Britain into imagined colonies, fails to inhabit the historical and cultural position already securely occupied by Shakespeare. *Ulysses* resolves the difficulties of an encyclopedia of a belated and marginal Irish culture by acknowledging the political marginality of its protagonist, while asserting the literary centrality and density of the book's relation to the larger culture of Europe.

This is not the occasion for a general theory of encyclopedic narrative, which I hope to supply elsewhere, but it may be useful to construct a model that will serve for the moment.[2] Encyclopedic narratives attempt to render the full range of knowledge and beliefs of a national culture, while identifying the ideological perspectives from which that culture shapes and interprets its knowledge. Because they are the products of an epoch in which the world's knowledge is larger than any one person can encompass, they necessarily make extensive use of synecdoche. No encyclopedic narrative can contain all of physical science, so examples from one or two sciences serve to represent the whole scientific sector of knowledge. One of many points of distinction between epic and encyclopedia is the epic writer's unconcern with fields of knowledge outside his experience. In the ancient epic, no such fields exist, or none of any importance; while in the modern epic, which is generally interiorized or miniature like *The Prelude*, the only knowledge that matters is the knowledge through which a mind creates itself.

Encyclopedic narrative evolves out of epic, and often uses epic structure as its organizing skeleton (Dante, Cervantes, Joyce), but the subjects of epic become increasingly vestigial to the encyclopedic form. Joyce wrote that *Ulysses* was "a sort of encyclopedia,"[3] and *Ulysses* probably shows the last extensive use of epic patterns in Western encyclopedic writing. Epics treat of the immediate culture in which they are written only allusively and analogically: epic action is set in a legendary past, and although that action may comment forcefully on the situation of the writer's "present," as does the *Aeneid*, the action takes few of its particulars from the facts of ordinary "present" experience. Encyclopedic narratives are set *near* the immediate present, but not in it. The main action of most of them occurs about twenty years before the time of writing, allowing the book to maintain a mimetic (or, more precisely, satiric) relation to the world of its readers, while permitting it also to include prophecies that are accurate, having been fulfilled between the time of the action and the time of writing. These "accurate" prophecies then claim implicitly to confer authority on other prophecies in the book which have not yet been fulfilled. Thus Dante begins writing around 1307 about events of 1300, and can easily make his characters prophesy the death of Pope Boniface VIII in 1303. Cervantes lets Don Quixote prophesy the writing of his own history, and Joyce prophesies the authorship of Stephen Dedalus. Pynchon sets the action of his book at the moment which he proposes as the originating instant of contemporary history, a gestative nine months at the end of the Second World War. Encyclopedic narrative thus achieves the double function of prophecy and satire: it predicts events that are, in reference to the book's action, in the unpredictable future, yet the action is sufficiently close to the moment of publication to allow the book to describe and encompass the familiar details of its readers' lives.

The prophetic quality of encyclopedic narrative — its openness in time — is echoed by its peculiar indeterminacy of form. Generic analysis of encyclopedic narratives yields far more limited results than may be gained from most other varieties of narrative. An encyclopedic narrative is, among other things, an encyclopedia *of* narrative, incorporating, but never limited to, the conventions of heroic epic, quest romance, symbolist poem, bourgeois novel, lyric interlude, drama, eclogue, and catalogue.

Encyclopedic narrative identifies itself not by special plot or structure, but by encompassing a special set of qualities. Almost all encyclopedic narratives share a range of characteristics peculiar to themselves, and these characteristics may, in summary form, be listed briefly. (Near-encyclopedias — *War and Peace, Middlemarch, Bouvard et Pécuchet, U.S.A., One Hundred Years of Solitude*, the work of Balzac and Quevedo — are excluded from the central genre not only by their lack of many or most of these characteristics, but also by their failure to occupy a special cultural position.)

All encyclopedic narratives include a full account of at least one technology or science. That is, they correlate the opposed worlds of aesthetic freedom (which is reflected in art) and natural necessity (which is reflected in science) far more elaborately than most other literary works. A complete medieval astronomy may be constructed out of the *Commedia*. Don Quixote explores the pharmacopeia and is an adept at the "science of arms." *Faust* expounds opposing geological theories, and anticipates evolutionary biology. *Moby-Dick* is an encyclopedia of cetology. A detailed summary of embryology is embedded in "The Oxen of the Sun" chapter of *Ulysses*, as is a theory of positivism in "Ithaca." *Gravity's Rainbow* is expert in ballistics, chemistry, and mathematics. An encyclopedic narrative normally also includes an account of an art outside the realm of written fiction: the carved bas-reliefs in the *Purgatorio*, the puppetry of *Don Quixote*, the Greek tragedy in *Faust*, whale-painting in *Moby-Dick*, the musical echoes in *Ulysses*'s "Sirens," film and opera in *Gravity's Rainbow*.[4]

Each encyclopedic narrative is an encyclopedia of literary styles, ranging from the most primitive and anonymous levels (all encyclopedias include compendia of proverb-lore, as *Gravity's Rainbow* lists the Proverbs for Paranoids) to the most esoteric of high styles. All encyclopedias metastasize the monstrousness of their own scale by including giants or gigantism: the giants who guard the pit of Hell in Dante, the eponymous heroes in Rabelais, the windmills which Don Quixote takes for giants, the mighty men whom Faust sends into battle, Moby Dick, the stylistic gigantism of Joyce's "Cyclops," the titans under the earth in *Gravity's Rainbow*, and the angel over Lübeck whose eyes went "towering for miles" (151).

Because encyclopedic narratives appear near the beginning of a culture's or a nation's sense of its own separate existence, and because Melville has already fulfilled the encyclopedic role in North America, Pynchon's international scope implies the existence of a new international culture, created by the technologies of instant communication and the economy of world markets. Pynchon implies that the contemporary era has developed the first common international culture since medieval Latin Europe separated into the national cultures of the Renaissance. The distinguishing character of Pynchon's new internationalism is its substitution of data for goods: "Is it any wonder the world's gone insane," someone asks in *Gravity's Rainbow*, "with information come to be the only real medium of exchange?" (258). Elsewhere, another character explains that the immediate postwar situation is "like the very earliest days of the mercantile system. We're back to that again" (336). The postwar proliferation of new systems and structures is made possible by the elimination of older systems that can no longer function, the collapse of social structures that have grown obsolete: "this War . . . just for the moment has wiped out the proliferation of little states that's prevailed in Germany for a thousand years. Wiped it clean. *Opened it*" (265, Pynchon's italics).

Pynchon's implied historical claims are enormous, and, in any sober reader, should inspire a healthy skepticism. But the book's ambition is essential to its design. No one could suppose that encyclopedic narratives are attractive or comfortable books. Like the giants whose histories they include, all encyclopedias are monstrous (as they are *monstra* in the oldest Latin sense — omens of dire change). None of their narratives culminates in a completed relation of sexual love. Dante's flesh cannot merge with Beatrice's soul; Panurge never gets around to marrying; Dulcinea either does not exist at all, or — if you happen to be reading a different part of the book — she does exist, but Don Quixote has never seen her; Faust loses Margarete a third of the way through the book, then marries and loses the bodiless Helen; Ahab's wife waits on shore for widowhood; Bloom and Molly do not resume the sexual relations they ended a decade ago; and, while Mexico loses Jessica, Slothrop, for all his sexual exuberance, disintegrates lovelessly. The encyclopedic impulse is both analytic and synthetic: in its analytic and archetypally masculine mode, it separates a culture into its disparate elements, while its synthetic, archetypally feminine mode merges them in the common texture of a single book: but it is a law of encyclopedic form that the synthetic mode cannot be localized in a single sexual relationship. Compared with other works by the same authors, encyclopedias find it exceptionally difficult to integrate their women characters into the narrative at any level more quotidian or humane than the levels of archetype and myth.

Encyclopedic narrative strains outwards from the brief moments of personal love towards the wider expanses of national and mythical history, and towards the history of its own medium. All encyclopedias are polyglot books, and all provide a history of language. Dante identifies the dialects of Italy and France and the degenerate language of Nimrod, and in Canto XXVI of the *Paradiso* Adam offers a religious history of language. Panurge begs bread from Pantagruel in thirteen languages (three of them invented for the occasion) before getting around to French. Don Quixote is expert in etymology, especially the effect of Arabic on Castilian. Faust educates Helen out of Greek hexameters into the rhymed stanzas of romance languages. Melville opens his book with a full range of etymologies. Joyce puns in at least seven languages. Pynchon uses French, German, Italian, Spanish, Middle Dutch, Latin, Japanese, Kirghiz, Herero,[5] various English and American dialects — all with their concentrated emblem in the German-Latin macaronic that Roger Mexico and Jessica Swan-lake hear in an English church at Christmas. Pynchon also asserts the inclusiveness of his vision through his development and use of three "national" styles: a dignified and elegiac manner employed for British characters and settings, a slangy American dialect that syncopates around Tyrone Slothrop and pretends to be a stream-of-mutterings, and a heightened solemn manner used for German scenes, one which I suspect is meant to recall the prose style of Rilke. (It is noteworthy that the only conventionally modernist sections of the book are the Slothrop sequences, with their private point of view and stream of consciousness. Slothrop's disintegration, Pynchon implies, summarizes the historical fate of literary modernism.)

The difference between the two twentieth-century encyclopedias in English, Joyce's and Pynchon's, appears in an especially emphatic manner in their opposing accounts of language. The *knowledge* of language in Pynchon and Joyce is entirely comparable, but their *histories* of language arise from drastically incompatible visions of both language and the larger world. "The Oxen of the Sun" chapter of *Ulysses* offers a linguistic history on an organic model derived from embryology. Joyce's history is primarily a history of style, and of the effects of style on social conventions. Like an embryo metamorphosing progressively from silent zygote to squalling infant, the styles of Joyce's chapter metamorphose historically from Old English to a drunken garble that staggers through the language of the present. The historical sequence is interrupted only by brief delays and anticipations based on corresponding anomalies in the development of the embryo. Pynchon's corresponding historical linguistics occupies the episode in *Gravity's Rainbow* that follows Tchitcherine to the Kirghiz (338–359), and is a history not of style but of the political *use* of language. It is also an exposition of the ways in which language is altered by political decisions, and of the modes in which language affects the world of life and death that lies ultimately outside language.

Read as if it were one element among the conventional structures of a novel, the Kirghiz episode seems disproportionate and anomalous. Its apparent goal, Tchitcherine's vision of the Kirghiz Light, does have analogical relations with other charismatic goals in the book; and the prehistoric city that lies below Tchitcherine "in mineral sleep" as he watches the Kirghiz Light gives local habitation to the strata and processes described by the spirit of Walter Rathenau in an earlier chapter (167). Tchitcherine's vision almost but (the narrator emphasizes) not quite induces in Tchitcherine himself the emptying and rebirth that takes place on a political level in the book's vision of a disordered Europe. But all the rest of the sequence, concerned as it is with the motives and consequences of the Soviet introduction of a Latin alphabet into illiterate Kazakhstan — what can that have to do with the rest of the book?

Yet once the encyclopedic nature of the book is recognized,

the Kirghiz interlude moves from its apparent place at the book's periphery to its ideological and thematic center. Virtually every event in *Gravity's Rainbow* is involved in a political process: specifically, the transformation of charismatic energy into the controlled and rationalized routine of a bureaucracy. These terms are of course borrowed from Max Weber, to whom Pynchon twice attributes the phrase "the routinization of charisma" (325, 364). The history of language in *Gravity's Rainbow* illustrates one version of this process of political organization. For the Kirghiz people, before the arrival of Tchitcherine and his bureaucracy, language "was purely speech, gesture, touch . . . not even an Arabic script to replace" (338). With the introduction of the New Turkic Alphabet, or NTA, whole systems of committees, subcommittees, various divisions of labor and authority now organize and reticulate themselves over the buried strata of the local folk culture. Unlike the language of Joyce's "Oxen of the Sun," the NTA does not develop according to an organic model, but is shaped deliberately by the forces of government, forces which are themselves ultimately directed and initiated by the cartels which organize the book's secular world.

The processes that shape the NTA, and with it the Kirghiz language, are enactments, at a relatively modest scale, of world-processes that function throughout the book. But the events of the book cannot be blamed entirely on the political intentions of cartels and governments: the processes that shape events in *Gravity's Rainbow* operate continuously on all levels of the book's reality, including the mythic levels of titans, the bodiless world of the dead, and the submicroscopic level of chemical structure, all of which even the powerful cartels can neither recognize nor control.[6] One of the NTA functionaries, Igor Blobadjian, has a vision in which he is reduced to the size of molecules, and discovers that the political processes in which he participates at the level of the world "above" have their molecular counterparts in the chemical politics of the world "below."

The NTA is shaped by processes that are not merely linguistic, and its effects are felt outside of language. The availability of a written language permits more than the simple act of writing: it makes possible new events not limited to the realm of signs. Pynchon's parenthetical joke gets to the heart of the matter:

> On sidewalks and walls the very first printed slogans start to show up, the first Central Asian . . . kill-the-police-commissioner signs (and somebody does! this alphabet is really something!) and so the magic that the shamans, out in the wind, have always known, begins to operate now in a political way. . . . (355–356)

The shamans worked curses and blessings through incantations or spells, but now language, formulated into writing, operates "in a political way." The consequences of this realization have a tragic force. All the book's efforts at truth-telling, all its thrusts at the increase of freedom through the revelation of necessity, are *infected* by the inevitable fact that the book itself must use a language that is, unavoidably, a system shaped by the very powers and orders that it hopes to reveal. Language can never be liberated from lies. One cannot speak outside of language, and one cannot directly speak the truth within it — this not only in the reflexive sense proclaimed by recent critical theory, but in a political sense as well. To separate oneself from language, in an attempt to be free from its imposed order, is to enter a world of chaos and vacancy. This tragic realization is at the ideological center as well as on the stylistic surface of the book. *Gravity's Rainbow* does not propose — with the romantic fervor appropriate to such proposals — that you escape the systems of pain and control that occupy and shape the world: the book insists that it is impossible to escape those systems yet retain any decency, memory, or even life — just as it is impossible to escape from language yet communicate. If the connectedness of the world has its metonym in paranoia — "nothing less than the onset, the leading edge, of the discovery that *everything is connected*, everything in the Creation" (703) — then Slothrop's detachment from the world's order and the order of language (he is in the end unable to speak or even to hear) may be called "anti-paranoia, where nothing is connected to anything, a condition not many of us can bear for long" (434).

The NTA episode proposes the linguistic basis for *Gravity's*

Rainbow, but it also fortuitously provides us with our first extended glance into Pynchon's workshop. Although the organizing historical intelligence behind each of Pynchon's books may be identified with little difficulty — Henry Adams is named in *V.*, as Weber is named in *Gravity's Rainbow*, and I have presented elsewhere the evidence for Mircea Eliade's shaping presence behind *The Crying of Lot 49* — no one has yet identified a source for any of the *local* clusters of data in Pynchon's work.[7] The NTA episode, if it is in fact as typical of the rest of the book as it appears to be, demonstrates how little of Pynchon's world is built from nothing. In fact, virtually all the historical and linguistic details in the episode derive directly from an article by Thomas G. Winner, "Problems of Alphabetic Reform among the Turkic Peoples of Soviet Central Asia, 1920–1941," in the *Slavonic and East European Review*, 31 (1952), 133–147. And the Kirghiz folklore, the ajtys, the aqyn, and all the Kirghiz vocabulary of the episode, derive from Professor Winner's book, *The Oral Art and Literature of the Kazakhs of Russian Central Asia* (Durham, 1958). As far as I can determine, however, the Kirghiz Light is Pynchon's own invention.

The scale of the source and the fiction are of course entirely different: Pynchon selects from, and elaborates on, some of the smallest of Professor Winner's details. Pynchon invents a bureaucratic dispute over the spelling of "stenography," a word required in the Kirghiz language only as a consequence of the politically motivated introduction of an alphabet. You don't need a word for stenography if you can't write. The dispute — "a crisis over which kind of g to use" (353), whether a roman g or an ad hoc letter resembling a reversed cyrillic g — exfoliates from a footnote in which Professor Winner lists loan-words in Kirghiz, of which the word for stenography is the only one using the unusual letter. By the end of the episode the whole matter has become embedded in the texture of the narrative: Tchitcherine takes down the Aqyn's song of the Kirghiz Light "in stenography" (357).

One almost hesitates to report a discovery of this kind. Charismatic books tend, like other loci of charisma, to develop a routinized critical bureaucracy around them. Who, witnessing the enormous multinational operations of the IG Joyce cartel, would choose to open an office in the Pynchon industry? Fortunately, the identification of a source in Pynchon does not lead in circular fashion to a curious bit of antiquariana that illuminates nothing outside the work or its literary tradition. Behind Pynchon stands Weber, whose concepts and vocabulary have articulated structures by which the world has actually been affected. Behind Joyce stands Victor Bérard, whose *Les Phéniciens et l'Odysée* is an interesting work of scholarly reconstruction, but nothing more. And where Pynchon uses social, political, and economic systems which actually affect our lives, Joyce uses not even the historical illuminations of Bérard but the arbitrary speculations of Madame Blavatsky and the occult "sciences."

Pynchon, in choosing one aspect of the history of language to serve metonymically for the whole, selected the most inescapably political aspect he could find. The introduction of the NTA involves a complex of political motives arising in the decisions of a central authority, and shaped by political circumstances. When Joyce offers a history of language linked metaphorically to embryology, he implies that the development of language is entirely a natural process, its variety and change deriving from a process of evolution substantially unaffected by locality or motive. (Joyce's connection between language and its representative is a metaphoric not a metonymic one: relations in Joyce are analogical and aesthetic, in Pynchon etiological and historic.) For Pynchon, as for the rest of us, the separation of language from the world it alters and describes is not an unchanging ontological problem, but a political one, whose recognition ultimately permits the possibility of voluntary action and response.

II

The political history of language in *Gravity's Rainbow* has antecedents in the accounts of statecraft that inform all encyclopedic narratives, whether explicitly as in Don Quixote's instructions for

Sancho Panza's governorship, or by inversion as in the rules of the Abbey of Thélème or the decrees of the New Bloomusalem. Statecraft is a larger matter than social observation. Almost all novels, until recently at least, concern themselves not only with character but also with a descriptive account (in some cases prescriptive) of the specific society in which the characters live. Upon such description encyclopedic narrative superimposes a theory of social organization, normally a theory which offers itself implicitly for *use* outside the book. The writing of an encyclopedic narrative proves to be a political act, and the narrative itself tends sooner or later to be co-opted for political purposes — of which some, certainly, have been alien to the book's author. Dante's use of his native Tuscan in preference to international Latin had political consequences for Italian nationalism — or at least provided a focus for later political acts. In *Le Conflit des Interprétations*, Paul Ricoeur writes that the display of a world and the positioning of an ego are symmetrical and reciprocal. Encyclopedic narrative not only locates an ego, it also locates a culture or a nation.

Furthermore, the development of a nation's self-recognition, and its identification of an encyclopedic narrative or author as its central cultural monument, are also reciprocal processes. The idea of Italian or German nationality makes use of Dante or Goethe while at the same time canonizing them (in the original senses of the word). But encyclopedic narratives begin their history from a position *outside* the culture whose literary focus they become; they only gradually find a secure place in a national or critical order. Dante writes the *Commedia* in exile; Rabelais's books fall under the interdict of the Sorbonne, and their author has to go into hiding; Cervantes refers to *Don Quixote* as "just what might be begotten in a prison"; Goethe allows publication of Part II of *Faust* only after his death; *Moby-Dick* receives most of its early recognition in England; the last words printed in the encyclopedia of Dublin are "Trieste-Zürich-Paris." To an extent unknown among other works that have become cultural monuments, encyclopedic narratives begin their career *illegally*.

Short of committing a crime, there is little a modern writer in

Western Europe or North America can do, as writer, to put himself in an illegal position. In any case, the illegality of encyclopedic narratives is never deliberately *sought* by their authors. The West's wide range of toleration leaves, paradoxically, only a narrow area for dissent — which Pynchon has managed to occupy. His elusive near-anonymity, which entirely predates his encyclopedic efforts, is a stance alien to our literary culture; and *Gravity's Rainbow*'s drastic violations of what remains of the tattered fabric of literary decorum assert a further distance from officialdom. Critics who praise Pynchon tend to gloss over the uncomfortable fact that he writes quite a few stomach-turning pages. Slothrop's nightmare of a descent through the sewers, Brigadier Pudding's coprophilia, Mexico and Bodine's verbal disruption of officialdom at the dinner table — or Mexico's urinary dissolution of the solemnity of an official meeting — are all gross violations of literary and social decorum. When critics blithely quote such passages, as if they were as innocuous as Longfellow, they do Pynchon a disservice in ignoring the uncomfortable fact that his language retains an unmistakable power to shock and disgust, without ever allowing itself to be dismissed as infantilism or mere noise. Only a false sophistication — or a terminally brutalized sensibility — can claim not to be repelled by many pages of *Gravity's Rainbow*.

The illegality of Pynchon's vision has already been illuminated by a critic who never heard of Pynchon: Mikhail Bakhtin in *Rabelais and His World*. Bakhtin provides the finest available introduction to the decorum of *Gravity's Rainbow*, and, in consequence, demonstrates the deep historical roots of Pynchon's literary mode. Bakhtin observes that Rabelais's laughter stands assertively outside the realm of dogma and law, and that Rabelais writes at a moment when a received hierarchical system suffers the strains that will ultimately shatter it. Pynchon, like Rabelais, proposes a grotesquerie that governance can never acknowledge, a vital energy that officialdom must always seek to rationalize or destroy (*cf.* 688). Bakhtin's discussion of Rabelais's use of the common perception that urine has a power both debasing and generating brings Mexico's gesture of revolt in Mossmoon's office into sharper focus. Bakhtin's analysis of the use of excrement in the feast of fools rescues Katje's debasement of Brigadier Pudding from its narrow place in a catalogue of perversions, and allows it to serve as a vision of the temporary, but recurring, reversals that restore energy to the sullen bureaucracies of the rationalized world.

In a *positive*, or affirming, illegality Roger Mexico and Jessica Swanlake (whose first initials recall two earlier illegal lovers in Verona) enjoy their love only during the chaotic disorder of the war. They come together in forbidden territory, an evacuated village under barrage balloons. After the war, "in the rationalized power-ritual that will be the coming peace," Jessica will return to an empty legality, and lose "her cheeky indifference to death-institutions" (126); she "will take her husband's orders . . . will become a domestic bureaucrat" (177). Wretched at his loss, Mexico resorts to *negative* illegality, gestures of revolt that save him from living within an empty legal order, but otherwise do little more than satisfy a nose-thumbing impulse, and establish no alternate enterprise of love or understanding. On a larger scale, the negative illegality of the book's black markets establishes false and betraying systems, whose agents and organizers end in blithering inanity. Tyrone Slothrop ends in a condition of *a*legality, neither in revolt against social organization, nor, certainly, in concord with it, but in absolute separation from all systems of organization whatever.

An encyclopedic narrative is a work of positive illegality, originating in moments of hierarchical strain and cultural distress. But some years after its author sends it out into the world, and after literary orthodoxy has expended much energy in attempting to exile or dismiss the book's outrageousness, the book itself, now safely settled in the literary-historical past, becomes an element in a centripetal network of official cultural self-consciousness and the focus of an organized bureaucracy of textual and historical scholarship. The cartels of Goethe G.m.b.H., Dante Internazionale S.A., and IG Joyce are continuing organizations, where specialization and the division of labor are (below certain high levels of management) well-observed procedures, in which recognized authorities deliver written verdicts on the work of lesser figures in the organization, and in which, more often than not, a position in the firm guarantees a lifetime of steady work and reliable remuneration. These are, of course, the characteristics Weber assigns to legal bureaucracies in general. And the process by which an encyclopedic narrative becomes integrated into its culture — becomes, in fact, the focus of an organized culture of its own — is a version of the pandemic Weberian process in *Gravity's Rainbow*, the process through which charismatic eruptions, originating in moments of cultural distress, become rationalized into legal bureaucracy.

Charisma, in Pynchon studies, is not only about to be rationalized, it is about to become a very tired subject indeed. It is not, however, Pynchon's only inheritance from Weber. Pynchon's pervasive insistence on the reality of *process* finds theoretical justification in Weber's social analyses, which pursue a dynamic understanding of society rather than a reified one. At a séance early in *Gravity's Rainbow*, the spirit of Walter Rathenau refers to the successions of geologic strata — "epoch on top of epoch, city on top of ruined city." "These signs are real," Rathenau (or Pynchon's extension of him) continues. "They are also symptoms of a process. The process follows the same form, the same structure. To apprehend it you will follow the signs. All talk of cause and effect is secular history, and secular history is a diversionary tactic" (167). The signs we are to follow are only signs, but they are the shells and the consequence of sacred (not secular) processes: "Names by themselves may be empty, but the *act of naming* . . ." (366, Pynchon's italics and evocative ellipsis).

Like the hieratic language of *The Crying of Lot 49*, Weberian processes and terminology invade even the smallest crevices in the texture of *Gravity's Rainbow*. When Mexico envisions Jessica as "a domestic bureaucrat," he echoes Weber, as does Squalidozzi in explaining the control of "the center" (Weber's Central Zone) in ordinary times. Blicero's carefully separated technicians, each with his function in the *Schwarzgerät* project, make up a textbook example of the division of labor. A universal obsession in *Gravity's Rainbow* is *control*, Pynchon's translation of Weber's

Herrschaft. Weber distinguishes three pure types of authority or control, for each of which Pynchon provides a parody or a representation. The three types are *legal* domination, accomplished through a bureaucratic administrative staff (exemplified by "the Firm" and all the acronymic branches of the Allied war effort), *traditional* domination by patriarchies or by military leaderships with relatively independent surrogates (as in Tchitcherine's relation to Stalin), and *charismatic* authority centered on the exceptional qualities or powers of a leader's personality (as in Enzian's authority over the Schwarzkommando, an authority ultimately to be fulfilled "after" the end of the book, through his sacrificial ascension in the rocket).[8]

Slothrop himself embodies a parody of charismatic authority that Weber never anticipated: the mock-charismatic figure entirely victimized by an authority he neither wants nor understands. Slothrop first distinguishes himself when it is noticed that a map he keeps of his sexual adventures (real or fantasized) corresponds in a statistically significant manner with a map of V-2 strikes on London. To make the matter more perplexing, the stars on Slothrop's map *precede* by a few days the stars on a map of rocket strikes. Slothrop eventually becomes aware of a relation between his sexual impulses and the V-2 rocket, but the *precise* nature and cause of that relation never emerges in the book, and it remains entirely a mystery. Pointsman, committed to the use of bureaucracy and the rationalized world of Pavlovian psychology, thinks Slothrop a "monster" whose continued subjugation to official *Herrschaft* is necessary for the maintenance of order in the large: "*We must never lose control.* The thought of him lost in the world of men, after the war, fills me with a deep dread I cannot extinguish" (144; the last word recalls Pavlov's "extinguishing" of conditioned reflexes). But Slothrop escapes into the chaos of the Zone. Weber emphasizes that charisma appears at times of political, economic, social, religious, and cultural distress (legal and traditional domination are adequate to ordinary times), and it is at the chaotic end of the war that Slothrop's mock-charisma becomes most manifest. In Berlin he tries on the costume of a

Wagnerian tenor, and looks a bit like the V-2 rocket whose special (charismatic) qualities he has been seeking to identify. Those around him immediately call him Rocketman, and take for granted his attainment of the charismatic powers that belong to any comic-book hero: "No job is too tough for Rocketman" (371). By mere accident Slothrop's presence manages to confound officialdom — without Slothrop even being aware of it — and he is elevated into a "force": "There is a counterforce in the Zone," Tchitcherine is convinced (611). Eventually Slothrop adopts the costume of the charismatic pig-hero of a German town. When Russian police enter a melee on the day of the annual celebration of the pig's heroic feats, Slothrop wonders if he is "expected to repel *real* foreign invaders now?" (570).

Weber applies the term "charisma" to "a certain quality of an individual personality by virtue of which he is set apart from ordinary men and treated as endowed with supernatural, super-human, or at least specifically exceptional powers or qualities." So far, this description fits Slothrop precisely, but Weber goes on to say that a charismatic figure, in consequence of his special powers, is "treated as a leader," as Slothrop decidedly is not. "The Schwarzgerät is no Grail, Ace. . . . And you no knightly hero" (364). Far from being led by Slothrop, every official organization in Europe seems to think that he is the agent of their own interests. And the Counterforce that organizes around its desire to rescue him from dissolution becomes at last a bureaucracy committed to denying Slothrop's charismatic authority, not maintaining it: "We were never that concerned with Slothrop *qua* Slothrop" (738).[9]

Gravity's Rainbow, then, is *about* the rationalization of charis-matic authority, but, as an encyclopedic narrative, it is also the most recent member of a class of books that *enact* the same process in their own history. The process by which illegal charisma, originating in a moment of distress, becomes rationalized into legal bureaucratic organization, is precisely the process by which encyclopedic narrative, conceived outside the received sys-tems of literary culture, becomes a central element in successor organizations, the focus of new bureaucracies. And so *Gravity's*

Rainbow prophesies not only Western history between the time of its action and the time of its publication, but also its own history, the history of its own reception.

III

From his position at the edge of a culture, an encyclopedist redefines that culture's sense of what it means to be human. An encyclopedic narrative prophesies the modes of human action and perception that its culture will later discover to be its own central concerns. The disturbing "illegal" strangeness of most encyclopedic narratives at the time of their publication, the differences between the book and its culture's self-conceptions, are the result of the encyclopedist's understanding of modes of meaning that a culture has already begun to use but has not yet learned to acknowledge.

It is the interior world that has dominated the most noteworthy sophisticated fiction in the English language during this century, and the most precisely detailed literary presentation of interior experience is its encyclopedia: Joyce's *Ulysses*. The assumptions made in *Ulysses* as to what is significant in the world of reality, and what is not, have become the generally unexamined assumptions in most British and American fiction during the past fifty years. *Ulysses* is in no way the cause of the depressingly universal acceptance of the assumptions it embodies, but its massive authority has given special sanction to the literary modes — many of them not at all "Joycean" — of which it is the most notable exemplar.

The emergence of a writer whose authority is comparable to Joyce's, but who breaks radically with Joyce's assumptions — as Mexico suggests to Pointsman that science must "have the courage to junk cause-and-effect entirely, and strike off at some other angle" (89) — allows us to recognize that Joyce's perspective is a special one, without conclusive authority for the modern era.

My point here is hardly to diminish Joyce: I hope instead that an account of his successor-encyclopedist will inevitably suggest ways in which both Joyce's and Pynchon's work may be *located* more accurately than criticism has been able to do until now. *Gravity's Rainbow* provides an encyclopedic presentation of the world from a perspective that permits inclusion of fields of data and realms of experience that Joyce's perspective excludes. To locate the perspectives of *Gravity's Rainbow* is to demonstrate the possibility of perspectives radically different from those of most modern fiction, yet allowing comparable or greater intellectual range, aesthetic amplitude, and emotional depth.

I will begin with a little-understood aspect of *Gravity's Rainbow* which is perhaps its single greatest technical achievement in the art of writing. Pynchon's characters live *in their work* and in their relations to large social and economic systems. (Hence the emphasis, early in the book, on the concept of the *interface*.) In *Gravity's Rainbow*, as in life, people think about the world in ways related to the work they do much of the day. Pynchon's sample of professions tends to be highly educated and specialized, but his sample is certainly less askew than Joyce's sampling of a Dublin where no one seems to do much work at all. (The only kinds of work observed in any detail in most modern literature are reflexive variations on the work of writers themselves: the "work" of psychiatrists, poets, or, as in the case of Leopold Bloom, the advertising canvasser. The census bureau is correct in refusing to include in its list of job categories "forge in the smithy of my soul the uncreated conscience of my race.") We are accustomed to fictional characters whose work is all done "offstage," or in an office that is nothing but a backdrop for personal dramas that could take place anywhere, and we fail to notice that the elements chosen by a novelist for the presentation of such characters exclude an enormous segment of the data which, in our own daily lives, is essential to our knowledge of self and others. Joyce, who serves as the clearinghouse for the technical means of presenting character in modern fiction, saw no need to associate personality with work, and the older technical means of doing so have by now mostly been forgotten. Through a corollary of the modern prejudice that gives primacy to the affective aspects of personality, characters who live in their work tend to be dismissed by readers as "types," lacking in any substantial distinction or interest. All literary innovations are in part recoveries of lost techniques, and Pynchon's radical analysis of character includes recollections of such lost modes as the seventeenth-century developments of the Theophrastian character, and the allegorical type. But Pynchon modifies his recollection of older modes by acknowledging modern modes of psychological complexity (which he does not, however, place at the center of his presentation of character). Pynchon's world looks at first like a world we can never enter, a world lacking in the kind of people we know (or know about). But Pynchon knows more than his readers: eventually one realizes that the world which seems strange in Pynchon contains major elements of our own world that, although familiar to the language of politics and economics, have not yet adequately been named or assimilated in the language of fiction.

Pynchon signaled his redefinition of character in *The Crying of Lot 49*. There the name Oedipa refers not to the psychological permutations of the Oedipal complex, but to the social and ethical convolutions of responsibility in which the Sophoclean Oedipus found himself implicated. So, in *Gravity's Rainbow*, character is defined not only by interior affective considerations, but by action within a complex system of meanings — Weber's *Sinnzusammenhang* — which cannot be understood (as Freud understood society) to be merely a projection or extension of private categories and internal organizations.[10]

Pynchon's vision of the world of politics is integral with his rendering of the nature of personality. His political world is made up of cartels, corporations, bureaucracies, multinational and historically extended systems that are larger than the personalities involved in them, and whose organization is independent of private concerns. Joyce is equally consistent in his politics and his psychology: the politics in *Ulysses*, for all its wealth of local detail, are effectively large projections of *family* politics. Anything more elaborate would violate the formulae of paternity around which the book is organized. But as a solution to the political problem of encyclopedic organization — precisely the organization that Joyce claimed for his book — it is far too naïve and inadequate for anyone except literary critics to take seriously. Joyce comforts with his comic vision of the human scale and human correlation of all things, Pynchon disturbs and rebukes with his insistence on the real power of forces too enormous for us to influence or too minuscule or too patient and slow for us to recognize.

On the surface, of course, Joyce's politics seem to have wisdom, rationality, and weight, while Pynchon's seem obsessive, aberrant, and crazed. But Pynchon, here as elsewhere, adheres to the law by which self-conscious narrative can admit serious meanings only through indirection. Knowing the limits of fiction's power to persuade — and its ethical responsibility *not* to persuade that a fiction can be sufficient to the truth of the world — Pynchon consistently alters a serious vision of society through the distorting lens of paranoia. Yet if you "correct" for this distortion as the brain corrects the inverted image on the retina, and as Pynchon's strictures on paranoia *insist* that the distortion be corrected — the book yields a complex, dynamic, and plausible account of the social world. But no matter how hard you try to correct for the apparently reasonable lens of paternity in *Ulysses* (paternity or its counterpart metempsychosis in Joyce corresponding to paranoia in Pynchon), you cannot produce a recognizable vision of the social world larger than the family. Joyce's lens, although it transmits detail with vivid accuracy, permanently alters the structure of the image of the world outside the book; Pynchon's only bends it temporarily.

Joyce's ideal reader is an insomniac who spends all his time reading Joyce. Although the opening chapters of *Ulysses* propose to correct the heroic formality of the *Odyssey* through the daily quiddities of Dublin, the later chapters turn obsessively inward, to their own structure and verbal display. Pynchon, far from trying to seduce his readers and critics into a permanent relation with his texts, constantly urges us to distrust the enveloping embrace of fiction — to *use* fiction to call attention to the knowledge we need for making choices in the world outside. Pynchon's distrust of texts has a long ancestry: encyclopedic narratives all exhibit a love-hate relation with other books. For all his admiration for Virgil, Dante knows that secular literature cannot lead him to a vision of Paradise. Cervantes blames Don Quixote's madness entirely on his confusion of the fictional excitement of the romances with the ethical requirements of the world. *Gravity's Rainbow* constantly offers similar counter-examples against its own fascinations: texts that offer themselves for a reader's cathexis, but are emphatically not "the real Text" (520).

The clearest example is The Book — always capitalized and bearing too sacred an aura for its seven owners ever to name — bought by Pointsman and company, and passed ritually among them. It bears, Pointsman supposes, a "terrible curse." The title of The Book never appears in *Gravity's Rainbow*, but it is Pavlov's second series of "Lectures on Conditioned Reflexes," *Conditioned Reflexes and Psychiatry* (1941). (The pervasive presence of this book in *Gravity's Rainbow* illuminates, among many other matters, Pointsman's attempt to have Slothrop castrated, the relation for Pavlov of social systems to physiological systems, and the relation of paranoia to "pathological inertness" of the kind displayed by Slothrop before he disintegrates.) This sacred object has, for Pointsman, the effect only of limiting his understanding, forcing his perception of extraordinary events into the sterile categories that Pavlov proposes. But Pointsman is not the only victim of too great a reliance on a text's version of reality. The Schwarzkommando who construct their own rocket, the successor to the charismatic V-2 that carried the Schwarzgerät, come to think of the rocket as a "Text," but a text that "seduced us while the real Text persisted, somewhere else, in its darkness, in our darkness" (520). The Counterforce that fails to save Slothrop replaces him with a carefully numbered and organized "Book of Memorabilia." In *Gravity's Rainbow* films have the same seductive falseness as written texts. An erotic scene in *Alpdrücken* is the occasion for erotic impulses in the film's viewers, and the children conceived as a product of the film become reduced to fictional counters in the eyes of their parents (see the story of Ilse Pökler). Pynchon leaves Gerhardt von Göll immersed in the making of a film that he will never finish. Pynchon's own buffoonery, the puns[11] and pie-throwing that occur whenever matters threaten to become too serious, is a way of insisting that *Gravity's Rainbow* not be confused, even locally, with the world it illuminates.

Slothrop's disintegration at the end of the book is accompanied by his own confusion between the events in his past and a "text" that transforms and — inadequately — interprets those events. Slothrop progressively forgets the particularity of his past, and replaces his memory of past events with garish and crude comic-book versions of them. His disintegration of memory is not the work of those who oppose or betray him, but is the consequence of his own betrayals, his own loss of interest in the world, his own failures to relate and connect. Near the beginning of the book, when he first meets Katje, his past is still with him: "It's the past that makes demands here" (208). But when he has entered his isolation in the Zone, his sense that acts have consequences in time begins to diminish; he forgets that he exists in a realm of responsibility where relations extend into the past and future. With Bianca on the *Anubis*, "Sure he'll stay for a while, but eventually he'll go, and for this he is to be counted, after all, among the Zone's lost. . . . He creates a bureaucracy of departure . . . but coming back is something he's already forgotten about" (470–471). What Slothrop no longer remembers is that his actions occur not for their own sake, or for his, but in a complex of meaning, a *Sinnzusammenhang* of ethical responsibility. The engineer Kurt Mondaugen postulates Mondaugen's Law: "Personal density is directly proportional to temporal bandwidth" (509). Separated by his own escape and his own empty freedom from an originating past or a future to which he could be responsible, Slothrop can only diminish and disintegrate. As his "temporal bandwidth" — the degree to which he "dwell[s] in the past and in the future" — diminishes, so must all his relations to the world. When he forgets the world to which, if he could exist coherently, he would be somehow related, he does so by replacing his recollections with a text derived from popular culture. Slothrop himself has recognized that responsibility depends on memory and knowledge: when Säure Bummer makes a remark that reminds him of the Berkshire of his childhood, he decides that Bummer "can't possibly be on the Bad Guys' side. Whoever They are, Their game has been to extinguish, not remind" (438). "They," everyone for whom Slothrop is a convenient victim, try to extinguish different elements of his mental structure: Jamf extinguished the conditioned reflex of "infant Tyrone" twenty years before; Pointsman, in trying to have Slothrop castrated, hopes to extinguish his mysterious relation to the rocket. But the only extinguishing that succeeds is Slothrop's own increasing inability to remember who and where he is. Near the end of the book, Slothrop, already "corrupted" (627), yields the remnants of his memory to patterns picked up from comic books. In a long passage set in Slothrop's comic-book construction of the Raketen-Stadt, he thinks of his relation to his parents in terms of a fantasy of the Floundering Four *vs.* Pernicious Pop and his Parental Peril. Finally, his disintegration all but complete, he can remember neither his parents nor even the etiolated images that have supplanted them.

Gravity's Rainbow has on occasion been misunderstood as an endorsement of popular culture in preference to "high" culture, but Pynchon is equally insistent on the potential dangers that lie in absorption at either extreme. The popular modes that Pynchon assimilates into his encyclopedia of styles are never modes of liberation from the systems of oppression, but are instead a *means* of oppression and extinguishing. In his references to popular forms, Pynchon incidentally commits historical errors of a kind absent from his allusions to Rossini or Rilke: he is not, for example, sufficiently interested in a film like *The Return of Jack Slade* to notice that its inclusion in *Gravity's Rainbow* is a ten-year anachronism.[12]

IV

Gravity's Rainbow is a book that recalls origins and foresees endings, but it insists on the continuing responsibility of those who live in the present that lies between. Its attention to charisma is necessarily a concern with origins, for, in Weber, charisma in its pure form exists only in the process of originating. It cannot remain stable. *Gravity's Rainbow* explores a variety of originating moments, most vividly that of the rocket's ascent "on a promise, a prophecy of Escape" (758) from the distress that gives rise to charisma. But the ascent, "betrayed to Gravity," leads nowhere but to a dead end. Only during its originating moments of ascent does it appear to have a fiery "life," and only then can its direction be altered, through telemetry, by human control or *Herrschaft*. After its engine stops, the rocket becomes a piece of inanimate junk, its course irrevocably determined. *Gravity's Rainbow* perceives the contemporary era in terms of its first brief moments of origination and possibility, when the means of control, Pynchon suggests, were engaged and the political and technological character of our time determined once and for all.

Yet the book insists that we are not determined, as the inanimate rocket is determined, unless, paradoxically, we *choose* to be, by submitting to Pavlovian brain-mechanics or to the hopeless linkages of cause and effect. The possibilities of freedom, the whole range of probabilities that lie between and outside the one and the zero, exist in the book, but are always difficult to locate or achieve. Everyone in *Gravity's Rainbow* who confronts the agonies of choice and decision tries to dream instead of a world in which all difficulties of choice are removed — in which the condition of the world has miraculously been altered for the better — in which an illusory and easy "freedom" *from* the problems of responsibility and the anxiety of human limitation somehow replaces the true and difficult freedom *to* act and choose.

Enzian dreams that "Somewhere, among the wastes of the World, is the key that will bring us back, restore us to our Earth and to our freedom" (525), or that there might be "an Aether sea to bear us world-to-world [to] bring us back a continuity, show us a kinder universe" (726). And Slothrop imagines that "somewhere in the waste" of the disordered Zone might be "a single set of coordinates from which to proceed, without elect, without preterite, without even nationality" (556).

But these are exiles' fantasies of Eden and Utopia, evasions of responsibility in the immediate world of time. Faced with responsibility, Pynchon's characters can choose either to escape it in voluntary servitude to legal authority or the authority of a text, or to enact it, through free relations with others. Free relations are built on language, but language in Pynchon is the means of both freedom and oppression (as metaphor in *The Crying of Lot 49* is both "a thrust at truth and a lie" — *Lot 49*, 129/95). In *The Crying of Lot 49* Oedipa's discovery of the positive illegality of the Tristero postal system is the means by which she achieves the possibility of vital and unfamilar relations that she may freely enter. In *Gravity's Rainbow*, where conditions are more difficult, the affirmative and "true" aspects of communications cluster, like almost all the book's moments of hope and love, around the character of Roger Mexico. (In this drug-ridden book, marked throughout with sexual cruelty and betrayal, it is Roger Mexico who never even lights a cigarette — the nicotine on his teeth at one point in the narrative is only in Bodine's imagination — who is neither sadist nor masochist, and who betrays no one. The day after Christmas, 1944, Mexico realizes that his love for Jessica has broken down the barriers of self and even the language of self. He thinks:

> I'm no longer sure which of all the words, images, dreams or ghosts are "yours" and which are "mine." It's past sorting out. We're both becoming someone new now. . . .

Immediately the narrator identifies Mexico's feelings in a charged phrase: they are "His act of faith." And in the next sentence the children in the street are singing:

Hark the herald angels sing:
Mrs. Simpson's pinched our King . . . (177)

What is this topical carol doing here? The events of the abdication, to which it refers, occurred eight years earlier. Yet its juxtaposition to Mexico's uncertainty over what is "mine" or "yours" makes a specific point. This fractured carol is used by Iona and Peter Opie, near the opening of their classic book *The Lore and Language of Schoolchildren*, to illustrate the possibility of communication in a manner "little short of miraculous." The children's version of the carol, which could not have been broadcast or printed or repeated in music halls, managed to spread across all of England in the course of a few weeks, during school term, when there could have been little traveling that might speed its oral transmission. The children singing the verses could have no idea that they were enacting what *The Crying of Lot 49* calls the "secular miracle of communication."

But in other manifestations, communication can dislocate and destroy. The network of cartels that maintains observations on Slothrop is one whose activities are neither edifying nor miraculous. Among the varieties of connectedness in the world of *Gravity's Rainbow*, the connected communications of cartels and black markets are always profitable, but they are false. And the mechanist science that, in league with the empty legality of the Firm, hopes to eliminate hope, is a limited and false science that ultimately fails (as Pointsman, following his narrow logic, becomes "an ex-scientist now, one who'll never get Into It far enough to talk about God . . . left only with Cause and Effect and the rest of his sterile armamentarium" — 752). The true and vitalizing connectedness of sympathy and memory is always fragile. The quantum leap that Mexico must make to achieve his "act of faith" is a dangerous one, but only through vulnerability and risk can the book's true relations be achieved.

As all of Pynchon's books implicate their readers in the processes they describe, so *Gravity's Rainbow* invites its readers to make quantum leaps towards relationship in the very act of reading. *The Crying of Lot 49*, which is short enough to read at a sitting and hold in one's memory, allows its reader to make the unique binary choice of finding in the book either relation and indicative meaning, or chaos and subjunctive fantasy. But *Gravity's Rainbow* is far too large and complex for any adequate unified response. The zero/one choice available — demanded — in *Lot 49* is transformed, in the wider field of *Gravity's Rainbow*, to its empty opposite: the limiting matrix of Pointsman's Pavlovian brain-mechanics in which a stimulus produces either a response or none, and in which any issue that cannot be reduced to the control of binary notation is not worthy of attention. To read the encyclopedic *Gravity's Rainbow* is, necessarily, to read *among* the various probable interpretations of the book. There is no unavoidable choice to be found among the various networks of *Gravity's Rainbow*, but there are many varieties of probable relationships along which to find your way. Pynchon expounds the matter with reference, once again, to Roger Mexico:

> If ever the Antipointsman existed, Roger Mexico is the man. . . .
> [I]n the domain of zero to one, not-something to something,
> Pointsman can only possess the zero and the one. He cannot,
> like Mexico, survive anyplace in between. Like his master I. P.
> Pavlov before him, [Pointsman] imagines the cortex of the brain
> as a mosaic of tiny on/off elements. . . . But to Mexico belongs
> the domain *between* the zero and the one — the middle Points-
> man has excluded from his persuasion — the probabilities. (55)

(Incidentally, the transformation of binary choice, from the vitalizing choice of *Lot 49* to the restrictive mechanism of *Gravity's Rainbow*, continues Pynchon's procedure of inverting his central metaphors from one book to the next. In *V.* thermodynamic entropy increases, to the detriment of the world; while in *Lot 49* it is information entropy that increases, to the enrichment of those who live in the world.)

But there is a warning in this praise of Mexico, as well as encouragement. To know the probabilities is not necessarily to act on them. At the beginning of the book, for example, Mexico has not yet learned to recognize the full consequence of actions — see his exchange with Paul de la Nuit (56) on sacrality and the *use* of probabilities — but he will learn. Mere understanding is inadequate to action — as art is not enough.

For although Mexico and the Counterforce of which he is a part achieve some understanding of the world-processes that affect their lives, they are finally unable or unwilling to do very much about it. Knowledge alone insures neither courage nor triumph. The Counterforce fails: "They are as schizoid, as double-minded in the massive presence of money, as any of the rest of us, and that's the hard fact.[13] The Man has a branch office in each of our brains, his corporate emblem is a white albatross, each local rep has a cover known as the Ego. . . . We do know what's going on and we let it go on" (712–713). Faced with the knowledge of "Their" power, Mexico is free to choose, but his choice is, by necessity, between life as "Their pet" and defiance leading to death. "It is not a question he has ever imagined himself asking seriously. It has come by surprise, but there's no sending it away now, for he really does have to decide. . . . Letting it sit for a while is no compromise, but a decision to live, on Their terms" (713).

The solution — and there does prove to be a solution — to this tragic choice is a comic disruption of "Their" necessity, as Mexico and his ally, Seaman Bodine, disrupt the most official of dinner parties with the most nauseous and unofficial language. They escape unharmed because they have wrenched the realm of language away from its official manipulators, the western counterparts of the makers of the NTA, and have brought to the surface the unrationalizable physical disorder and illegal energy that officialdom keeps under restraint. Their use of language cannot alter the world, but it can save them for another battle. After this scene, Mexico disappears from the book.

Gravity's Rainbow's knowledge of language is encyclopedic and deep, but it insists that language is not all. The kill-the-police-commissioner sign in Central Asia erupts out of the closed and static world of written "signs" into the world of irreversible acts, the world of life and death. To insist that language is separate from the world of acts (or, more subtly, that the world of acts consists only of linguistic acts) is to keep language at a safe distance from our lives. The worst, most dangerous moments in *Gravity's Rainbow* are the moments when words *act* on the world, when they are translated into lethal action. In a sequence set in Peenemünde, when Slothrop and others are in a dispute with some Russian soldiers, the narrator interrupts the action with this extraordinary address to Slothrop, to the reader, and to himself:

> But . . . what might that have been just now, waiting in this broken moonlight, camouflage paint from fins to point crazed into jigsaw . . . is it, then, really never to find you again? Not even in your worst times of night, with pencil words on your page only Δt from the things they stand for? And inside the victim is twitching, fingering beads, touching wood, avoiding any Operational Word. Will it really never come to take you, now? (510)

So Slothrop, searching for the rocket ("fins to point") as if for the Grail, will never again be found *by* it — as all true searchers and authentic goals find and are found — not even at the "worst times of night" when words and things are separated infinitesimally, not in space but in *time*, by an unimaginably small time differential (delta-t). For Slothrop, living in a chaos of vacancy and dissociation, words and things will never find each other again. For the rest of us, the relation of words and things is often terrifying, but is crucial to our lives. Our most difficult and vertiginous moments can be those when our words of hatred or love change the vulnerable lives of others and ourselves, when the words of others permanently alter our own knowledge and identity. In those moments events are separated by only the smallest gap, the smallest delta-t, from words; and those words — we sense with some relief — immediately fall away into the safety and permanence of memory or writing. The rocket's sacrificial victim avoids Words that Operate, words that have immediate effect, for when words act on the world, when the last delta-t is crossed, they have sufficient power to cause the direst of consequences. But Slothrop is no longer vulnerable even to words. His difficulty, predicted in this passage, is his eventual dissociation from *all* systems in which words have effect, or could have effect. The victim, in the rocket, is in the dangerous position where his words *can* have an effect — and a fatal one. But Slothrop, denied even the dignity of sacrifice, will be reduced to a fictional world of comic-book images and kabbalistic elaboration in which words are fluid and meanings arbitrary, where Slothrop will lose all real and potential relation to *any* world, whether of language or of act.[14]

Moments of distress and disorder, uncrossable interfaces of delta-t, such as the dissolution of Germany or the scattering of Slothrop, are only temporary. States and bureaucracies immediately fill the disordered void. The charismatic ascent of a Gottfried or an Enzian is succeeded by the bureaucracy of the rocket-cartel (566). The mock-charisma of Slothrop generates the system of the Counterforce, and Slothrop's dissolution is simultaneous with "his time's assembly" (738). The world is never finally altered — and all is never gained nor lost. Total annihilation occurs only at the end of time. Within the world of time we know, there are crises and transformations, but total cataclysm cannot occur. In *Gravity's Rainbow*, as always in fiction, the devil has the best lines: it is Wernher von Braun who opens the book by asserting his conviction that "nature does not know extinction; all it knows is transformation."

Yet *Gravity's Rainbow* is, in a profound sense, a book about endings as well as about charismatic origins. Like William Slothrop, going westward in Imperial style, the book moves westward, in the direction of endings, the direction of the tragic necessity of the *Abendland*'s decline. Slothrop's dream of Crutchfield the westwardman (67) resonates against the book's westward vision of the next war, whose first bomb explodes over the western city of Los Angeles. The final pages of the book rush forwards towards the west and towards endings, but, almost simultaneously, the book rushes backwards through time, and eastwards through space, to Abraham and Isaac and the Judaic origins of the civilization of the west. In the last pages of the book "we" sit in the Los Angeles theatre on which the rocket is about to fall — as it "reaches its last unmeasurable gap above the roof of this old theatre, the last delta-t." But the final ending is delayed: "there is time" to sing William Slothrop's forgotten hymn, now miraculously remembered, as the hymn itself recalls the "light that hath brought the Towers low," and all the Preterite of "our crippl'd Zone." And the hymn anticipates the ultimate cataclysm that has not arrived, the end of things in the parousia, when the transfigured world will bear "a face on ev'ry mountainside, / And a soul in ev'ry stone."

But the book only anticipates this last postponed transfiguration. For us, as readers, nothing has changed. The book's prediction of the eschaton is a metaphor of its own ending: for us, all that has been concluded is our reading of a book. The last delta-t is not crossed by fiction. The rocket falls *after* the book's last words, outside the book's world. And within that world, where all events exist simultaneously in written words now unaffected by time, we find evidence that we have survived the explosion. The book's first sentence reads, "A screaming comes across the sky." If we have heard the rocket, we are safe: the sound that reaches us follows a destruction elsewhere. So, as readers, destruction has passed over us, and we have survived. But we have more of the knowledge that is required if we are to act freely outside the world of writing — in the world where acts have consequences, time is real, and our safety is far from certain.

Notes

1. To keep this essay only unreasonably — rather than impossibly — long, I have assumed the reader has some familiarity with the book, and will need little exposition of events and characters. The parenthetical page references refer to both hardback and paperback Viking editions (the Bantam paperback references may be found by multiplying the number given by seven-sixths). With the permission of the editor of the *Yale Review* I have taken over a few phrases from my review of *Gravity's Rainbow* in the issue for Summer 1973.

2. I have deliberately blurred some generic questions in the discussion that follows, but hope to resolve them in another place.

3. In a letter to Carlo Linati, 21 September 1920.

4. This is a good occasion to dispose of a bit of misinformation that seems to be growing popular: the square "frames" that separate the chapters of *Gravity's Rainbow* are the work of the publisher's production department, and were *not* suggested by Pynchon himself.

5. Pynchon's Herero vocabulary — including its precise distinctions of size, source, and freshness of different varieties of excrement (325) — derives entirely from the preface and text of F. W. Kolbe's *An English-Herero Dictionary* (Capetown, 1883).

6. But Dr. Jamf hopes even to reorganize the molecules of living matter, in order to achieve greater control over them. He proposes to substitute chemical bonds built on the *seizure* of electrons for the existing bonds built on the *sharing* of electrons, and to replace analogues for voluntary relations with analogues of power relations.

7. Cf. my essay "The Sacred, the Profane, and *The Crying of Lot 49*," in *Individual and Community: Variations on a Theme in American Fiction*, edited by Kenneth H. Baldwin and David K. Kirby (Durham, N.C.: Duke University Press, 1975), pp. 182–222.

8. Enzian's succession by Christian, who preserves the sacred utterances of his predecessor, is an example of charismatic succession (525, 728–729). Weber's theoretical account of charisma may be found in the translation of the first part of his *Wirtschaft und Gesellschaft*, published as *The Theory of Social and Economic Organization* (New York, 1947), pp. 358–392.

9. In reference to the Counterforce, this might be the occasion to note that the presence in the book of extraordinary events is usually preceded (perhaps *triggered*) by a mistaken verbal or "textual" reference. Osbie Feel makes a film of faked Schwarzkommando before we encounter the real ones. Tchitcherine wrongly supposes there is a "counterforce in the Zone" — he has been misled by the accidents around Slothrop — before there actually is a Counterforce.

10. The manifestation of a *Sinnzusammenhang* in *Gravity's Rainbow* is the *city*. There could easily be a long essay on the subject, but I will restrict this note to a few observations. Cities in the book range from Ant City underfoot (399) and the conurbations of Slothrop's body ("His fingers are cities, his biceps is a province" — 330) through the historical London and Berlin, to the cities of intention constructed by men and women out of their own motives. As the book proceeds from London and Berlin into the disorder of the Zone, cities whose names are on maps increasingly become supplanted by such imagined cities as the mandala-shaped Raketen-Stadt that accommodates the vectors of intention focused on the V-2; Rilke's Leidstadt; the City Dactylic "where every soul is known, and there is no place to hide" (566); the Hexes-Stadt (an especially clear example of bureaucratization — 718); and the Happyville of ignorant complacence. (For Pointsman the Nobel Prize is imaged only through its metonymic city, Stockholm.) Unlike the cities of history, Pynchon's cities of intention vary in form

according to the perception and motives of those who participate in them. In a notoriously obscure chapter, when some of the characters escape the They-Systems of oppression to fumble towards the good through a We-System, a Counterforce, they find themselves in a "disquieting structure . . . a place of many levels, and new wings that generate like living tissue" (537). Pirate Prentice and Katje Borgesius, who enter this structure (which is reminiscent of comic-book cities elsewhere in the book), find they have not, after all, been able to escape from *all* systems, as Slothrop has done: to act in the world, for any motive, requires a system of meaning in which to act. The system into which they escape is not only built upon the structure of their previous actions, whose consequences cannot be undone, but also differs according to their perceptions of their own motives. Prentice, always an organization man, and Katje, who revolts out of despair over the deaths she caused, see the world of their meeting in entirely different terms, neither of which is fully "correct":

"What did it look like out there, Katje? [Prentice asks.] I saw an organized convention. Someone else saw it as a garden. . . ." But he knows what she'll say.

"There was nothing out there. It was a barren place. . . ." (547)

11. Among these, the Hobbesian law firm of Salitieri, Poore, Nash, De Brutus, and Short is justly celebrated. But has anyone noted the even more elaborate moment of Francophilia in Bloody Chiclitz's "For De Mille, young fur-henchmen can't be rowing" (559)?

12. Pynchon's historical expertise does not protect him from other venial errors. *Gravity's Rainbow* makes quite a few mistakes in German, mostly through the use of copulative rather than excretory expletives. And there is a curious "mistake" in the plot of *The Crying of Lot 49* (pointed out to me by Eliot Krieger): in Chapter 5, Oedipa parks her car in San Francisco's North Beach, then spends the night wandering through the Bay Area on foot and by bus, ending up the next morning at her hotel in Berkeley; after a short sleep she "checked out of the hotel and drove down the peninsula." How did her car get from San Francisco to Berkeley? *Aliquando dormitat Pynchon.*

13. It is notable that the empty bureaucracies in *Gravity's Rainbow* are directed towards the acquisition of money (and even the Counterforce has become a matter of interest to *The Wall Street Journal*). In contrast, Weber notes, "Pure charisma is specifically foreign to economic considerations."

14. The whole issue of kabbala in *Gravity's Rainbow* is, for the moment, best banished to a footnote. (One critic has already misread the book as a kabbalistic document.) The subject does, however, deserve balanced study: the planetoid Katspiel, for example, source of pinballs (584), takes its name from an Archon in prekabbalistic Jewish mysticism. Pynchon is imaginatively correct in assigning to the exiled Herero a modern form of cosmological speculation that can neither be disproved nor confirmed by the internal test of consistency and logic or the external test of adequacy to experience. Kabbalistic speculation, with which the diaspora compensated for exile, leads in *Gravity's*

Rainbow not to any version of the truth, but to private visions of inadequate segments of the truth, and, ultimately, to self-destruction. Enzian's opposition to the Empty Ones' program for tribal suicide is doomed, for all his anticipations of an exfoliating rocket-kabbala, by his own commitment, not to a sacred center but to the death-machinery of the V-2 rocket.

Brünnhilde and the Chemists: Women in Gravity's Rainbow

Marjorie Kaufman

In exalted apocalypse, with holy promises of ritual renewal, Wagner brings on die Götterdämmerung and returns, at last, der Ring des Nibelungen to the Rhinemaidens.[1] In *Gravity's Rainbow*, we witness a post-Wagnerian holocaust of love and death. For Thomas Pynchon, our twilight and the twilight of the gods begins when the nineteenth-century German chemist, Kekulé von Stradonitz, interprets his dream of the ancient hermetic symbol of unity and renewal — the Serpent with its tail in its mouth, surrounding the world — to be a vision of the model of the benzene ring, which makes it possible to pervert natural elements into the man-made molecular structures of plastics and rocketry. To Pynchon, the first perpetrators of the perversion, and the augurs of the curse we put on when we grasp the ring of such knowledge and such power, were the officers of General von Trotha, in Deutsch-Südwestafrika, when, in 1904, they conducted the first programmatic genocidal drive of this century against the pantheistic Hottentots and Hereros. As Captain Weissmann, one of the characters who links *V.* to *Gravity's Rainbow*, records the experience, it was a subtle replacement of the old human emotions — love, hate — by a kind of a-feeling he calls "operational sympathy." From that "de-vital" turn (the rejection of chaotic passions for "functional agreement" with *orderly* means), comes the consequent shift in manners and morals from "random" and "picaresque acts" to "a logic . . . that substituted capability for character, deliberate scheme for political epiphany," and a bleak, wind-driven sterile shore for the greening landscape that once dignified human suffering and enabled our ancient Dance of Death.[2] Now, in the last years of the Second World War, the Curse of the Ring begins to fulfill its promise: the dead heroes and the gods again sit formally and dispassionately watching, as the flames of the funeral pyre. reach the new Valhalla — already in Wagner, a rainbow bridge spreads to their feet as a causeway.

This time, however, there is no redemption, because no love, and the Wagnerian ecstasy and full orchestra are not ours; the death of this world is played on harmonica or kazoo or sung to a simple tune. But whether heard as "just a song at twilight" or the cry of an ex-Valkyrie, its meaning is the same: it's all over with the end of either song. In the terrible "name" of love we have all made the new death, not the grisly but grand old gate to the eternally returning ("love's old sweet song"), but to the perpetuity of the links of bioundegradable plastics, spreading their deathlessness to the antechambers of the Throne Room. The gods who stole the Ring made from the old Rhine treasure knew the price of the cosmic power it gave them — the foreswearing forever of love. Only those innocent trilling Rhinemaidens could have thought the price too great to tempt them or us. In a world where the gods have become an anonymous "They" — not a Pantheon but a System, a Corporation, an Establishment, a multinational cartel, a Masonry that has connections beyond the grave — and where the pretty swimmers themselves have turned into a beer promotion, annually elected to their title, the price has long since been paid. MENE MENE TEKEL on the walls of the old Weimar Republic has already announced "AN ARMY OF LOVERS CAN BE BEATEN." From the traffic flowing over the Santa Monica Freeway to the screen of the Orpheus Theatre, gone suddenly blank, under a sky the color of taffy pulled only once or twice, the brown fog of Eliot's Waste Land is a rosy glow. In very truth, we "had not thought death had undone so many" or so much.

To inquire of the maker of such a fiction (and I have barely suggested its dimensions) if he perceives the role of women as richly and as dreadfully, as comically and as tenderly, with as equal a share of hate and fear and pity as he views the role of men is the question I have been asked to explore in this paper. With no puns on Forster's distinctions intended, are the female characters of *Gravity's Rainbow* as "round" as the male? Or are they assigned only the male-oriented stereotypical role: La Belle Dame Sans Merci and, for that matter, the flipped coin of that powerfully destructive, monstrous beauty, the equally stereotypical role perceived by the raised consciousness of NOW, the passive, even willingly enslaved object of male sexual gratification? Does Thomas Pynchon, given the epic leisure of over seven hundred and fifty pages, a view of space that makes use of a larger telescope than any yet designed and the minute pryings of Nuclear Magnetic Resonance, and a view of time that forbids mention of the first V-2 rocket falling over London at "6:43:16 British Double Summer Time" without taking into account the knowledge that the final countdown began somewhere in the 1620s, in the single-steepled white churches of New England and their doctrine of the Elect — given such leisure, such space, such time, does he also give a fair shake to his women characters, to the female sex?

An immediate answer has seemed obvious to me, and consistent, for Pynchon's three novels: yes, of course, he does. A full and considered response, however, has proved more labyrinthine than I was wise enough to suspect; though fundamentally unchanged, it can at least serve the purpose of running us deep into the ways and whys of *Gravity's Rainbow*, to its center, as cold as the last circle of Dante's Hell or of Wernher von Braun's outer space with its certifiably sterile moon.

Seven women occupy enough room in the novel, and in London, the Riviera, and the "demilitarized" Zone, to be considered major characters, even if their roles are not equally significant. In order of appearance, they are Jessica Swanlake, Katje Borgesius, Leni Pökler and her daughter Ilse, Geli Tripping, Greta ("Margherita") Erdmann and her daughter Bianca. With all these women, young and old, except Jessica and Ilse Pökler, the novel's hero (to use the language of the old dispensation) has more or less intense encounters. Because it is a "given" of *Gravity's Rainbow* that if you are a woman in its world, to meet American Army Intelligence Lieutenant Tyrone Slothrop is joyously to bed down with him, these encounters include a variety of, again more or less, bizarre sexual couplings.

Other women recur frequently enough to get full names but are of less central or lasting concern: the English women, Nora Dodson-Truck and Scorpia Mossmoon, the Polish Stefania Procalowska, and the Argentinian Graciela Imago Portales. Of these Slothrop actually meets only Stefania — and, if I'm not mistaken, she is virtually the only attractive woman he does meet, under even remotely favorable circumstances, with whom no physical intercourse occurs.

In addition, literally dozens of other women cross these pages, some to linger for a paragraph or two — some even to stay on and play a not insignificant role in a single episode — then to disappear utterly or return a hundred pages or so later, perhaps just to walk across a sentence. They are usually given first names or titles, and, along with their even more numerous and anonymous sisters, seem to gather into three not-very-tight categories: the young, pretty, nubile, well-intentioned; the generally older, generally aristocratic, rather thoroughly decadent; and Mothers. Also, lots of children, many of whom are little girls. And a goodly crew of females who are not even technically human: two relatively important animals, Ursula, a lemming, and Frieda, a pig; a bit part for a Siamese cat who is also a Mother ("Sooty"); an "older" melanocyte; two light bulbs — Brenda, who keeps conventional hours, and Beatriz, an immortal; Miss Enola Gay, the plane that carried the Hiroshima bomb, and the A-Bomb itself; "Lady London," the War, this Earth, and the Rocket, though the Rocket is probably androgynous, if that is the word for a phallic object equipped with clitoris and womb.

Despite the fact that probably the entire range of human (and inhuman) sexual behavior as noted by Krafft-Ebing or invented by the Marquis de Sade also occurs in the novel, the final effect of such variety is to reduce the importance of physical gender and intensify that of sexual energy. I think Pynchon intends this effect. Further, once we examine the functions of the major women in the novel, we often see female-ness balanced by a parallel masculine figure or act; *Gravity's Rainbow* is an extraordinary web of links among characters and actions, doubles, role-playing and role-reversing. Images of coordinating systems, parallel ideas, cross it at every point and at every level of theme and plot. When one recalls that it is by analogy — "the six carbon atoms of benzene are in fact curled around into a closed ring, *just like that snake with its tail in its mouth*, GET IT?"[3] — that Kekulé forged the Ring, the central and pervasive significance of the figure to the novel is evident.

Whatever the doublings, the links, the parallels, however, there are the "girls, girls, girls, girls, girls" of *Gravity's Rainbow* and primarily of Slothrop's.

> "I know there is wilde love and joy enough in the world," preached Thomas Hooker, "as there are wilde Thyme, and other herbes; but we would have garden love, and garden joy, of Gods owne planting." How Slothrop's garden grows. Teems with virgin's-bower, with forget-me-nots, with rue — and all over the place, purple and yellow as hickeys, a prevalence of love-in-idleness. (22)

Tyrone's London map, recording in varicolored stars the sites of his affairs, starts one of the major threads of the novel; for with frightening consistency, though never known to Slothrop, the stars precede by a day or two (near the end of his London stay, only by minutes) the bomb sites of the silent death of the V-2 rocket, the pair making perfectly matched Poisson Distributions. How Slothrop *knows* becomes one of the preoccupying questions of the madly assorted group of psycho-, astro- and natural scientists, working out of PISCES (Psychological Intelligence Schemes for Expediting Surrender) and their research facility, "The White Visitation." Yet long after Slothrop has left London and his map for the Riviera, after the bombs have stopped and he is deep within the Zone, the "girls" are there.

> "Tits 'n' ass," mutter the girls, "tits 'n' ass. That's all we are around here."

"Ah, shaddap," snarls G. M. B. Haftung, which is his usual
way of dealing with the help. (507)

This little chorus line, their chant anachronistically echoing a
Lenny Bruce "bit," has just been ordered to lead an attack on the
Russian soldiers occupying the firing site, at Peenemünde, of the
Super-Rocket 00000, by providing "diversionary tactics." They
will do their jobs and pass on, like their sisters, equally anonymous, conventionally pretty and, despite the momentary protest
of that chorus, congenial. Nurses, stenographers, shoppers, pros-
titutes — on streets, in fields, in offices, in dreams or out, in 1930
or 1945 — at office parties or in subways or on little old-world
village squares, they are mostly there to fill a scene or two, their
bottoms inevitably pinched, their breasts squeezed.

These young women form the largest group of supernumeraries
in *Gravity's Rainbow*; of that cast of thousands, they seem to
cluster particularly at moments of change: recovery, location,
season. When the earth's axis tips into the spring of 1945, they
are a simple link in the allusory chain that records the full complexity of the season's coming:

> The great cusp — green equinox and turning, dreaming fishes
> to young ram, watersleep to firewaking, bears down on us.
> Across the Western Front, up in the Harz in Bleicheröde,
> Wernher von Braun [. . .] prepares to celebrate his 33rd birth-
> day. Artillery thunders through the afternoon. Russian tanks
> raise dust phantoms far away over the German leas. The storks
> are home, and the first violets have appeared.
> At "The White Visitation," days along the chalk piece of
> seacoast now are fine and clear. The office girls are bundling into
> fewer sweaters, and breasts peaking through into visibility again.
> March has come in like a lamb. Lloyd George is dying. (236–237)

The increase of the girls' mammalian visibility is as natural and
as inevitable as zodiacal turn and migratory flight, a part of what
joyous life there is left among the equally manifest harbingers of
death.

When one or two of these extras are momentarily fitted out
with a name of her own, she usually has more (not, of course,
other) to do "around here" than proffer "Zitch and Asch." Among

the girls whose liberated awareness the phrase suggests, we know
only "Hilda." But to know her is also to watch her help Tyrone
make "Phoney Phirebombs" and listen sympathetically to Silent
Otto Gnahb's "views of The Mother Conspiracy." Of the three
girls from César Flebótomo's chorus line at the Casino Hermann
Goering on the Riviera, who go on the octopus-rescue picnic,
Ghislaine, "tiny and slender, pin-up girl legs, long hair brushed
behind her ears falling all the way down her back, shifts [of
course] her round bottom in the sand" (188); but she also risks
giving Slothrop his first external confirmation that "They" are
"conniving." And her act is large enough to earn her disappearance on the same night as Tantivy's, Slothrop's only friend who
also dared offer him a hand later that evening.

There really are dozens of such bit players — Trudi and Magda,
who help convert Tyrone into Raketemensch with odds and
ends of stolen Wagnerian costumes; the anonymous daughter of
an old Wobbly printer, herself adept at setting type, who takes
Slothrop, now become a "trudging pig in motley," to her bed,
and gives him food and safety for the night. And Frieda, a ver-
itable pig, "very fat and pink," who "grunts and smiles amiably,
blinking long eyelashes" (573), as she leads our hero to water and
eggs and the information Franz Pökler, the plastics expert, has
for him about the mysterious Imipolex-G.

These "pretty young things," in short, nurture life, offer a
moment of warmth, light, safety, truth, wherever we find them.
Preterites, given bottom billing on the program, they offer what
they can and what they have, passing Slothrop along from hand to
bed humbly, generously, hilariously, into that final Humility
which Enzian, the Herero-Nguarorerue, knows he is to be denied
and envies deeply. As reward, they are spared Pynchon's satire
and given his gaiety and tenderness and compassion. It is not, I
think, a male chauvinist pig who leaves the "docile girl" at the
gate, knowing someone else will show up for the Schweinheld
next year. Nor an author filled with the shoulder-padding of
American machismo who draws back to view Frieda and Tyrone
nestled down together for the night, amidst pines covered with
tinfoil to "fox the German radars," and finds them "asleep under

the decorated trees, the pig a wandering eastern magus, Slothrop in his costume a gaudy present waiting for morning and a child to claim him" (575).

Yet the "girls" have no representative among the major female characters of the novel. They really do serve as "moments" — the *little* life-flow that Slothrop first understands them to be. Numerous as they are, they can unite in no lasting resistance to the breeding death. Their breasts warm hands in cold doorways; and the light they throw against the raging dark has energy no stronger than an "English firefly," Slothrop's metaphor for their peaceful postcoital cigarettes. Though least of all expendable, they are expended. Darlene, the most fully viewed of the London girls, scrounges the markets after work to find limes for her old landlady's scurvy; but when a postwar search is made for the girls behind Slothrop's stars, only the old landlady is found. The Rocket does parallel the path of Slothrop's pleasing penis, and the London girls, far more vulnerable than Milton's Eve, "ingorg'd [happily] without restraint / And knew not eating death."

Geli Tripping, the delightful novice witch whom Slothrop meets in the Zone, is a unique species of the genus. She, and her chocolate-bar-eating Owl, Wernher, provide diverting links between widely separated characters in northern Europe; she gives Slothrop shelter and sex and boots he badly needs; she gaily dances with him on the Brocken and sends him off in a balloon when his life is threatened. But Slothrop's fatal magic, unlike its effect on the London girls, is powerless in the aura of Geli's own. Though she likes him and treats him kindly, she is not really interested in charming Slothrop. Her power is reserved for Tchitcherine, a Russian Secret Intelligence officer who is searching for his half-brother Enzian, with, as Geli explains to Slothrop, an "old-time, pure, personal hate" (331). On Tchitcherine, her "Attila," the little witch spreads the full enchantment of her love. As he confronts his own unreality, his long delusion of useful service to the Party — as he realizes his Preterition, in short — Geli casts her spell over his isolation and pain; bewitched, he fails to recognize Enzian when they meet at last, and so takes bread and cigarettes from his brother instead of his life. Geli Tripping's nurture is clearly special and specialized; open to every natural and supernatural force of the universe, loving, "World-choosing," her magic is some antique survival, come undiluted from the fruitful past.

On the prism of creative force, between the burning green of Geli's primal magic and the flickering flames of the London girls, is Jessica Swanlake — on the one hand, just another "young rosy girl in the uniform of an ATS private" (30); on the other, a power strong enough to waken the dead. Jessica, unlike Geli who is far out of this world, is in it and of it. Her magic, human and full of life, is as tamed as the English countryside from which she draws her strength; her memories of the prewar past are full of the sights and smells of innocent, peaceful, domestic concretions: "Games, pinafores, girl friends, a black alley kitten with white little feet, holidays all the family by the sea, brine, frying fish, donkey rides, peach taffeta, a boy named Robin . . ." (59). When she dreams of a future with *her* lover, Roger Mexico, it is no Tripping dream of a carefree nomadic idyll through heath and Pan-filled grove, but rather a "flash of several children, a garden, a window, voices *Mummy, what's* . . . cucumbers and brown onions on a chopping board, wild carrot blossoms sprinkling with brilliant yellow a reach of deep, very green lawn and [Roger's] voice — " (59). The brightly colored perceptions, the happiness, the health of body and mind she brings her love are vital, but they are rooted in an assumption of residential safety, Ishmael's "attainable felicity" — "the wife, the hearth, the bed, the table, the saddle, the fire-side, the country."

It is, therefore and ironically, only during the visible extremis of uprooting war that Jessica's wild life-breeding passion can be fully released. At its apex of freedom, she rides, topless, bare-breasted, to Roger's delighted chagrin, down a trunkroad to London — such a vision of the goddess Freia, of Youth and Beauty, stripped of her mufti and returned to rejuvenate the earth, that even the ubiquitous midgets of *Gravity's Rainbow*, who sporadically appear to parody its scenes of pain and joy, the Niebelungen of this world, stare and drool from their passing lorry. At such moments, Jessica is "as good as gold." Forced by the war from the upper middle-class comforts and habits that once secured her from the world, Jessica nevertheless retains the specificities of that life; her imagination, fed by its accoutrements, paradoxically, enables her own magic; she makes secure nooks in disaster areas and perceives the dismantled lives that echo from death-abandoned things. Standing amidst the rubble of a recent explosion, in "some woman's long-gathered nest, taken back to separate straws, flung again to this wind and this darkness," Jessica sees, "twined" around a "brass bedpost," "someone's brassiere, a white, prewar confection of lace and satin, simply left tangled. . . . For an instant, in a vertigo she can't control, all the pity laid up in her heart flies to it, as it would to a small animal stranded and forgotten. [. . .] She knows she must not cry [. . .] But the poor lost flimsy thing . . . waiting in the night and rain for its owner, for its room to reassemble round it . . ." (43). And, not surprisingly then, among all those in the novel who know of Roger's grids and equations, of Slothrop's clustered stars, it is Jessica who first asks about the human beings their abstractions successfully neutralize.

> [I]n the house [the lovers have made a home] at the edge of the stay-away town, Jessica, snuggling, afloat, just before sleep was to take them, whispered, "Roger . . . what about the girls?" That was all she said. But it brought Roger wide awake. And bone-tired as he was, he lay staring for another hour, wondering about the girls. (87)

Although one can already read in their divergent responses to the implicit answer — Jessica, snuggling; Roger, wide-awake and staring — the inevitable end of their affair when the war is officially over, the essential question is not new to Jessica, only newly directed. In the most undramatic, most ordinary domestic terms, at *such* moments, Jessica wants OUT. And her fatal alternative to Roger, Jeremy ("Beaver"), offers the stiff-upper-lip safety, the undisturbing protective affection, of an English officer who does his duty, never questions, *is* the Establishment, is "death-by-government." "He is," thinks the Jessica-enlivened Roger, "every assertion the fucking War has ever made — that we are meant for work and [. . .] for austerity: and these shall take priority over love, dreams, the spirit, the senses and the other second-class trivia that are found among the idle and mindless hours of the day . . ." (177). But for Jessie, when rocket falls wake her from the warmth of her post-orgasm sleep with Roger, when her dream of "herself in a chair, old-fashioned bonneted, looking west over the deck of Earth, inferno red at its edges, and further in the brown and gold clouds," suddenly shifts to "night: The empty rocking chair lit staring chalk blue by — is it the moon or some other light from the sky?" (123), when she feels that flood of pity at the sight of the forever breastless bra — then she cries:

> "I've lost my mind. I ought to be cuddling someplace with Beaver this very minute, watching him light up his Pipe, and here instead I'm with this *gillie* or something, this spiritualist, statistician, what *are* you anyway — "
> "Cuddling?" Roger has a tendency to scream. "*Cuddling?*"
> (43)

For the duration, Jessica has, in fact, lost her mind; against the deadly undertow of fear and habit, she swims, wildly and wittily strong in the enchanting passion of human love and the joyful, death-defying gifts its magic allows her to bestow on Roger. Their brief last-winter-of-the-war affair has a Lawrentian ideality: "Together they are a long skin interface,[5] flowing sweat, close as muscles and bones can press, hardly a word beyond her name, or his" (121) — "a joint creature unaware of itself. . . . In a life [Roger] has cursed, again and again, for its need to believe in so much that was trans-observable, here is the first, the very first real magic; data he can't argue away" (38).

As Roger makes "his act of faith" in the terrible Christmas of '45 — "We're both someone new now, someone incredible" — Pynchon bitterly puts children "in the street," chanting, "Hark, the herald angels sing: / Mrs. Simpson's pinched our King . . ." (177). For the hope in the heraldic message of a real-life abdication of power and security for love is a deception. Roger and Jessica are not royally free. Jessica's magic is encumbered, and the Roger she has loved and warmed into life has a heritage she is not equipped to fight. Without Jessica, Roger wanders among his equations with no myths to sustain him, no illusion of cause and effect, no temptation to belief in natural force — just a terrible lonely ease *"between* zero and one" with a numbed acceptance and aesthetic awe of the statistical probabilities he charts.

> He'd seen himself a point on a moving wavefront, propagating through sterile history — a known past, a projectable future. But Jessica was the breaking of the wave. Suddenly there was a beach, the unpredictable . . . new life. [. . .] [H]e wanted to believe it too, [. . .] believe that no matter how bad the time, nothing was fixed, everything could be changed and she could always deny the dark sea at his back, love it away. (126)

Yet as Roger tells Jessica repeatedly, "My mother is the war"; and from that lady he carries, no matter how innocently, the genes of death. She has already, Pynchon adds, "leached at all the soft, the vulnerable inclusions of hope and praise scattered [. . .] through Roger's mineral, grave-marker self, washed it all moaning away on her gray tide" (39). And, ironically, it is just that Mother's son that renders Jessica's magic impotent. Away from him, Jessica finds

> he depresses and even frightens her. Why? On top of him in the wild nights riding [. . .] there's only room for *Roger, Roger, oh love* to the end of breath. But out of bed, walking, talking, his bitterness, his darkness, run deeper than the War, the winter; he hates England so, hates "the System," [. . .] stays inside his paper cynic's cave hating himself . . . and does she *want* to bring him out, really? Isn't it safer with Jeremy? She tries not to allow this question in too often, but it's there. (126)

So "from forth the fatal loins" of War and the Establishment, these "star-cross'd lovers take their life / . . . [and] the fearful passage of their death-marked love." But unlike the poisons of Romeo and Juliet, those of Roger and Jessica are not self-administered but taken at their mothers' breasts, and *their* passing promises no civil peace — although they too sense their own helplessness and the inevitable tragedy of the conclusion. Jessica, at the night window of the house in the stay-away zone, stands "filling with a need to cry because she can see so plainly her limits, knows she can never protect him as much as she must — from what may come out of the sky" (58). And Roger? Although he "is learning to recognize the times when nothing really holds her but his skinny, 20-pushup arms," yet "the coincidence of maps, girls, and rocketfalls has entered him silently, silent as ice, and Quisling molecules have shifted in latticelike ways to freeze him" (176).

Jessie, tearing the masks off the x's and y's of Roger's equations and exposing the people the little letters hid, has taught him to love and pity and care; and through his caring, she has freed him to join the Anti-System, "The Counterforce," even if she must remain behind with "Them." She has created a Roger who has not only dared to laugh and love but to weep and rage as well. If, then, she seems to the "gentle skimmer" of *Gravity's Rainbow* still a little conventional bitch, having her kicks and running out when the cards are down, I suspect it's because her course, as we see it in the novel, is *from* a fragilely held life *to* death, a less attractive change than Roger's partial thawing. After her transfer to Cuxhaven in the official peace, Jessica's "hair [is] much shorter, [she's] wearing a darker mouth of a different outline, harder lipstick" (708), and engaged to Jeremy. But at the lovers' last meeting, while Roger and the boys of "The Counterforce" turn the Kruppfest banquet into alliterative verbal nausea, Roger's old poison still works. Cynically he thinks "They" will use even the rebellion: "We help to legitimize Them" (713). Thus, as he first realizes he must seriously decide whether to live on as Their "pet freak" or make his own death, and Jessica leaves, "weeping on the arm of Jeremy her gentleman," Pynchon asks:

> Does Roger have a second of pain right here? Yes. Sure. You would too. You might even question the worth of your cause. (716)

The question and answer are terrible and terrifying, worse than Romeo's "lightening before death." As Jessica literally jumps into Roger's world as a bomb explodes at their first accidental meeting, so she has been allowed to bring him into life only so he can suffer dying. Like the wall-slogan of the Weimar Republic, the action suggests that it is *not*, in this world, better to have loved and lost, but deadly to have loved at all. And the war, triumphantly, is Roger's mother still.

With just enough exception to prove the rule, the war in fact is a fairly representative Pynchon mother. Until the "accident" of Jessica, she had drained Roger of hope and the joy of hope fulfilled — left him not heartless, but with a heart paralyzed, numb, uncommitted — given him, as he himself realizes, "a somber youth squarely founded on Death" (126),[6] and bequeathed him its component conviction that everything is predictable, unchangeable. The Mothers of *Gravity's Rainbow*, then, are a perversion of the "girls." Their wombs nourish life, but their children once born take from their breasts not only physical strength but a taste for death, an aptitude for dying. The little set piece of Otto Gnahb's version of the Mother Conspiracy is a comic microcosm of maternal action in the novel: "The Mothers get together once a year, in secret, at these giant conventions," Otto explains to Hilda, "and exchange information."

Recipes, games, key phrases to use on their children. "What did yours use to say when she wanted to make you feel guilty?"
" 'I've worked my fingers to the bone!' " sez the girl.
"Right! [. . .] You see, you see? That *can't* be accidental! They have a contest, for Mother of the Year, breast-feeding, diaper-changing, they *time* them, casserole competitions, ja — then, toward the end, they actually begin to use the *children*. The State Prosecutor comes out on stage. 'In a moment, Albrecht, we are going to bring your mother on. Here is a Luger, fully loaded. The State will guarantee you absolute immunity from prosecution. Do whatever you wish to do — anything at all. Good luck, my boy.' [. . .] Only the mothers who get shot at qualify for the finals. Here they bring in psychiatrists, and judges sit with stop-watches to see how quickly the children will crack. 'Now then, Olga, wasn't it *nice* of Mutti to break up your affair with that long-haired poet?' 'We understand your mother and you are, ah, *quite close*, Hermann. Remember the time she caught you *masturbating into her glove*? Eh?' Hospital attendants stand by to drag the children off, drooling, screaming, having clonic convulsions. Finally there is only one Mother left on stage. They put the traditional flowered hat on her head, and

hand her the orb and scepter, which in this case are a gilded pot roast and a whip, and the orchestra plays *Tristan und Isolde*." (505)

Here, at Mother's knee, the children learn that love means pain and shame, guilt and despair. The mothers are destroyers; they belong to "Them." Otto's own mother, Frau Gnahb, with all the vigor of Marie Dressler's "Tugboat Annie," runs a pirate barge for the black marketeers of the Zone, hell-bent at every turn of the sea passage through which she ferries, "bellowing" as she goes "a blood thirsty SEA CHANTY":

> I'm the Pirate Queen of the Baltic Run, and nobody fucks with me — And those who've tried are bones and skulls, and lie beneath the sea.
> And the little fish like messengers swim in and out their eyes, Singing, "Fuck ye not with Gory Gnahb and her desperate enterprise!" (497–498)

Fair warning.

To wither further the old life-giving adage, it is, then, not only better *not* to have loved, but, best of all, not even to have been born. And Pynchon's concern with origins, with discovering where we first took the terrible turn into the nonhuman twentieth century, leads him to worry not only about the effects of such mothers on the child but how Mothers came to be converted from the loving "girls." If one can look upon *V.* in relation to *Gravity's Rainbow* as one views Joyce's *Portrait* in relation to *Ulysses*, as my colleague Richard Johnson suggests we do, we can discover passages in *V.* that explicate what *Gravity's Rainbow* directly renders. As *V.*'s Maltese-born Fausto Maijstral, in his "Confessions," tries to chart the past's relation to the postwar present, the course we have taken from "the quick to the inanimate," he at first closely echoes Yeats:

> Does any mother anticipate the future; acknowledge when the time comes that a son is now a man and must leave her to make whatever peace he can alone on a treacherous earth. No, it's the same Maltese timelessness. They don't feel the fingers of years jittering age, fallibility, blindness into face, heart and eyes. A son is a son, fixed always in the red and wrinkled image as they first see it. (*V.*, 321/300)

So, Pynchon's mothers participate in those Yeatsian "Presences" — "self-born mockers of man's enterprise" — because they too reject change. But change, the possibility of altering an apparently preset course, is vital to Pynchon's view (hardly unique) of what makes life, living. Maijstral notes that he has been "learning life's single lesson: that there is more accident to it than a man can ever admit to in a lifetime and stay sane" (*V.*, 320–321/300).

It is just that terrifying unpredictability of accident and its power in the act of creation, that inscrutable life-giving force, operating on no rule of cause and effect or any other rational principle, that drives mothers, as the Pynchon of *V.* sees it, into secret alliance, ironically serving the Establishment of *un*rejuvenating death. "Mothers are closer than anyone to accident," Maijstral continues.

> They are painfully conscious of the fertilized egg; as Mary knew the moment of conception. But the zygote has no soul. Is matter. [. . .]
>   Their babies always seem to come by happenstance; a random conjunction of events. Mothers close ranks, and perpetrate a fictional mystery about motherhood. It's only a way of compensating for an inability to live with the truth. Truth being that they do not understand what is going on inside them; that it is a mechanical and alien growth which at some point acquires a soul. They are possessed. Or: the same forces which dictate the bomb's trajectory, the deaths of stars, the wind and the waterspout have focussed somewhere inside the pelvic frontiers without their consent, to generate one more mighty accident. It frightens them *to death*. It would frighten anyone. (*V.*, 321–322/301, italics mine)

I've quoted all this from *V.*, not only because it demonstrates an amazing prescience of the action and imagery of *Gravity's Rainbow*, but because I think it makes explicit what the later novel may at first conceal: the vampire mothers are not Philip Wylie's simplistic "Moms" nor formed from Fiedler's view of the tradition of death in the American novel. They are, instead, as much the tragically disfigured catastrophes of events gone out of human control as any other set of characters in *Gravity's Rainbow*.

Although it is startling, it is not then surprising to see the

mothers linked, as early as *V.*, to the "bomb's trajectory," nor to
find that the Rocket itself is an equally helpless mother, carrying
its Schwarzgërat as the womb its fetus. Neither is it surprising to
find the mothers, again explicitly in *V.*, dramatically in *Gravity's
Rainbow*, soldered to the sterile perversions of decadence.

> Decadence, decadence. What is it? Only a clear movement
> toward death or, preferably, non-humanity. As Fausto . . . like
> [his] island, became more inanimate, [he] moved closer to the
> time when like any dead leaf or fragment of metal [he'd] be
> finally subject to the laws of physics. . . .
> Is it only because Malta is a matriarchal island that Fausto
> felt so strongly that connection between mother-rule and deca-
> dence? (*V.*, 321/301)

Thus for the child to love the Mother "They" made, it must
love death-in-life and must hate or fear the fragile self that
would oppose her. To love Mother is to love tyranny and oppression and wish to emulate its power, or to love the submission and
humiliation the oppressor demands.

In summary, then, a girl, to *endure* the terrifying knowledge
that her sexual joy is used by impersonal forces to convert her,
will-she won't-she, into an incubator of life, has conspired to
conceal her helplessness, her lack of control over the most inti-
mate processes of her being, by creating the stultifying myths of
Motherhood. And so that her children will succeed, she has
taught them "cunning," as Maijstral puts it, and with it, betrayal,
lying, and the concomitant *r*eactions of shame and guilt, as a
"way of life" that has become (at least by the end of the First
World War in Western society) a way of joyless sterility or recurrent, fecund death.

Hence Greta/Margherita Erdmann, the Queen-Mother of the
"decky-dance" in *Gravity's Rainbow*, doing her act in prewar
German movies, with a touring company to entertain the troops
at concentration camps, at the launching site of the Rocket, and
finally aboard the good ship *Anubis*. But despite the allusive echoing of her names, she is merely the porno-films' black-and-white
type of Willing Victim of Man's Sexual Rage, "less," says Pynchon, "than the images of herself that survive in an indeterminate

number of release prints [. . .] about the Zone, and even across
the sea" (364). She is all that is left, in this world, of Wotan's
Erda; and her daughter (no Valkyrie) is fittingly conceived
amidst a mass orgy of bit players, "the jackal men," whose
celluloid-induced sexual drives, at the end of Greta's most notorious movie, *Alpdrücken*, run beyond the limits of the scenario
but not beyond the camera's continuously recording film. Only
Bianca, the sexually precocious and adept prenubile child of that
cinematic copulation, is allowed to get off the wheel (reel?) of
recycling replication, "Their" deadly parody of the continuing
fecundity of life.

"We can get away," Bianca urges Slothrop, after their pecu-
liarly satisfying intercourse — in Pynchon's imagery, a foretaste
of the womb-filled Rocket's rise into the Void — "I know how
to hide. I can hide you too" (470). But when his eyes fail her,
as they have failed the pleading eyes of Berkshire girls in roadside
diners glimpsed from Greyhound bus windows long ago, fail
because it is less painful to suppress his "Eurydice-obsession, this
bringing back out of" (472), than to respond, Bianca recognizes
(her alternative escape) the certain horror ahead: "In her ruined
towers now the bells gong back and forth in the wind. [. . .]
sails on the sea too small and distant to matter . . . water too
steel and cold . . ." (471).[7] When we and Slothrop see her again,
she hangs from a pipe, as fittingly entombed as she was born, in
the bowels of the *Anubis*, the white, jackal-headed yacht that,
with its cargo of Central European aristocratic Nazi decadents,
plows the fogged sea passages of the North, running the interface
between light and dark, living and dead — old Anubis, usher in
Limbo, judger and embalmer of the dead.

Whether Bianca hangs there as the resigned victim of her
mother's sexual jealousy or as yet another sacrifice of Greta's
mad demands in her role as "Shekhinah, queen, daughter, bride,
and mother of God" (478) or, simply, as her own final solution
hardly matters. She has in any case torn through the iron gate,
has made her own death run.

That Pynchon finds Slothrop as implicated as Greta is abundantly clear. Slothrop is not only an Orpheus who didn't even
try, he is also — to Greta *and* her child — a Tannhäuser for whom

the Pope's staff never flowers (364, 470), who never frees himself from the Venusberg of this novel, but wanders near its perimeters, the Lunesberg Heath, where the only underground orgies are rocket-assemblies. In fact, Greta and Slothrop have much in common: they have each known the ultimate sexual ecstasy of "Their" world, the magnetic embrace of its Superplastic. And although Greta once incestuously mistakes him for one of her murdered children, rising from the mud of Bad Karma, she knows he carries the identity card of Max Schlepzig, her leading man in *Alpdrücken*, the Grand Inquisitor, the first rapist at the disassembling that created Bianca. "Of all her putative fathers," intones Pynchon, "Bianca is closest [. . .] closest to you [. . .] you [. . .] you, alone [. . .]. She favors you, most of all." And with the reiterations of the pronoun, Pynchon expands its referent outward; not only to Slothrop, but to the reader, also. "You'll never get to see her. So somebody has to tell you" (472).

So, not just Slothrop, then, or Greta, but all of us have joined in the corporate act of the murder of exploitable innocence. Yet the pointing finger of those lines, despite the bitter paradox implied, counts Greta, too, among the innocents — "No Dietrich [. . .] not destroyer of men but doll" (393–394). Greta, the most fallen, the least human of Pynchon's mothers,[8] is, after all, "Their" creation, "Their" tool. If Slothrop is weakened and used here by the debilitating morality of his Puritanic judgments (*"sure I know them* [. . .] *probably some hooker"* — 472), Greta is vulnerable because "she always enjoyed it too much, chained up in those torture rooms" (461). Though both characters sense the horror of their destructive acts, neither really understands enough to reverse or restrain his moves. Slothrop, the less plasticized, is visited by flashes of yearning and, near the end of the novel, is granted one wish-fulfillment dream of Bianca, "smiling," and himself, riding the wheel of the old self-rejuvenating life-cycle, in a closed system where trees grow and birds sing (609–610); Greta, too synthetic and inanimate for even such unreal comforts, sits on a toilet of the *Anubis*, spook-ridden, terror-filled, destroyed by a preconditioned titillating fascination with her own, sporadically recognized, frightfulness.

Still, the immensity of Pynchon's sorrowing love for the universally anthropomorphized beings[9] of *Gravity's Rainbow* extends easily to the human shard that is Greta. Never one of "the girls," but dead as Bianca long before she was impregnated, she is nonetheless one of the novel's many Gretels, who, with their Hansels (for Greta, Thanatz, her equally decadent husband), wander, lost babes, in the witch-filled woods of the Zone (485); she is the Minnesinger's fragile and doomed image of sacred love, and Faust's pure village maiden, deserted, death-dealing and death-dealt. The allusiveness of her names and acts generously lend her damnation all the significance it can hold; in this world, every old tale the language evokes comes back mutilated — shorn of the promise of its happy ending or its "*redeeming* cataclysm," its ultimate, perhaps only, fiction.

Except for the narrating voice of the novel and the voices of those beyond the interface that separates what-we-agree-to-call-life from physical death, only Leni Pökler understands how "They" manipulate, how the Mothers, the Fathers, are made for Their purposes, *and* only Leni has the strength to resist Them, to fight to break away — Leni, wife of Franz, a German chemical engineer, and herself a mother, whose daughter Ilse is conceived under the same film-induced sexual itch that produces Bianca.

> Thus Pökler's whole front surface, eyes to knees: flooded with tonight's image of the delicious victim bound on her dungeon rack, filling the movie screen — close-ups of her twisting face, nipples under the silk gown amazingly erect, making lies of her announcements of pain — *bitch!* she loves it . . . and Leni no longer solemn wife, embittered source of strength, but Margherita Erdmann underneath him, on the bottom for a change, as Pökler drives in again, into her again, yes, bitch, yes. . . . (397)

Leni, an activist of the already-suppressed Communist Revolution in the last days of the Weimar Republic, has utopian dreams of what might have been but no illusions of how it is. In this context, Pynchon suggestively introduces her into the novel through the loving, extrasensory perceptive eyes of Peter Sachsa, a medium who channels the *true* shape of things to come from the spirit of the assassinated Walter Rathenau to "the corporate Nazi crowd" of generals and scientists who attend his séances (162–167).

Each night [Leni] came he wanted to cry at the sight of her captivity. In her smudged eyes was clear hatred of a life she would not leave: a husband she didn't love, a child she had not learned to escape feeling guilty for not loving enough. (153–154)

Yet as Peter is unconscious of the words spoken through him from "The Other Side," so his vision of Leni is blurred.

When Leni herself enters the novel a few paragraphs later, she, with Ilse, has already made her break from Franz and is about to join Sachsa, wondering only if Peter will "accept that she is not *his*, any more than she belonged to Franz" (164). Just as she will not be owned, even by her lovers, she also rejects the temptation to possess those she loves. She leaves Franz when she is convinced he will never be more than a "dead weight" in her arms. "She has talked to psychiatrists [Wilhelm Reich?, whom Pynchon clearly has also read], she knows about the German male at puberty." Wandervogel, lying passively "in meadows and mountains" waiting for the betraying, inevitable stroke of Destiny to send them flying "from pain to duty, from joy to work, from commitment to neutrality."

> Franz loved her neurotically, masochistically, he belonged to her and believed that she would carry him on her back, away to a place Destiny couldn't reach. As if it were gravity. He had half-awakened one night burrowing his face into her armpit mumbling, "your wings . . . oh, Leni, your wings . . ."
> But her wings can only carry her own weight, and she hopes Ilse's, for a while. (162)

In the arguments that precede her departure, as she tries *not* to condition Franz to despair but to make him "grow up" (162), she carries one of the major expository burdens of *Gravity's Rainbow*.

She argues for the natural wheeling of the astrological heavens against Pökler's scientific insistence on causal relationships; she describes, in answer to Franz's fear of violence, the fear-free tranquility of losing oneself in "the moment, and its possibilities," the exhilaration to be found, in his vocabulary, of "Δt approaching zero, eternally approaching" (158–159). She tries, futilely for Franz but significantly for Pynchon's reader, to explain that the signs — hers, Crab; his, Pisces, for instance — don't "cause," don't "produce" but rather

"It all goes together. Parallel, not series. Metaphor. Signs and symptoms. Mapping on to different coordinate systems. [. . .]" (159)

" 'Try to design anything that way and have it work,' " says Franz. (I assume that the whole of *Gravity's Rainbow*, and, in Mark Schorer's old encompassing sense, its technique, is Pynchon's answer to that challenge.) Leni's long daydream, which begins with a Lesbian fantasy, reflecting a primitive sexual attraction as part of her anti-Semitism, quickly dissolves itself into the *life* that might have been, a workers' paradise of sexual equality and joy: chaste, healthy, naked bodies, laughing, teasing, in the common bath — and Leni's childhood sweetheart back from France, virgin as she, and as loving — gentle as she, and as strong, shy, blond, their union bound by the slow "reach" of his hand "to hold her face" and (perhaps most touchingly) the President, breaking off his speech on war — *Fickt es*, and Rosa Luxemburg about to be elected in his place. "Incredible joy at the baths, among the friends. True joy: events in the dialectical process cannot bring this explosion of the heart. Everyone is in love . . ." (158). But, of course, Rosa Luxemburg was murdered more than a decade ago. And Leni's thankless expository task goes on. "They're using you to kill people," she tells Franz; "That's their only job, and you're helping them." "Kadavergehorsamkeit," she calls him. To every rational explanation, every suggestion of ultimate idealistic uses for rocketry, or of suggestions that means (i.e., money) are irrelevant to ends, Leni cries, "*No!*" (400–401).

When Leni leaves him, Franz sees himself helplessly exposed to the very world whose existence, with her, he denied — "an unemployed servant," "a Victim in a Vacuum!" (414), and, as he becomes Blicero's "best ally," he recognizes he has only two choices: "personal identity and impersonal salvation" (406). Yet, although he has been drawn by the charismatic death-force of Blicero and the Rocket, manifested in a tendency to drift away —

"some assumption of Pökler into the calculations, drawings, graphs" (405) — a flicker of Leni's life-force has also touched him. Not that he doesn't continue to serve Them, but he has taken enough of Leni to face the quality of his submission, to confront at the last, the human horror of the concentration camp, to offer a single act of repentance and charity without romanticizing its effect. Seen last, a part now of the great Humility, he sits on the ground with Frieda, his pig and Slothrop's benefactor, in the deserted children's play-city of Zwölfkinder, waiting for the improbable return of Ilse, and telling Slothrop tales of Imipolex-G and his old professor Laszlo Jamf (577ff.).

As Leni Pökler has refused to play the domineering, sadistic wife-mother to her husband, she also refuses to carry the orb of the gilded pot roast for Ilse, fiercely determined that her daughter will not be used (156). To do so, she rejects her own "daydreaming child's face [. . .], exactly the sort of fat-softened, unfocused weakness that causes men to read her as Dependent Little Girl" (156), and the "dream of gentleness, light, her criminal heart redeemed" — the dream of peace and safety and joy. Leni knows the price of resistance; "she knows what she has to impersonate" (156). In bitter paradox, while the dead of *Gravity's Rainbow* try desperately to impersonate the living, Leni, to live and to give life to her child, understands she must play the dead-at-heart, "Especially with Ilse watching her more." Her answer to Peter Sachsa's concern about Ilse, if Leni is arrested, records not only her own accurate perceptions of "Them" but comments on the movement of Pynchon's thought in the decade since the passages from Maijstral's journal quoted earlier from *V.*:

> "[. . .] Peter can't you see, they *want* a great swollen tit with some atrophied excuse for a human, bleating around somewhere in its shadows. How can I be *human* for her? Not her *mother*. 'Mother,' that's a civil-service category, Mothers work for *Them!* They're the policemen of the soul . . ." her face darkened, Judaized by the words she speaks, not because it's out loud but because she means it, and she's right. (219–220)

Pynchon nowhere softens or dilutes the solemnity and terrible courage of Leni's lonely struggle in the endless, shelterless streets.

To save her soul, she must be kept constantly at war, barely afforded an unvigilant moment (such as Pynchon does allow Katje, for instance, with Slothrop on the Riviera); she cannot slip into the comforting illusions of myth or story or practice the conventional habits by which we are bound. As she is given no joy except in the forbidden dream, itself more prosaic than most dreams in the novel, so she is given no sentence of even potential sentimentality. When Leni and Ilse are confined to the "reeducation" camp Dora, we hear of Leni selling her body to survive, only indirectly, remotely. She has, in fact, few direct scenes of her own; her recurrent voice in the novel reaches us primarily through the remembered phrases or imagined scenes in the memories of Franz and Sachsa. Perhaps, by keeping her offstage, by shielding the scenes of her pain from direct presentation, Pynchon intends to preserve her from the too-easy pity of his readers. For whatever reason, in the Leni passages his prose is at its most ordinary, least witty, least allusive, least imaginative.

As a result, Leni seems to me one of the least attractive characters in the novel — quick, it is true, with hard-fought-for life and highly admirable, she nevertheless emerges two-dimensional, unlovable, unpitiable, cold. How much then is Pynchon saying, if his stylistic treatment of the most fully and consciously liberated woman in the novel strikes other readers as it does me? First of all, as I've already suggested, that the price for preserving one's humanity in this world is the *apparent* loss of it; second (and I'm less sure here), that the repression of dream and the rejection of traditional roles cannot help also half-killing the heart. If one adds to this Franz's observation (though his analyses of Leni's behavior are not always reliable) as he sits in the postwar ruins of the Zwölfkinder, that perhaps she had "some desire to be actually destroyed. . . . She went out to her street-theatre each time expecting not to come back, but he never really knew that" (399), then perhaps Pynchon is drawing close to Hawthorne's view of Hester Prynne. As Hawthorne contemplates the cost of *his* heroine's spiritual and intellectual independence and isolation in a world not ready for her ideas, he thinks:

[S]he might have come down to us in history, hand in hand with Ann Hutchinson, as the foundress of a religious sect. She might . . . have been a prophetess. She might, and not improbably would, have suffered death from the stern tribunals of the period, for attempting to undermine the foundations of the Puritan establishment. (*The Scarlet Letter*, Chapter 13)

Perhaps, says Hawthorne, she would have killed herself, if it had not been for little Pearl. Suggestively, too, the Hawthorne chapter occurs when Hester is least alive and is also hidden from his reader's direct observation.

When Leni reappears near the end of the novel, her name is now "Solange," (*Ger.*, "as long as"), and she works as a "masseuse" at Putzi's in Cuxhaven, after the Armistice. Brought by Seaman Bodine, one of the "good guys" in *Gravity's Rainbow* and greatly matured since his appearance in *V.*, to Slothrop, still pig-costumed, hiding in a closet, she is "a child brought to visit the weird pig in his cave." Her face continues perhaps to reflect her human heart. With Bodine, she clarifies the escape-routes of the humble to Slothrop:

[It] is Slothrop's first news, out loud, that the Zone can sustain many other plots besides those polarized upon himself [. . .] and that by riding each branch [of the enormous transit system] the proper distance, knowing when to transfer, keeping some state of minimum grace though it might often look like he's headed the wrong way, this network of all plots may yet carry him to freedom. He understands that he should not be so paranoid of either Bodine or Solange, but ride instead their kind underground awhile, see where it takes him. . . . (603)

Then, says Pynchon, "Solange leads Slothrop off to the Baths" (ah, Leni's dreams!) and later, as he lies "curl[ed]" beside her "in a wide crisp-sheeted bed," himself dreaming the happy dream of Bianca I mentioned earlier,

And "Solange," oddly enough, is dreaming of Bianca too, though under a different aspect: it's of her own child, Ilse, riding lost through the Zone on a long freight train that never seems to come to rest. She isn't unhappy, nor is she searching, exactly, for her father. But Leni's early dream for her is coming true. She will not be used. There is change, and departure: but there is also help when least looked for from the strangers of the day, and hiding, out among the accidents of this drifting Humility, never quite to be extinguished, a few small chances for mercy. . . . (610)

So Leni's kind of maternity, whatever cost to her character or characterization, *is* creative — her daughter, "Bianca under a different aspect," is Ilse, alive; and her final dream, the most reliably, realistically hopeful moment in the novel.

There is little more to add in viewing the remaining major woman character, Katje Borgesius, the counterspy. Although she is central to *Gravity's Rainbow*, Katje, for the purposes of this essay, represents but a variant of themes and types, a new combination of attitudes and attributes, previously explored.

In addition to all the other explicit doublings of the elegant Katje with Bianca, Gottfried (her Hansel when she is Gretel), Enzian, Margherita, she has an almost perfect male counterpart in "Pirate" Prentice, a captain in British Intelligence. Slightly ominous characters, with underlying "good intentions," both serve the System, wittingly, and endure their slavery by carefully preserving an illusion of independence from it: on the one hand, by a frank recognition of that dependence and its destructive capacity — and, on the other, by faith in their myth of a secret self-control. Unlike Greta Erdmann, who knows she has no identity beyond the roles she plays, Katje and Prentice delude themselves into a belief that behind their official masks a heart still beats that can, when the war is won, function freely and openly.

Yet that proud delusion is not as absolute as I have made it seem. Intelligent, sophisticated, they are pecked at by the fear that they may have become too tarnished by the nonhuman personae they inhabit ever to be wiped wholly clean and shining. So driven by the loneliness of their insight and their fear, incapable of loving, except some frozen form of it they can share with each other, tempted by an exquisitely developed taste for decadence, they are ultimately weakened by their own flawed and rationalized knowledge of themselves. Thus, they too fail to break away, enchained not only by "Their" orders and a certain pride in an illusory success as double agents, but also by a blindness to the fact that the self each so secretly harbors has already suffered a death of the heart, "a leeching of the soul."

When Katje is "dropped" by the Dutch underground, it is because they understand that she "seriously" believes "there's a real conversion factor between information and lives" (105). Katje's training in higher mathematics is not incidental but functional; she *believes* in the relation between abstract numbers and men, and if a Jessica asked *her*, "But what about the girls?" Katje, unlike Roger, would simply fail to understand the question — or, worse, find it a sentimental one.

In a parody of Slothrop's failure to "bring out" Bianca, Captain Prentice succeeds in taking Katje out of Enemy Territory only to send her, voluntarily of course, to "The White Visitation" in England. When something about her makes him uneasy, he finds he can not only quickly dispel the difficulty but convert it to a sympathetic quality he also recognizes in himself: "it's a lapse of character then, a crotchet. Like carrying the bloody Mendoza" (107), the outdated gun he carries, despite its "extra weight," in place of the government-issued regulation Sten. Yet by his defining example of "crotchet," he has debased that lovely old word for an intensity of *human* individuality, a distinguishing insistence on unique *person*ality — the cherished eccentricity — and converted it, with unconscious irony, into a penchant ("yes, most likely it's love these days") for an inanimate object, a deadly weapon, in fact. And he deepens the already comforting delusion as he enlarges the voluntary burden of its *weight* into a metaphor for his acceptance of responsibility for Katje: " 'Am I going to let the extra weight make a difference? It's my *crotchet*, I'm indifferent to weight, or I wouldn't have brought the girl back out, would I' " (107). The identification between Katje and "Pirate" is virtually completed, then, early in the novel, when, as a final stroke, Pynchon connects that "crotchet," in almost identical phrases, to the one beloved by Katje's equally conscious, equally destructive and self-deluded ancestor, the seventeenth-century killer of Dodos on the island of Mauritius, who "knew a snaphaan would weigh less [. . .] but [who] felt a nostalgia about the haakbus . . . he didn't mind the extra weight, it was *his* crotchet" (111).

So, Katje and Prentice pass through the action, melancholy but doing what must be done, rather like Bergman and Bogart under orders from Claude Raines. But for Katje, Prentice will never turn into the Cary Grant who, under "Their" very eyes, will carry her safely from the room.

Both Katje and Pirate are doomed, as Enzian tells Katje, "to survive" — when they meet in the many-chambered house of Pynchon's Eliotic, Dantesque Hell, in the circle of political informers, double agents, pseudo-defectors, "people who kill each other" (542), they are forced to see themselves as they are: betrayers of men, without honor, without love, without a molecule of secretly preserved humanity. Interestingly, it is Prentice, not Katje, whom Pynchon shows as more resistant to the truth — he weeps, sentimentally, over clichéd images of a lost past and future (544); it is Katje who enters with eyes already open: " 'Is there room here for the dead? [. . .] I mean the ones who owe their deadness directly to me' " (544–545). "They are here," says Pynchon, "to trade some pain and a few truths." And Katje will lead Prentice all the way. Looking over "a graceful railing," *down* into the Street (where the Lenis endlessly run), they watch a continuing "chronicle" of *How I Came to Love the People.*

> "But the People will never love you," [Katje] whispers, "or me. However bad and good are arranged for them, we will *always* be bad. Do you know where that puts us?" (547–548)

So as Pirate "lifts his long, his guilty, his permanently enslaved face to the illusion of the sky, to the reality of [. . .] the hardness and absolute cruelty of it" and Katje's face takes on the look "of truce, of horror come to a détente with," Pynchon extends what compassionate words he can find for them, as he has comforted the others: "they dissolve now," he says, "into the race and swarm of this dancing Preterition, and their faces, the dear, comical faces they have put on for this ball, fade, as innocence fades, grimly flirtatious, and striving to be kind . . ." (548).

When we see them last, they have joined the "delusionary"

Counterforce. Now happily ineffective, Pirate is flying a hijacked P-47, looking for Slothrop but missing him, still too high to see the Humility. And Katje, too numb to feel the icy darkness Enzian shows her, is traveling North with the Hereros to take part in the Secret Assembly but hearing inaccurately the Sacred Texts Enzian utters en route.

Well, what to make of *all* this? In a letter protesting Susan Sontag's apparent failure to make "important sexual/political connections," the poet Adrienne Rich asks a series of questions, felicitously pertinent to this novel:

> What *are* the themes of domination and enslavement, prurience and idealism, male physical perfection and death, "control, submissive behavior, and extravagant effort," "the turning of people into things." . . . the objectification of the body as separate from the emotions — what are these but masculinist, virilist, patriarchal values? Isn't the black-leather, brothel, ecstasy-in-death fantasy far less a lesbian fantasy than a fantasy of heterosexual males and the male homosexuals they oppress?[10]

If what Ms. Rich means is that male-oriented literature supports those "themes" as *positive* values, then Pynchon's *Gravity's Rainbow*, as a whole, can be read as a thinly disguised treatise written to support the views of radical feminism and its analyses of "patriarchal history" and "patriarchal society." It is downright anti-"masculinist," and Thomas Pynchon differs from Rich's view only in the depth of his compassion and love for victor and victim alike. But such a reading commits violence to the novel. As the grimmer of Pynchon's characters insist on perverting coordinating systems into cause-and-effect relationships, so Ms. Rich's conflation of events turns the complex world into a simplistic dogma of sexual means and ends. Pynchon's questions and values are of a different order: Why have we grown afraid of the good Death, of the Earth? Why have we placed that old revitalizing sexual energy at the service of the state and, man and woman alike, become mere copulating machines?

In other words, and more to the point of the novel if less to the point of this essay, *Gravity's Rainbow* creates a world, a moving frighteningly close image of our own, gone "bad" because it once failed in love, once refused to understand that the true function of the Preterite was to define the election of the Elect, and so, misunderstanding, failed to love them and damned them instead to loneliness, fright, and a life-denying hunger to feel safe — and thereby replaced the wheel of life, the fecund cycle of rejuvenating death on which both Preterite and Saint might joyously have ridden, with the gear's mechanical imitation of movement and its continuing replication of depletion, pollution, death-engendering death. In such a world, what is it to say that, after all, the contributions of the sexes are equally dismaying? For I've meant to show they *are* viewed as equal collaborators — knowingly, willingly, or not. If Leni Pökler seems to resist more bravely and strongly than any male character, her resistance has no more power than Katje's "détente." Brünnhilde's fearless ride into the burning pyre doesn't keep the flames from spreading to Valhalla. Whether or not the armies are ignorant, or led by Hippolyta or Hercules, they still clash by night. And we end, both with a bang and a whimper, singing "to a pleasant air" of a bygone time, and all together, that "Though thy Glass today be run" (760), yet "everything that lives is holy."

Notes

1. The parallels between Wagner's Ring operas and *Gravity's Rainbow* are extraordinary. I recommend a good plot summary. See, for example, Henry W. Simon, *100 Great Operas and Their Stories (Festival of Opera*, 1957; Garden City, N.Y.: Dolphin Ref.–Doubleday, 1960), pp. 439–440. Although it may seem pretentious to add "acknowledgments" to an essay, perhaps one way of describing the complexity of *GR* is to note that I could not have written this paper without the patience of David Collette (Electrical Engineer), Professors Kathryn Eschenberg (Biological Sciences), Thomas Moore (Physics), Harry Seelig (German), Jean Sudrann and Richard Johnson (English), Robert Weaver (Mathematics), and two librarians of the Williston Memorial Library at Mount Holyoke College: Nancy Devine (Research) and Marilyn Dunn (Hermetic expert).

2. *V.* (New York: Lippincott, 1963; New York: Bantam, 1964), pp. 262/243, 273/254.
3. Pagination for the Viking edition of *GR* (New York, 1973) will subsequently be cited in the text. Pages in the Bantam paperback (New York, 1974) can be determined by multiplying the Viking reference by 7/6.
4. Because Pynchon habitually uses the conventional sign for an ellipsis within his own text, I will distinguish mine by placing the periods within brackets.
5. By "interface," I take Pynchon to mean something more than "a surface forming a common boundary between adjacent regions" (*American Heritage Dictionary*), but a partition, a line, not necessarily visible, at which people or things reach their greatest intensity, and at which any attempt to cross may mean repulsion, destruction, or resolution into a new whole. Interfaces abound in *Gravity's Rainbow.* Everywhere their presence challenges the occupants of the novel to risk a crossing. And by their acceptance or refusal, we shall know them.
6. In the context of this reflection, Roger thinks, "how fanatically his mother the War must disapprove of [Jessica's] beauty, her cheeky indifference to death institutions he'd not long ago believed in" (126).
7. Interestingly, Jessica Swanlake seems to be the first of the rejecting "Eurydice-obsessed" lovers; cf. quotation on p. 208.
8. The alcoholic Nalline Slothrop, Tyrone's mother, friend of old Naziphile Joe Kennedy, somehow lacks a theater large enough to fulfill *her* promise.
9. Pynchon seems aware of the literal pathos in the rhetorical figure; throughout his novels "things" grow animate as people become "nonhuman."
10. "Feminism and Fascism: An Exchange," *New York Review of Books*, 22, No. 4 (20 March 1975), 31.

On Trying to Read
Gravity's Rainbow

David Leverenz

... the gray river, hissing and spiculed with the rain. (*GR*, 433)

I

Like most academics interested in contemporary literature, I eagerly bought *Gravity's Rainbow*. But the first twenty pages cooled my interest from curiosity to baffled boredom. By page fifty I had put the book down, and during the rest of that summer I haphazardly skimmed through it, looking for funny limericks or quotable lines. Having no special interest in detective stories and no special bent for paranoid conspiracies, I gave up on Slothrop, idled over the sexy little girls, giggled at the toilet bowls and Giant Adenoids, and wondered why the characters didn't seem ... well, complex, richly human and all that. The sequences of words and paragraphs made no sense to me, seemed in no special order, accrued no momentum.

But I was shamed into reading it a second time. Friends read passages aloud with passion and flair. They seemed to have made sense of it, at least to their own satisfaction. I was assured that Pynchon's intimidating mastery of nonliterary languages was self-explicated within the text. Besides, his vision of the world was more "real" than my illusion of subjectivity. His was the vanguard of the anti-identity novel, the multinational novel, the novel of post-industrial plots and systems that overwhelm all character. No matter how well-intentioned and honest our confessionals, we speak in a world where "a million bureaucrats are diligently plotting death and some of them even know it" (17). *Gravity's Rainbow* jars the ego into seeing how much waste and destruction can come from the I's passion for centering energies, whether as self, nation, corporation, or Elect. The story's undergraduate defenses against seriousness are themselves part of a more terrible seriousness. Screwed to the sticking post by these arguments, I slogged through it again, this time carefully, though dutifully.

Now I was hooked on Slothrop, the he-ness I thought was my own. Through him, I would find out What This Book Is About. For six hundred pages I followed his quest, avid like him to discover what Laszlo Jamf really did to his poor little penis with Imipolex G, what Imipolex G really was anyway, how Slothrop's penis is in love with death, how fathers betray sons and create waste by their orderly transcendence into the Firm. Yet while all sorts of nonanswers were emerging for these questions, why wasn't Slothrop paying attention? Why all this drug-running and partying, all these Argentinian anarchists and Tugboat Annies? Why the White Knight, the movies, the glorification of the Rocket? What was this "Counterforce" that enlisted Pirate Prentice and Katje and perhaps even Enzian, while Slothrop was being co-opted by everybody's petty needs? How come the Kenosha Kid was disappearing?

No longer bored, I now realized I was annoyed. Pynchon had toyed with my subjectivist temperament. He had seduced me into liking Slothrop, only to rob me of that novelistic coherence. The one quester whom I could understand had become a jumble of other people's quests. Worse, the entire structure of the novel had been deliberately fragged into random pigs, lemmings, immortal light bulbs, Masonic symbols, Tarot signs, ur-Christian uprisings, aether theories and other "singularities." My involvement with Slothrop, like my need to understand, had shown my membership in the Firm. The book was an act of calculated hostility against my own need to find out what it was about. In fact, *that* was what it was about. Anything organized, including narrative or interpretation, signified co-optation by waste-making forces. Abandon all systems, ye Bliceros who enter here, and joyously accept the anarchic redemptive rainbow of waste, death, and poor preterite anonymity. My initial boredom had been a mask for these more unsettling feelings of guilt, intimidation, and anger. The book had cunningly constructed, then destroyed, my basic trust.

That was taking it rather personally, I reflected. A point for Pynchon. There were levels and levels of Slothrop in me to be confronted. In mulling over my vehement reaction, I realized how dutifully I had followed the quest, underlining each new item of information and waiting in vain for the ah hah! of full recognition. Yet all that time my real interest had been slipping toward the periphery: to Pökler's lonely dilemma, to Bianca's fate, to Katje's changes, to the lovely singing-duel before the Kirghiz Light (so different from the limericks! could Pynchon be right about different states of consciousness?), to Enzian's relentless self-probing, to irrepressible Frau Gnahb and her "bloody enterprise," and above all to the language, especially the poignant images of nature that suffuse these human scenes. I'd had far more "singular" responses than I supposed, though I had stifled them at every point to conform to what I thought the structure expected.

Now I began to see that not only is the novel a prolonged act of seductive hostility to re-educate such responses, but it also establishes a covert structure, at odds with the dominant structure of the quest. *Gravity's Rainbow* is actually a dualistic melodrama, one side tending toward order, transcendence, and evil, the other tending toward disorder, death, and redemptive human feeling. Slothrop, too accommodating at the beginning of his life as at the end, becomes the victim of whichever side he happens to be passing through.

At this point my reading habits took on a feverish birdlike air. I tirelessly flapped across underlined pages to peck at these covert themes.

II

At one pole is the Firm. The benzene ring discovered by Kekulé not only made possible the invention of plastics, freeing chemists from "the mercy of Nature" (249), but it also brought into being a vast interplay of organizations, bureaucracies, corporations, "with no real country, no side in any war, no specific face or heritage" (243). This is the world of "the Führer-principle," of Pointsman and Blicero, whose goal is a rational universe and whose hope is that "personalities could be replaced by abstractions of power" (81). Those who enter this world find homosexuality and anal sadism inextricably mixed with power and manipulation, with paper at the root of it all, though some men look in vain for a simple love-child, as Jessica is for Roger or Ilse for Pökler, to hide with at the periphery.

White parents, fathers especially, staff the Firm, and white mothers too " 'work for *Them*! They're the policemen of the soul' " (219). As the frequent references to Hansel and Gretel imply, Slothropian children are regularly sacrificed to the "oven" of the Firm's needs. Yet there are no villains here. Walter Rathenau speaks wisdom from the dead, Lyle Bland achieves an orderly transcendence, and even Blicero becomes richly sympathetic in his Rilke-like longings. Not people but the "needs of technology" are the final Führers. Like the monsters of a thousand movies the Firm's secret cry is, *"dawn is nearly here, I need my night's blood, my funding, funding, ahh more, more . . ."* (521).

A motley, disorganized crew stands by the other pole, all enlisted under the banner of "loveable but scatterbrained Mother Nature" (324). Gaucho anarchists, dispossessed black South Africans, little girls, lone lemmings and pigs, bureaucrats with secret mysticisms in their souls, self-hating triple agents, ur-Christian revolutionaries, and finally the Earth herself work in various "singular" ways to undercut the entropy-making forces of market organization. This battle goes on under cover of the war, which itself is simply "a celebration of markets" (105). "The War does not appear to want a folk-consciousness," we're told; "it wants a machine of many separate parts" (130–131). Names like "Earth, Soil, Folk" can easily be co-opted by Nazi filmmakers (395). Yet by the book's end, which is really a kind of Lost and Found, Earth gathers all these "preterite" wasted ones to her bosom, where they suck the "Mindless Pleasures" of the book's original title. Having given up on their hunger for power, order, and permanence, they simply seek death and the milk of transient kindnesses — the best that Earth can bestow. Slothrop, on his way to becoming a "crossroad," has a vision of rainbow sexuality (626), though his own sexuality has already been possessed by the Firm.

Though World War II provides the "plot," in all three senses (story, land, conspiracy), *Gravity's Rainbow* is really about this wider war: between what is "firm" and what is "natural." It's a war between white and colored, the "White Visitation" and the spirits of rainbow place. So Squalidozzi thinks: *"We tried to exterminate our Indians, like you: we wanted the closed white version of reality we got — but . . . the land has never let us forget. . . .* We cannot abide that *openness*: it is terror to us. Look at Borges" (264). Tchitcherine, obsessed with the fact that his soul-brother was conceived by the same white father but of a black woman, can't abide such openness either. As Geli Tripping tells Slothrop, Tchitcherine " 'thinks of Enzian as . . . another *part* of him — a black version of something inside *himself*. A something he needs to . . . liquidate' " (499, Pynchon's ellipses). By the close of his destructive quest, he has become pure failed machine, alone "with the plastic family toothbrushes" (706) and his steel body, "A passive solenoid waiting to be sprung" (734). Unable to accept his family rainbow, he has become imprisoned in the machine-making destructive urge that powers the Firm.

It's also a war between central government and anarchist dispersion (386). Weissman (White Man), alias Blicero (Bleached One), discovers very early that "every true god must be both organizer and destroyer" (99). For him the Rocket "was an entire system *won*, away from the feminine darkness," in a war where love and manhood have to do "with masculine technologies, with contracts, with winning and losing" (324). The world of the pleasure boat, the *Anubis*, moves toward the arcane sexual replications of the benzene ring that first allowed these centralizing forces to gather. Watched by Ensign ("We Who Are About to Die") Morituri, everyone is sucking or fucking in a gigantic daisy chain — a final perversion of the closed system. Meanwhile Frau Gnahb pilots her uppity tugboat through decentralizing anarchist seas, for which Squalidozzi calls (265). She offers an open, spontaneous counterpart to the closed world of dominance and submission.

The war takes on larger sexual meanings as well. From the beginning, the Argentinian anarchists are free of the European passion for manhood and dominance. We see them first in a political cartoon that shows "a line of middle-aged men wearing dresses and wigs, inside the police station where a cop is holding a loaf of white" (263). Their image of "the infant revolution" is explicitly described as a virgin birth, "free from the stain of Original Sin" that White Poppa has induced worldwide. Though Buenos Aires, or the Firm, has gathered people into its "neuroses about property," the Argentinian heart still longs for "that anarchic oneness of pampas and sky" (264). Much later, Graciela Imago Portales is able to reach a perspective beyond manhood. Though her man "will stake everything on this anarchist experiment," "dealt him by something he calls Chance and Graciela calls God," she can break the European fantasy of God-Power down even further "to see really how much she needs the others, how little use, unsupported, she could ever be" (613). While men are calling for anarchy and fearing Chance, women consistently perceive the possibilities for oneness and rebirth in natural processes.

The war takes on national overtones too, as America and fascist Europe stand against the exploited colonies. "American voices, country voices, high-pitched and without mercy," Slothrop thinks as MPs knock on his door (256); "what surprised him most was the fanaticism, the reliance not just on flat force but on the *rightness* of what they planned to do. . . ." America itself had been given to Europe "when the land was still free and the eye innocent . . . a purity begging to be polluted" (214). So "of course Empire took its way westward, what other way was there but into those virgin sunsets to penetrate and to foul?" The German extermination of the Hereros and Jews, the American war on Indians, the Dutch massacre of the Dodos, are Pynchon's historical metaphors for white consciousness, that " 'order of Analysis and Death' " (722), the closed system that stands in fear of its "dark, secret children" (75).

Other polarities expand these contexts: perverted sex against natural love, machinery against animal life, Beethoven against Rossini, form against change (96), bureaucratic work against childhood, abstraction against detail, city against country (661), shit, money, and the Word (28) against Love and Silence (650). In all of them, Pynchon's allegiances are clear. He opposes any "fiction and lie" that would "subvert love in favor of work, abstraction, required pain, bitter death" (41). There are love values and there are war values, with no interface and much co-optation, as his last two adjectives imply. Roger Mexico, whose name itself indicates the border he tries to straddle, sees clearly that Jessica's other lover, the Beaver,

> *is* the War, he is every assertion the fucking War has ever made — that we are meant for work and government, for austerity: and these shall take priority over love, dreams, the spirit, the senses and the other second-class trivia that are found among the idle and mindless hours of the day. (177)

Just to put the polarities in such dualistic form, in fact, shows my own system-making bent. Even the Counterforce fails, at the end, by getting organized. "The Man has a branch office in each of our brains, his corporate emblem is a white albatross, each local rep has a cover known as the Ego, and their mission in this world is Bad Shit" (712–713). In such a world, Pynchon continues, what can we be but children, pets, or dead?

Within these wars, the emotional theme of the book is betrayal, especially of children by parents. Children, who have those simple human urges toward love and kindness, are unremittingly bought, used, co-opted, fucked, corrupted by various aspects of the Firm.

Slothrop's father allowed little Tyrone to be used for Laszlo Jamf's experimentation in return for $5,000 so the boy could go to Harvard. Blicero enlists Gottfried and Katje as his Hansel and Gretel, and sends Gottfried aloft in his rocket as a self-immolating monument to his pederasty. Though Ensign Morituri stops Margherita from killing yet another Jewish boy, World War II happens to begin the next day, killing children en masse. In the midst of Pökler's incest fantasy, he has no way of even knowing if his daughter Ilse is really his, or just some ringer sent to keep him doing the Firm's work.

There's almost a *Catcher in the Rye* flavor to some of the later dialogues, as between Katje and Pirate Prentice (545), where children caught on the interface struggle toward shelter and mutual protection from self-betrayal, vainly hoping for salvation. We know from the start, though, that "[u]nderfoot crunches the oldest of city dirt, last crystallizations of all the city had denied, threatened, lied to its children" (4). At the end, the earth does hold some promise of renewal, if not salvation. Rockets can become Holy Trees, white penises can become Crosses (694) or at the very least a rainbow of Pirate's bananas. Even in the city, "in each of these streets, some vestige of humanity, of Earth, has to remain. No matter what has been done to it, no matter what it's been used for" (693). But death and betrayal are the givens, abandonment the common experience, and forced separation the outcome of any nourishing relationship.

Why, then, the striking lack of anger? Here is the classic Oedipal situation: "Pernicious Pop," as Pynchon calls him (682), clearly "a villain" (674), betraying sons and raping daughters while co-opting Mom into the Firm.

> How Pointsman lusts after them, pretty children. Those drab undershorts of his are full to bursting with need humorlessly, worldly to use their innocence, to write on them new words of himself, his own brown Realpolitik dreams. . . . (50)

Yet at points where that anger might focus clearly, the language turns comic (674), or explanations surface to account for betrayal through nonhuman forces — technology, the market, transcendence — rather than human evil. *Everybody*, as in a Kurt Vonnegut novel, is being used, by greater and greater levels of mechanical abstractions. Fathers are castrating, of course. Though "Marvy's Mothers" do the actual chasing, Blicero and Pointsman manage the energies of death. "Fathers are carriers of the virus of Death, and sons are the infected," says Blicero (723). Yet as Slothrop knows, "Mothers and fathers are conditioned into deliberately dying . . . leaving their children alone in the forest" (176). Perhaps, he muses here, it's better to have father's absence, swallowed by the Firm, "than a father who still hasn't died yet, a man you love and have to watch it happening to." No scorn now, only sympathy. Even the city itself is an "inexhaustibly knotted victim" (93). The debate about whether it's "the needs of technology" or cruel individuals that create these betrayals goes on (521) without solution, while Slothrop dissipates into the Zone.

Maybe the lack of anger is Slothrop's problem, not the narrative's. He is a victim of his own accommodations. As the younger Schwarzkommando argue,

> ". . . Go ahead, capitalize the T on technology, deify it if it'll make you feel less responsible — but it puts you in with the neutered, brother, in with the eunuchs keeping the harem of our stolen Earth for the numb and joyless hardons of human sultans, human elite with no right at all to be where they are — " (521)

Slothrop never dares that kind of voice. In fact, his disintegration begins when he feels "less anxious about betraying those who trust him. . . . a general loss of emotion, a numbness he ought to be alarmed at, but can't quite" (490–491). Though he sucks on eggs (526) and rises from eggshells (598), he has failed to be reborn. Tchitcherine, who similarly failed to be reborn (359), failed out of fear, and also fades into abstracted dispersal. Great love takes great anger, as the folk song says, and the failure of one leads to the failure of the other.

Pynchon is enough of a Puritan to know that spiritual rebirth means shattering the old self completely, to experience "a nova of heart that will turn us all, change us forever to the very forgotten roots of who we are" (134), to "sense all Earth like a baby" (358). For Slothrop, it would mean not just renewing anger but also giving up his quest to find the penis that never was his own. He would have to stop trying to "get it up," like the Rocket, and just get it down. His penis must become a Holy Tree (694, 747), abandoning the old Slothrop heritage of making paper and profit from cutting trees out of their rightful creaturely place (552–553). He would have to abdicate from his search for erect white maleness, which means death-dealing, and join the gravity-prone rainbow preterite, which means simply death. "Somewhere, among the wastes of the World, is the key that will bring us back, restore us to our Earth and to our freedom" (525). To relinquish the lust for ownership, as in Faulkner's *The Bear* or Mailer's *Why Are We in Vietnam?*, is a prerequisite for any kind of communion with nature on her own terms.

Otherwise Slothrop is condemned, at best, to a Firm transcendence. " 'The real movement,' " Walter Rathenau tells the séance (166) and Wernher von Braun tells us in the epigraph, " 'is not from death to any rebirth. It is from death to death-transfigured.' " Lyle Bland, after making sure that "all the family finances were in perfect order" (591), has such a transcendence, even discovers the trans-anarchist awareness of Earth as "a living critter" at the moment that he passes on. The waste required for the few to be elected, however, is enormous. Slothrop's moment of truth comes, in several senses, at the moment of entering Bianca's pubescent body, when he discovers that "he was somehow, actually, well, *inside his own cock.*" The self-encapsulating, pornographic, mercilessly unloving quality of that transcendence shows in Pynchon's explication: "Yes, inside the metropolitan organ entirely, all other colonial tissue forgotten and left to fend for itself" (470). Here is Firmness with a vengeance, a self-transformation that Slothrop is much too limp (and human) to hold on to for long.

If the worst sin is this "dead white" against "the living green" (268), the first step away from identifying with these systems is simply to give up power. While Rathenau seized Kekulé's benzene ring and made it the vehicle for a worldwide cartel, Pökler gives his gold wedding ring to "a random woman" in the concentration camp that took his daughter. "If she lived, the ring would be good for a few meals, or a blanket, or a night indoors, or a ride home" (433). Home is the need, the dying fall of too many fade-outs, but transience is the certainty, and possessive manhood is what has to be overcome. To make the bombs stop killing innocent girls, Slothrop must give up his branding iron.

"Mother" seems the harbor for this transparent though many-faced Oedipal voyage. As Nature, or trust, or the enduring green or brown female, she receives men in all their stages of power, betrayal, manipulation, and fear, to transform those who are ready. The book offers a comic array of men entering enclosures — caves, vaginas, toilet bowls, noses — to seek or to retreat. Byron the Bulb finds immortality by being screwed into "Mütter," meaning socket or mother, as Pynchon tells us several times (299, 653). Slothrop dreams of a middle-class lady being fucked by a grand panoply of animals (446–447), then drowning, yet teeming with life — "octopuses, reindeer, kangaroos." The dream ends in green, with frank lyricism about "proper love." Men teem with death while women, so long as white men aren't involved, teem with life.

Much later the Argentinian anarchists, who of all the characters most understand Earth's random fruitfulnesses, remember a similar tale, an old legend of a baby surviving in the wilderness by nursing from its mother's corpse. At this point (612) rocks are coming alive, becoming animate, while lemmings and pigs are taking on more personality than the main characters have ever had. The moral drawn from this legend is that "we must also look to the untold, to the silence around us, to the passage of the next rock we notice — to its aeons of history under the long and female persistence of water and air" (612–613). In Pynchon's endless series of concluding clues to the buried texts that only seekers can see, "these things of Earth's deep breast we were never told" (726) are the rock on which new faith is built.

Yet Roger Mexico's mother is the War. Etzel Ölsch's mother named him after Attila the Hun (298). Bloody Chiclitz's mother, even worse, named him Clayton (558). Nalline Slothrop is a

parody of the Tupperware party Oedipa Maas came home from
to start *The Crying of Lot 49*. Anti-Momma jokes abound, with
Mrs. Quoad's bonbons (116–118), Nalline's letter to Joe Kennedy
(682–683), the antimother of the year contest (505), a random
pie-at-Momma song (740). Katje plays "Domina Nocturna . . .
shining mother and last love" to Ernest Pudding, whose proof is
in his eating what drops from her buttocks (232). As Earth,
enclosure, green sustenance, and gravity, Mother asserts and re-
generates. But as person, Momma (at least white Momma) is
simply someone who "has submitted" (223) rather than fought.
She is at the "Mom's-argyle-socked sublevel of these conspirators
above" (637).

What can be co-opted, Pynchon tells us, will be. Trees will
be cut for Slothrop's family to grow rich (553), paper will flow
with "shit, money, and the Word," rockets will fly, and mothers
will do the Greater Daddy's will. Yet Pynchon's tone is elegiac,
sympathetic, more like Slothrop than like the younger Schwarz-
kommandos. "The Oedipal situation in the Zone these days is
terrible," he concludes.

> There is no dignity. The mothers have been masculinized to old
> worn moneybags. . . . The fathers have no power today and
> never did. . . . So generation after generation of men in love
> with pain and passivity serve out their time in the Zone, silent,
> redolent of faded sperm, terrified of dying, . . . willing to have
> life defined for them by men whose only talent is for death. (747)

But Pynchon throws these parental sadisms and masochisms into
comic insignificance. His "Titans and Fathers" finish by "belting
each other with gigantic (7 or 8 feet long) foam rubber penises"
(708) for circus entertainment. Meanwhile Geli Tripping has a
more serious vision of "the World just before men. Too vio-
lently pitched alive in constant flow ever to be seen by men
directly. They are meant only to look at it dead, in still strata,
transputrefied to oil or coal" (720).

It is man's mission "to promote death," she realizes. That
mission is "nearly as strong as life, holding down the green
uprising. But only nearly as strong." Here is the real "faith" that
Katje, Pirate Prentice, even Enzian are looking for, that Roger

Mexico hopes for through his probabilities, that Slothrop comes close to seeing through his eggshells and speaking trees, that Nora Dodson-Truck can discover through planetary psychics (639). White women can see it, dark women can begin to enact it, but the Earth itself must bear its fruit. William Slothrop was inspired to write *On Preterition* by the thought of his pigs, "possessed not by demons but by trust for men, which the men kept betraying," and whose simple "gift for finding comfort in the mud on a hot day" (555) stands for all the mindless pleasures men deny themselves.

Gravity's Rainbow is about trusts, in several contrary senses. At the simplest mother-and-child level of human feeding, however, the phrase that runs through Slothrop's head (as Pökler points a Luger at him) is, " *unto thee I pledge my trough*" (576). Though Mrs. Quoad and her bonbons almost carry the day, Frieda the Pig, who occasions both the Luger and the phrase, is the most down-to-earth female symbol for the book's basic trust: that ecology will (barely) beat bureaucracy (almost) every time.

Everyone is caught on the interface between these vast opposing values, especially Enzian, who replaces Slothrop as the book's agonized moral center. Born of the interface between a black woman and a white man temporarily fleeing power, he knows his dilemma to the full, and can't escape to either side. Struck in the face by "Christian," Enzian fills with "meekness" and redirects his quest from Blicero and the Rocket to Christian's lost sister "Maria" (525). Though he knows, as he later tells Katje, that "There is no heart, anywhere now, no human heart left in which I exist" (660), he at least has the capacity to admit his lostness.

> He knows how phony it looks. Who will believe that in his heart he wants to belong to them out there, the vast Humility sleepless, dying, in pain tonight across the Zone? the preterite he loves, knowing he's always to be a stranger. . . . (731)

Others will be reborn, other texts ambiguously appear. But these are the people Pynchon unabashedly loves, the lost anonymous dying ones, used and discarded without hope of transcendence or salvation, stranded, abandoned, voiceless with their simple needs and feelings.

III

Having got my responses in order at last, I found several modes of satisfaction. First, here was the discovery that the book did make sense. Second, I at last felt comfortably in control. Third, I could turn the tables. From having been first intimidated, then annoyed, I could dismiss the book as a sermon that was, quite simply, wrong. No longer did I have to accept Pynchon's anti-organization bias, his hostility to the white male Establishment, his equation of Europe with "Analysis and Death" or Original Sin with "Modern Analysis" (722). At last I had enough clarity to refuse the guilt and self-hatred that *Gravity's Rainbow* required of me.

Pynchon has a clear vision of the ecological and human contexts for modern history, as far-reaching in his way as Fernand Braudel's extraordinary investigations into earlier Mediterranean times.[1] But instead of showing the symbiotic interplay of all these forces, he imposes a Manichaean fantasy of oppositions and apocalyptic fragmentation. Like Hawthorne, he is most appalled by the sin of righteousness and the specter of tyrannical fathers betraying and raping the innocence of their children. Though Henry Adams is a more conscious analogue, Pynchon's real affinities are with the author of "Rappaccini's Daughter" or "The Birthmark." But unlike Hawthorne, he takes sin and guilt away from humans and attributes it to systems. *Gravity's Rainbow* has no center; it moves away from human realities to a series of mixed signals and pulled punches. We put down the book laden with sympathy for *everybody*, and hostility only for human organization (and analysis) of any kind. Blicero isn't guilty, nor Pointsman, though Hawthorne would say they are. Only the reader is, for trying to make sense of it all. The book should be read under a tree that whispers the Kabbala into where our penises used to be. Don't figure it out, says the whisper; grow a banana.

Against the twentieth-century complexities of bureaucracy, colonialism, markets, technology, interest groups, nations, Pynchon offers only the nineteenth-century fantasies (and they were fantasies even then) of anarchic individualism, momentary utopian communities, and the cult of Nature, which, as D. H. Lawrence said, is absolutely the safest thing to love.[2] In his cry for Redemptive Mom he writes in the somewhat lesser American tradition of Charles Brockden Brown's *Alcuin* and Sherwood Anderson's *Perhaps Women*. To be out of mind, out of history, into the timeless romantic ideal of the uncorrupted child in the virgin wilderness; to be free of systems and machines, because as his limericks say to fuck with machines is to be castrated, usurped, maimed, killed; to be out of the competitive struggle for manhood and control, and simply accept death and ordinary kindness as the only human basics — these may have been vivid dreams for a nineteenth-century elite, but they are nonsensical to invoke for contemporary preterite voices who Want In. They are peasant fantasies of a suburban alien. There's not much difference between Pynchon's call for a flight from manhood into Nature and any one of the late 1960s "Youth Culture" books (*Gravity's Rainbow* is dedicated to his late friend Richard Fariña), like Alan Watts's *Nature, Man, and Woman*. The sermon is similar. Vonnegut at least is clearer about the lines of power, abstraction, and manipulation, and both *The Sirens of Titan* and Joseph Heller's *Catch-22* are more bitter-funny about the war.

This dismissive response was a great release, an outpouring against my earlier frustrations. Yet it still couldn't account for the contrary depths of my feelings. The book's language and events lingered, irreducible, at odds with the overarching themes and frame. Though Pynchon often shows his hostility to the ordinary mind-set of the ordinary American reader — "You will want cause and effect. All right" (663) — there were singularities, disorganized moments of impact and power, as well as the co-editorship of this book, that compelled me back to read *Gravity's Rainbow* for a third time.

Now I was most aware of Enzian, Pökler, and the language. Both Enzian and Pökler at least strive to be good fathers; Enzian, to his lost and suicidal Hereros, Pökler, to the Ilse who visits him every year. Though he suspects she may not even be his daughter, he deliberately refuses to enact his fantasy of incest (421). He gives her comfort, inept but real, instead of dominance. "Close to losing control," we soon learn (430), "Pökler committed then his act of courage. He quit the game." Isolated, alone, bereft even of Ilse at the end, he nevertheless stands as the novel's most concentrated look at integrity within the Firm.

But beyond characterization, I rediscovered that my primary response lay with Pynchon's language, especially his aching tenderness for natural description. Though his theme is Earth's random plenitude, his language cries out at loss, separation, loneliness, moments of transient contact and imposition expressed with self-conscious exactitude. Little phrases, like "the white fracture of the rain passes" (37), or "the long, clonic, thick slices of night that pass over their bodies" (100), or the "icefields below and a cold smear of sun" (6), articulate this sense of sudden juxtaposition, the forced entry of human perception to the inviolate transience of natural things. In these three phrases, for instance, the intrusive words are "fracture," "clonic slices," "smear," each one attributing human impairment to natural fact. Yet they all "pass," leaving the Earth as it is.

Similarly, the epigraph to this essay has a "monster 88" tank angling down "to point at the gray river, hissing and spiculed with the rain." That sends me to the dictionary, where I find that a spicule is "a minute slender pointed, usually hard body," especially found in "the tissues of various invertebrates." Like "clonic," which has to do with muscle spasms, "spiculed" connotes something extraneous to the natural flow, something momentarily animate yet hard, permanent yet only for a moment, a human imposition by the narrator's tongue. We have at once a strong frieze-image of the river, and a dictionary reflex that makes us self-conscious of language as a separating act. Like many of our greatest writers, especially Melville and Wallace Stevens,

Pynchon makes us ache with the limits of our intrusive perceptions.[3]

In these and a thousand other such sentences, Pynchon makes us at once self-conscious of our language, aware of natural particularity, and sensitive to the jar between human perception and natural fact. There is a painfulness in each of these brief perceptions, a pain of potential betrayal and separation, and a pleasure of momentary union beyond our control. These feelings shape my positive response to Pynchon. Often his observations simply signify exact description, as when "thunder suddenly breaks in a blinding egg of sound" (479). Yet how is sound an egg, and how does an egg blind? The senses are disordered by this image, as by the thunder. Simultaneously we sense a larger disorder: the image's aptness, and the narrator's oxymoronic attention to language. Are we perceiving the thunder, or the narrator, or the act of perception? How close can language come to enacting nature? Or are they finally opposed? These questions, which are mirrored in the larger statements of Pynchon's dualistic frame, to me are more sharply put through these small descriptive gestures.

Pynchon's best opposition to the Firm doesn't take the form of preaching, which is the Firm's forte, but of these descriptive particularities. Nature becomes animate, babbling with voices and creatures, for those who see:

> Up on the bridge of the *Anubis*, the storm paws loudly on the glass, great wet flippers falling at random in out of the night *whap!* the living shape visible just for the rainbow edge of the sound — it takes a certain kind of maniac, at least a Polish cavalry officer, to stand in this pose behind such brittle thin separation, and stare each blow full in its muscularity. (488)

The storm is a big random seal, flapping at the windows of our perception to say Look at me, there's a rainbow here if you dare. Like the cavalry officer, Pynchon does dare. He confronts, and confronts us with, nature's muscularity and our separation.

His preoccupation with the sky shows all of this complex disordering perceptiveness. The first sentence fills the sky with "A screaming." We think that the screaming is the sound of the Rocket, or at least a collective fearful reaction to the Rocket. Yet it just as easily could be the sound of a baby coming into the world, the "rebirth" called for by the Kirghiz Light. Is the sky possessed by Poppa-Rocket or Mother Nature? Is it a "luminous breast" (501), or "hardness and absolute cruelty" (548)? Is it "this ancient sky, in its corroded evenness of tone" (67), or is it "pregnant with saints and slender heralds' trumpets" (131)? Is it a scream or a "streaming, a living plasma" (626)?

Slothrop shows "a peculiar sensitivity to what is revealed in the sky" (26), though the narrator questions whether a hardon is what revelation is all about. Jessica knows she had to protect Roger "from what may come out of the sky" (58). Yet that basic paranoid fear, initially associated with the Rocket, gives way to something more vast. Perhaps the sky is "where nothing is connected to anything," Slothrop wonders (434). Maybe we have to *invent* Rockets, and Enemies, to force these connections. Otherwise even cities are "roofless, vulnerable, uncentered," and Slothrop has "only pasteboard images now of the Listening Enemy left between him and the wet sky" (434). Melville's Ahab felt a more desperate need to lunge through his "pasteboard masks."

Yet the hand of Providence is there among the stars, "giving Slothrop the finger" (461). That finger elects, for those who see it rightly. It's not the lack of connection but the fear of being reborn, of choosing sides, that keeps Slothrop back. Forgive him, our narrator asks, "Forgive him as you forgave Tchitcherine at the Kirghiz Light." This plea is addressed, as a formal incantation, to the pregnant sky: "oh, Egg the flying Rocket hatched from, navel of the 50-meter radio sky, all proper ghosts of place" (509–510). Slothrop can't scream any more, and that's his final perdition. Even the Rocket hatches from an egg, however, and there will be other Slothrops, Enzians, Katjes, Byrons, thousands of other births to fight "the powdery wipe of Nothing's hand" (24). The sky holds gravity's rainbow as well as the Rocket. Though it enacts death and disorder, screams of life can "come" within the fact of death, like the "singularities" that the old-fashioned heroes can only describe as cancer (752). On some magic night, "the animals will talk, and the sky will be milk" (133).

The European consciouness can do its damnedest to pollute this virgin egg, and it does:

> It was one of those great iron afternoons in London: the yellow sun being teased apart by a thousand chimneys breathing, fawning upward without shame. This smoke is more than the day's breath, more than dark strength — it is an imperial presence that lives and moves. (26)

Here a simple description of smoke evokes Pynchon's world view: urban contamination, abstracted already from the day into an "iron afternoon" and "an imperial presence," with manipulative sexual innuendos of "teasing" and "fawning," all of it "without shame." Yet the "yellow sun" will stay untouched by all these separating, befouling "chimneys" that, like Slothrop's cock, generate their own self-enclosing atmosphere of power and death.

The unity of the egg cannot be broken, no matter how many Dutchmen aim for Dodos (109), though only disorderly anarchists and women can know that for sure. Others, like Roger and Jessica in church on Christmas Eve (128–136), can get a brief glimpse of "the New Baby":

> to raise the possibility of another night that could actually, with love and cockcrows, light the path home, banish the Adversary, destroy the boundaries between our lands, our bodies, our stories, all false, about who we are: for the one night, leaving only the clear way home and the memory of the infant you saw, almost too frail. . . . (135)

To be reconceived, "free from the stain of Original Sin" (263), is the virgin-birth wish that all Pynchon's oddball disestablishmentarian language conveys. The last hundred pages are just holy relics, fragments of a new language that only the initiate — "Check out Ishmael Reed" (588) — can fathom. Some birds can rise into the sky, silent, while their owners are "shut in by words, drifts and frost-patterns of white words" (339).

Since my own essay is shut squarely into the old language, what Pynchon calls "the latest name" for Original Sin, "Modern

Analysis" (722), and snuggled squarely onto paper to boot, I remain as much stainer as stained. So, too, does my response. *Gravity's Rainbow* leaves me with an inextricable jumble of empathies and quarrels. To the Pynchon who throws shit in my white male established American face and then calls it mine, I respond first with confused intimidation, even guilt, and then with annoyed dismissal, both to what he preaches and to the fact that he preaches. That response, once made sense of, is easy. But to the Pynchon who creates the most powerfully aching language for natural descriptions in our literature, who can make me feel so keenly the moments of loss, separation, impingement, and simple sheltering human gestures, I respond with astonished praise, again and again, for all the singular exactitudes of seeing. True, my participation in this language intricates me into the vision I so roundly disapprove of, though on the level of Lost rather than Found. But he hooks me nevertheless.

If my appreciation has to become a "mindless pleasure," then so much the worse for the book. If I'm forced into that "firm" a choice between gravity and the rainbow, then — though anything, including seriousness, can be suspended for a moment — gravity will win every time. "Nobody ever said a day has to be juggled into any kind of sense at day's end" (204), Pynchon tells us. We do ask that of novels, though, even if the clarification is that life can't be clarified.

Yet there are several kinds of "sense" that do emerge from *Gravity's Rainbow*, at the "stone resonance, where there is no good or evil" (720). Almost all of these senses have to do with the perverted manipulation of natural love. As the Puritans knew and Pynchon continually reminds us (though none of us really thinks it's true), "kindness is a sturdy enough ship for these oceans" (21). One of the early Separatists, John Robinson, who in fact never ventured across, once wrote that "love rather descends, than ascends; as streams of water do."[4] He was talking of the love of parents for children, but in Pynchon's world that kind of "descent" is what is most missing from his betrayed, abandoned, oven-prone lives.

In *Gravity's Rainbow* Pynchon's sense of descent, of loss and separation and victimization, precludes jaunty solutions. Animate ambiguities are all he gives us, as a brief stay against conclusion; a hope for simple human gestures, love without aggression, demand, or use. So Nora Dodson-Truck pulls Carroll Eventyr inside her five-pointed star, with "an instinctive, a motherly way, her way with anyone she loved" (145). So another lost one feels:

> He is suddenly, dodderer and ass, taken by an ache in his skin, a simple love for them both that asks nothing but their safety, and that he'll always manage to describe as something else — "concern," you know, "fondness. . . ." (35)

"He" is Pirate Prentice, man of a thousand empathies, but he could be anybody. That love could be anybody's too: simple, sheltering, protective. For Pynchon, no language — " 'concern,' you know, 'fondness' " — can convey it without distortion.

This "ache in the skin" is what is most powerful, and most limiting, about Pynchon's work. It mocks any sense of structure, and any but the most momentary commitments. But it also makes us feel our own descent, alone, imprisoned in our perceptiveness. As if we were his burned-out Königstiger tank, Pynchon points us too at the gray waste, spiculed with kindness.

Notes

1. Cf. Braudel's *The Mediterranean and the Mediterranean World in the Age of Philip II*, trans. Sian Reynolds (New York: Harper & Row, 1975), vols. I and II (first published in France in 1949).
2. Lawrence, *Studies in Classic American Literature* (New York: Viking, 1922), in his chapter on Crèvecoeur, writes: "Absolutely the safest thing to get your emotional reactions over is NATURE."
3. Cf. James Guetti's *The Limits of Metaphor* (Ithaca, N.Y.: Cornell University Press, 1967), a study of Melville, Conrad, and Faulkner.
4. Robinson, "Of Children and Their Education" (1628), reprinted in Philip J. Greven, Jr., *Child-Rearing Concepts, 1628–1861: Historical Sources* (Itasca, Ill.: F. E. Peacock Publishers, Inc., 1973), p. 13.

Appendix: The Quest for Pynchon

Mathew Winston

The statements contained herein are not guaranteed but have
been obtained from sources which we consider reliable.
Pynchon & Co., 1929

Shortly after the publication of V., *a friend of mine noticed a*
copy of the novel in a Manhattan apartment she was thinking of
renting. She asked the current occupant whether he liked the
book. "Yes," he replied, "but you know — Pynchon's a very
strange man. He doesn't allow any photographs of him to appear.
There's none on the book jacket and none in the advertising."
"Why, that's true," said my friend, "but how did you happen
to notice that? It never would have occurred to me if you hadn't
mentioned it." "Oh, I work for the FBI," he responded. "It's my
business to notice that sort of thing."

The paranoia that dominates Pynchon's fictions may be justified
in more ways than one. But it is another central motif of Pynchon's writing that most interests me: the quest. In 1974 I spent
a summer at Cornell University, where Pynchon had been an
undergraduate. The memory of my friend's story, access to
people who had known Pynchon, his continued secretiveness,
and the excitement of his novels led me to begin what I choose
to think of as a quest for Pynchon. I assumed that the process
of looking for information about the mysterious Thomas Pynchon should be almost as intricate and fascinating as following
the metamorphoses of V., the legacy of Pierce Inverarity, the
history of Rocket 00000. The assumption has proved valid. Like

the movement of the crowd at the beginning of *Gravity's Rainbow*, and like that of any Pynchon novel, my investigation has been "not a disentanglement from, but a progressive *knotting into*."

Since direct communication with the sequestered Pynchon was impossible, I started by consulting official documents, and I immediately encountered difficulties. Some records, such as his Cornell transcript, are confidential by nature. Others Pynchon has made so; for instance, he has asked the principal of his high school not to disclose anything by or about him. Some documents seem to have disappeared. Information about Pynchon's service in the Navy may have gone forever when a records office in St. Louis burned after an explosion. And his dossier at the Cornell College of Arts and Sciences has vanished, to the bewilderment of the staff there. I suspect that Pynchon, who has taken care to cover his tracks, may know what happened to it.

I also met with resistance from people who knew Pynchon. One example will suffice. In the midst of a pleasant conversation with an old acquaintance of mine, I remarked that he must have been in Ithaca at the same time as Pynchon. He suddenly turned to ice. Only after thawing him for about ten minutes did I learn that he had once shared an apartment with Pynchon. But that is about all I did learn. Pynchon has been either unusually fortunate or unusually careful in his choice of friends, for they are as eager to protect his privacy as he is. At first it seemed as though a group of initiates guarded the arcane and ineffable secret of Thomas Pynchon, but later I recognized that his friends demonstrate their friendship by respecting his aversion to publicity, even though they may not understand it.

If I knew Pynchon personally, I probably would not write this essay and display publicly the fragments of his life which I have gathered. As is, I am uneasy about infringing on his privacy, although I have found support in a letter written by one of Pynchon's nineteenth-century relatives, Peter Oliver, to Nathaniel Hawthorne: "The public life of any man cannot & should not be hidden under a bushel, but is fit material for the man of letters wherewith 'to point a moral & adorn a tale'. It is only when the sanctity of his heart is invaded, when his motives are impeached, & his private character distorted, that there can be reasonable ground for complaint."[1]

I am also uneasy because the nature of Pynchon's writings compels me to examine my own reasons for pursuing the information I have sought. As Herbert Stencil observes of his quest for V., "in this search the motive is part of the quarry." I am not sure that I have found either, but the hunt has been enjoyable and exciting, and along the way I have learned much about the talent Pynchon shares with Stencil, his gift for "inference, poetic license, forcible dislocation of personality into a past he didn't remember and had no right in, save the right of imaginative anxiety or historical care, which is recognized by no one."

The family of Thomas Ruggles Pynchon, Jr., can be traced back to the eleventh century. The earliest Pynchon on record is one Pinco, "sworn brother in war" to Endo, who came to England from Normandy with William the Conqueror. His son was "Hugh, fils Pinconis," whose name later appears as "Hugh fils Pinchonis" and "Hugh Fitz Pincheun." The branch of the family from which Pynchon is descended was established in Essex by the fourteen hundreds. In 1533 Nicholas Pynchon became High Sheriff of London. John Pynchon, apparently Nicholas's nephew, obtained the family's coat-of-arms — per bend argent and sable, three roundles within a border engrailed, all counter changed — and its crest, a tiger's head erased argent. Neither, alas, contains a muted post horn.[2]

John's grandson, William Pynchon, brought the family to the New World with him in 1630. He was a patentee and treasurer of the Massachusetts Bay Colony and a founder both of Roxbury and of Springfield, which was named after his birthplace in Essex. He acquired great wealth trading in beaver furs and was on good terms with the Mohawks, who for a time referred to all New Englanders as "Pynchon's men." William was a strong-willed man whose pique with the Connecticut General Court, which had issued a wrong judgment against him, led to Springfield's becoming part of Massachusetts. In his capacity as magistrate, he presided over the witchcraft trial of Hugh and Mary Parsons, whom he sent on to Boston for further examination. But he himself ran afoul of the authorities when he became the first Pynchon to turn author. In 1650 he published in England the first of several theological tracts, *The Meritorious Price of Our Redemption*, which is in the form of a discourse between a tradesman and a divine. The book asserts that Christ saved mankind through his perfect obedience to God, not through bearing Adam's curse, and "that Christ did not suffer for us those unutterable torments of Gods wrath, that commonly are called Hell-torments, to redeem our soules from them." The "common Errors" which Pynchon wished to correct were truths to the New England Puritans, who found his book "to shake the Fundamentals of Religion, and to wound the vitals of Christianity" and who condemned it "to be burned in the markett place at Boston."[3]

Thomas Pynchon derived his interest in unorthodox Calvinist theology from his first American ancestor and drew on miscellaneous details of his own family history for the background of the Slothrops in *Gravity's Rainbow*. William Slothrop, the "first American ancestor" of Tyrone Slothrop, is a transformed version of William Pynchon. Both men sailed to America with Governor Winthrop, Slothrop on the flagship *Arbella*, Pynchon on the *Ambrose* or the *Jewell*. William Slothrop wrote a religious tract entitled *On Preterition;* "it had to be published in England, and is among the first books to've been not only banned but also ceremonially burned in Boston." Slothrop and Pynchon each returned to England and safety not long after his book was published.

Like William Slothrop, William Pynchon had a son John. John Pynchon, trader, merchant, and land speculator, holder of numerous public offices, owner of mines, ships, and mills, remained in America and became one of the richest men in New England; at his funeral a sermon was preached on "Gods Frown in the Death of Usefull Men." His family produced a considerable number of merchants, doctors, clergymen, and academics. One of his eighteenth-century descendants, Joseph Pynchon, seemed likely to become governor of Connecticut until he backed the losing side in the American Revolution. Nevertheless, Joseph is important to our story through his marriage to Sarah Ruggles, a descendant of Thomas Ruggles, who was one of the original settlers of Roxbury. Their son, Thomas Ruggles Pynchon, was the first to bear the name that has remained in the Pynchon family since 1760; he served as a physician in Guilford, Connecticut, until he was killed by falling from a horse in 1796.

The Pynchons entered literary history, somewhat obliquely, when Nathaniel Hawthorne published *The House of the Seven Gables* in 1851. The novel sets forth the unsavory history of a family named Pyncheon (indeed, Hawthorne had contemplated calling the book "The Old Pyncheon Family"). Hawthorne knew of no extant Pynchons, and so was surprised to receive two letters of protest from members of the family. The first to write, Peter Oliver of Boston, feared that the novel might sully the reputation of the great-great-grandson of the founder of Springfield, William Pynchon (1723–1789), who was popularly known as Judge Pynchon and who had resided for a time in Salem.[4]

The second correspondent was Rev. Thomas Ruggles Pynchon, who was the grandson of the Guilford physician and was at that time rector of St. Paul's Church, Stockbridge, and Trinity Church, Lenox. He faulted Hawthorne for "holding up . . . the good name of our Ancestors to the derision and contempt of our countrymen." He explained that he was particularly upset because "our Family Circle is an exceedingly small one. Probably there are not more than 20 persons in the whole country bearing the name, all of whom are closely connected by blood: and all — known to each other: We know of no Pynchons not of our own little band."[5] Hawthorne responded temperately and even went so far as to pen a requested disclaimer to add to his preface (which, however, was never published). But his irritation with those who confused his fiction with their reality emerged in a letter he wrote to his publisher on June 5, 1851: "I have just received a letter from another claimant of the Pyncheon estate. I wonder if ever, and how soon, I shall get at a just estimate of how many jackasses there are in this ridiculous world. My correspondent, by the way, estimates the number of these Pyncheon jackanapes at about twenty; I am doubtless to be remonstrated with by each individual. After exchanging shots with all of them, I shall get you to publish the whole correspondence, in a style corresponding with that of my other works; and I anticipate a great run for the volume."

Despite his literal-mindedness with Hawthorne, Rev. Thomas Ruggles Pynchon (1823–1904) was a worthy spiritual ancestor of the novelist who bears his name, for he was master of many different fields. He taught chemistry, geology, zoology and theology at Trinity College, Hartford, of which he served as the ninth president. His numerous publications range from *The Chemical Forces: Heat, Light, Electricity . . . : An Introduction to Chemical Physics* (1870) to *Bishop Butler, A Religious Philosopher for All Time* (1889). To my disappointment, the index to *The Chemical Forces* mentions neither entropy nor James Clerk Maxwell and his Demon.[6] Still, the novelist might appreciate the coincidence that the copy of the book I consulted bears the signature of Andrew Dixon White, the first president of the university he was later to attend.

It goes without saying that the Pynchon family history contains many such coincidences; in Pynchonland one may almost presume that "*everything is connected.*" Admirers of Dr. Schoenmaker's nose job in *V.* may not be surprised to learn of a Dr. Edwin Pynchon (1856–1914), who invented numerous surgical instruments for operations on the nose, mouth, and throat and who wrote articles on "Surgical Correction of Deformities of the Nasal Septum" and on a "New Mechanical Saw for Intra-Nasal Operations." Nor is it altogether a shock, given Pynchon's interest in rockets and in the military-industrial complex, to discover that a prosperous stock brokerage called Pynchon & Co. (George M. Pynchon, senior partner) publshed a book, *The Aviation Industry* (1928, 1929), which provided information for people considering "aeronautical investments"; its closing words form the epigraph of this essay. Byron the Bulb might have been interested in another of their booklets, *Electric Light and Power: A Survey of World Development* (1930).

This is the matrix in which Thomas Ruggles Pynchon, Jr., the novelist, lives and writes. His father, Thomas Ruggles Pynchon, Sr., is the grandnephew of the president of Trinity College, after whom he was named. His mother is Katherine Frances Bennett Pynchon, and he has two younger siblings, Judith and John. Pynchon was born on the morning of May 8, 1937, in Glen Cove, Long Island, New York. When he was a child, the family moved to nearby East Norwich, where his father, an industrial surveyor, worked for an engineering firm, was chief of the volunteer fire department, led the local Republican club, and served as highway supervisor and then town supervisor of Oyster Bay. Thomas Pynchon was just sixteen when he graduated from Oyster Bay High School in 1953, was class salutatorian, and was presented with the Julia L. Thurston award as "the senior attaining the highest average in the study of English."

Pynchon won a scholarship to Cornell University and matriculated that fall in the division of Engineering Physics. He was already camera shy; the freshman register for his entering class carries a blank space instead of a photograph of him. Although he later transferred to the College of Arts and Sciences and took his degree in English, he never abandoned his interest in physics; "one of his teachers still wonderingly remembers his apparently voracious appetite for the complexities of elementary particle theory."[7]

I have heard a rumor that Pynchon was married for a short time during his sophomore year, which seems unlikely in light of his youth, but which might explain the presence of several disaffected husbands in his fiction and also his leaving Cornell for the Navy at the end of that year. Although no information is available about this period, one may infer from his writings that he served in the signal corps.

In the fall of 1957 he returned to Cornell, where he was "a constant reader — the type to read books on mathematics for fun . . . one who started the day at 1 P.M. with spaghetti and a soft drink . . . and one that read and worked on until 3 the next morning."[8] He took a course taught by Vladimir Nabokov, who does not recall him, although Mrs. Nabokov remembers Pynchon's "unusual handwriting: half printing, half script."[9] He was extremely unassuming; despite his excellent grades, his modesty kept him from participating in the honors program. A celebrated Cornell English professor asked Pynchon to stop by his office after Pynchon had submitted one of the best papers he had ever seen. A tall, lanky, mustached young man appeared. When asked why he was not in the honors program, Pynchon replied: "Oh, sir, I'm not bright enough. I have some friends in the honors program, and they're much more intelligent than I am." He received his B.A. in June 1959, appropriately enough "with distinction in all subjects."

As a junior and a senior, Pynchon was on the editorial staff of Cornell's undergraduate literary magazine, *The Cornell Writer,* which during that time published several stories and poems by his close friend Richard Fariña. Fariña had also studied both engineering and English. He was an extrovert who liked to stage what might later have been called Happenings, and Pynchon sometimes participated. One spring day in 1959 Pynchon and Fariña came to a garden party dressed as F. Scott Fitzgerald *circa* 1919 — straw boaters, Princeton jackets, rep ties — and insisted on carrying out the role all afternoon. Fariña later wrote about a visit from Pynchon, who had come to serve as best man at his wedding, in an essay called "The Monterey Fair" which was included in *Long Time Coming and a Long Time Gone.* He also based an instrumental composition on *V.* Pynchon in turn wrote an advertising blurb for Fariña's *Been Down So Long It Looks Like Up To Me* and dedicated *Gravity's Rainbow* to him.[10]

Most important, Pynchon wrote his earliest published stories during his last two years at Cornell: "Mortality and Mercy in Vienna" (*Epoch,* Spring 1959), "Low-lands" (*New World Writing,* 1960) and "Under the Rose" (*The Noble Savage,* May 1961), which in a revised form became chapter 3 of *V.* He also wrote several loosely connected stories which form a kind of picaresque novel about a down-and-outer named Meatball Mulligan. Of these, only "Entropy" has been published (*Kenyon Review,* Spring 1960); I am told that another is set at a revival meeting in Virginia.

Pynchon's very first publication, "The Small Rain" (*The Cornell Writer*, March 1959), has not been reissued or even mentioned in print until now. The story concerns three days in the life of Army Specialist 3/C Nathan "Lardass" Levine, formerly of CCNY and the Bronx, who is approaching the end of his enlistment. Levine is sent with some other soldiers from Fort Roach, Louisiana, to set up communications for a crisis center at a local college after a hurricane has annihilated a Louisiana town. Moved by the college setting, or perhaps simply because it is "time for a change," Levine is stirred out of his "closed circuit" of indifference. He makes "one of those spur-of-the-moment decisions which it is always fun to wonder about afterward," travels to the destroyed town and helps to collect the bloated corpses. That evening he beds a college girl he flirted with earlier; he wears a baseball cap and smokes a cigar throughout their thoroughly unromantic coupling. He then returns to the barracks, from which he hitches a ride for a delayed leave. Having remarked that rain "can stir dull roots" or "can rip them up, wash them away," Levine observes the rain descending on the truck, and then falls asleep. The story seems to contain at least some autobiographical elements. Pynchon's circumstances and Levine's were (allowing for artistic license) very similar during the summer of 1957, when the story takes place. Moreover, there was a hurricane, Audrey, which destroyed the southern Louisiana town of Cameron ("Creole" in the story) on June 27 ("around mid-July") of that year. Many specific details of the tragedy are used in the story without change: town residents were warned in advance but were told not to rush their evacuation because the hurricane, which struck in the early morning, was not supposed to arrive until nighttime; hundreds were dead or missing; only the courthouse remained intact; rescue operations were based at McNeese State College. Army troops were sent from Fort Polk ("Fort Roach") to assist. Pynchon may well have been among the naval forces which were also present.

When Pynchon graduated from college, he had his choice of several fellowships, including a Woodrow Wilson, and was invited to teach creative writing at Cornell. He thought about becoming a disc jockey, an interest which emerges in the character of Mucho Maas in *The Crying of Lot 49*. He was considered as a film critic by *Esquire*. But he chose instead to work on *V.* while living in Manhattan with friends in Greenwich Village and on Riverside Drive. After some months of this hand-to-mouth existence, he left New York to take a job with the Boeing Company in Seattle, Washington. He worked for Boeing from February 2, 1960, to September 13, 1962, not as editor of a house organ, as has commonly been reported, but as an "engineering aide" who collaborated with others on writing technical documents. He then lived in California and Mexico while he finished *V.*, for which "he kept one of his Village friends running to the library to look up data in the World Almanac of 1948."[11] *V.* appeared to enthusiastic reviews in 1963 and was awarded the William Faulkner Foundation Award as the best first novel of the year.

Pynchon's familiarity with the distinctive madness of Southern California is evident in his second novel, *The Crying of Lot 49*, which was published in 1966 and won the Richard and Hilda Rosenthal Foundation Award of the National Institute of Arts and Letters. A need for funds may have prompted Pynchon to release sections of the novel to popular magazines as short stories — "The World (This One), The Flesh (Mrs. Oedipa Maas), and The Testament of Pierce Inverarity" (*Esquire*, December 1965) and "The Shrink Flips" (*Cavalier*, March 1966) — and earlier to publish a story called "The Secret Integration" in *The Saturday Evening Post* (December 19, 1964).

His interest in the interaction between white and black, shown in "The Secret Integration" and elsewhere, and his knowledge of Los Angeles were brought together in "A Journey into the Mind of Watts," an essay which he wrote for the *New York Times Magazine* (June 12, 1966). One might expect Pynchon to reveal something of himself in his only piece of nonfiction, but, although his attitudes are clear and although he describes what he saw and quotes people he spoke with, the piece is remarkable in that the writer never refers to himself.

Indeed, Pynchon has been extraordinarily successful at keeping himself hidden from his admirers. He has never given an interview and allows no photographs to be released (the only photograph of Pynchon made public, one taken when he was a teenager, appeared in *New York Magazine* on May 13, 1974, and was reprinted in *Newsweek* the following week).

Although Thomas Pynchon does not emerge to meet the public, his books do. The latest was the monumental *Gravity's Rainbow*, originally entitled "Mindless Pleasures,"[12] which was published in 1973. The novel had its beginning in a museum in Greenvale, a Long Island town near Pynchon's home. Pynchon may have been led to it by an article that was printed in his local paper, the *Oyster Bay Guardian*, on July 2, 1954, while he was home for the summer after his freshman year at college and was working for the Nassau County Department of Public Works. It was headlined "Hitler's Secret Weapon Displayed at Greenvale."

> The dreaded "V-1 Rocket" or "Buzz Bomb," which could have changed the course of World War II, is now peacefully on exhibition in a private museum at Greenvale, L. I.
>
> The jet-propelled 3½-ton flying bomb is 17 feet wide and 25 feet long, and its war head carried 1,000 pounds of T.N.T. It was assembled by the Army from "V-1's" that actually fell on England, and was later used as model for present-day "Guided Missiles."
>
> Hitler called his secret weapon "Vergeltungswaffe Eins" or "Vengeance Weapon No. 1." With it he bragged that he would destroy all of England, but the continuous Allied bombings of the launching ramps delayed the actual flights until after the D-Day invasion of Normandy.
>
> The bomb started flying into England on June 13th, 1944, and in a period of 80 days it destroyed 870,000 homes, killed 5,817 people, and wounded 17,036. It caused the second evacuation of London.
>
> It had many "nicknames": "V-1 Rocket," "Buzz Bomb," "Doodlebug," "Flying Blow Torch," "Robomb," etc.[13]

Gravity's Rainbow was selected for three major literary prizes. It shared the National Book Award with a collection of stories by Isaac Bashevis Singer. Pynchon, of course, did not appear at the award presentation. In his place, his publisher provided "Professor" Irwin Corey, a master of comic double-talk, who accepted the prize amid considerable confusion in the audience.

Gravity's Rainbow was unanimously elected by the judges for the Pulitzer Prize in literature, but they were overruled by the Pulitzer advisory board, whose members called it "unreadable," "turgid," "overwritten," and "obscene." As a result, no prize was given. Finally, in 1975, the novel was awarded the Howells Medal of the National Institute of Arts and Letters and the American Academy of Arts and Letters, even though Pynchon declined and suggested the medal be given to some other author. "The Howells Medal is a great honor," he wrote, "and, being gold, probably a good hedge against inflation too. But I don't want it. Please don't impose on me something I don't want. It makes the Academy look arbitrary and me look rude. . . . I know I should behave with more class, but there appears to be only one way to say no, and that's no."

Like Oedipa Maas, I feel I am "left with only compiled memories of clues, announcements, intimations, but never the central truth itself." There are still many paths to explore and discoveries to make in the quest for Pynchon. I have provided a few signposts. Whether the roads they point to and the trespassing they involve are worth the journey, I do not pretend to say. The search concludes for me, not with a revelation of Thomas Pynchon, but with a fresh sense of my own preterite spirit and a renewed appreciation of the magical interface between the reader and the book.

Notes

1. All quotations from the Hawthorne correspondence are from Norman Holmes Pearson, "The Pynchons and Judge Pyncheon," *Essex Institute Historical Collections*, 100 (1964), 235–255.
2. My information about the history of the family derives mainly from standard biographical sources: Henry F. Waters, *Genealogical Gleanings in England*, 2 (Boston: New-England Historic Genealogical Society, 1901), 845–867; Joseph Charles Pynchon, *Record of the Pynchon*

Family in England and America (1885; rev. W. F. Adams, Springfield: Old Corner Book Store, 1898); Hazel Kraft Eilers, " 'At the Sign of the Crest': Pynchon Coat-of-Arms," *Hobbies*, 73 (February 1969), 112–113; and several town histories, of which the most useful is Mason A. Green's *Springfield: 1636–1886* (Boston: Nichols, 1888).

3. Joseph H. Smith provides well-documented chapters on William Pynchon and his son John in *Colonial Justice in Western Massachusetts (1639–1702): The Pynchon Court Record* (Cambridge: Harvard University Press, 1961), and Samuel Eliot Morison includes a chapter on William in the revised edition of his *Builders of the Bay Colony* (Boston: Houghton Mifflin, 1964).

4. *The Diary of William Pynchon of Salem* has been edited by Fitch Edward Oliver (Boston: Riverside, 1890).

5. In a commentary in Waters's *Genealogical Gleanings*, p. 867, T. R. Pynchon notes that from the seventeenth-century John Pynchon "are descended all who bear the name in America."

6. Maxwell had published many important scientific papers before 1870, but did not hypothesize the sorting demon until 1871, in his *Theory of Heat*; see W. Ehrenberg, "Maxwell's Demon," *Scientific American*, 217 (November 1967), 103–110, and Anne Mangel, "Maxwell's Demon, Entropy, Information: *The Crying of Lot 49*," *TriQuarterly*, 20 (Winter 1971), 194–208, reprinted in this volume. T. R. Pynchon's revised edition of *The Chemical Forces*, entitled *Introduction to Chemical Physics* (1873), continued to ignore Maxwell.

7. Frank D. McConnell, "Thomas Pynchon," *Contemporary Novelists*, ed. James Vinson (New York: St. Martin's, 1972), p. 1034.

8. Lewis Nichols, "In and Out of Books," *New York Times Book Review*, 28 April 1963, p. 8.

9. Alfred Appel, Jr., "An Interview with Vladimir Nabokov," *Wisconsin Studies in Contemporary Literature*, 8 (Spring 1967), 139.

10. I was directed to "The Monterey Fair" by Joseph W. Slade, *Thomas Pynchon* (New York: Warner, 1974), p. 14. Fariña's composition is mentioned in the essay on Pynchon in *Contemporary Authors*, 19–20 (1968), 353.

11. Nichols, p. 8.

12. W. T. Lhamon, "The Most Irresponsible Bastard," *The New Republic*, 168 (14 April 1973), 27.

13. I have made several minor emendations in the article.

Bibliography

Bruce Herzberg

The following bibliography is intended only as a supplement to the exhaustive one by Joseph Weixlmann (in *Critique*, 14 [1972], 34-43). It does not pretend to exhaustiveness but to serve, rather, as a useful guide for readers interested in finding out yet more about Pynchon. In particular, we have not attempted to list all the reviews of *Gravity's Rainbow*, as Weixlmann tried to list all those of the earlier novels. Those we list strike us as being of some lasting importance as criticism of Pynchon.

Works by Thomas Pynchon

SHORT FICTION

"Mortality and Mercy in Vienna." *Epoch* 9 (Spring 1959): 195-213.

"Low-Lands." *New World Writing* 16 (1960): 85-108.

"Entropy." *Kenyon Review* 22 (1960): 277-292.

"Under the Rose." *Noble Savage* 3 (1961): 223-251.

"The Secret Integration." *Saturday Evening Post* 237 (December 19, 1964): 36-37, 39, 42-44, 46-49, 51.

"The World (This One), The Flesh (Mrs. Oedipa Maas), and The Testament of Pierce Inverarity." *Esquire* 64 (December 1965): 170-173, 296, 298-303.

"The Shrink Flips." *Cavalier* 16 (March 1966): 32-33, 88-92.

ARTICLE

"A Journey Into the Mind of Watts." *New York Times Magazine,*
June 12, 1966, pp. 34–35, 78, 80–82, 84.

NOVELS

V.
   Philadelphia: J. B. Lippincott, 1963.
   London: Jonathan Cape, 1963.
   Toronto: McClelland and Stewart, 1963.
   New York: Bantam, 1964.
   New York: Modern Library, 1966.
   Hammondsworth, Middlesex: Penguin, 1966.
   Paris: Plon, 1967 (in French).

The Crying of Lot 49
   Philadelphia: J. B. Lippincott, 1966.
   Toronto: McClelland and Stewart, 1966.
   London: Jonathan Cape, 1967.
   New York: Bantam, 1967.

Gravity's Rainbow
   New York: Viking, 1973.
   New York: Bantam, 1974.

Critical Articles (1972 to Fall 1975)

V.

Golden, Robert E. "Mass Man and Modernism: Violence in
Pynchon's *V.*" *Critique* 14, No. 2 (1972), 5–17.
   Lhamon, W. T., Jr. "Pentecost, Promiscuity, and Pynchon's *V.*:
From the Scaffold to the Impulsive." *Twentieth Century Literature*
21, No. 2 (May 1975), 163–176.
   Patteson, Richard. "What Stencil Knew: Structure and Certitude
in Pynchon's *V.*" *Critique* 16, No. 2 (1974), 30–44.

Richardson, Robert O. "The Absurd Animate in Thomas Pynchon's *V.: A Novel.*" *Studies in the Twentieth Century* No. 9 (1972), 35–58.
Richter, D. H. "The Failure of Completeness: Pynchon's *V.*" In *Fable's End: Completeness and Closure in Rhetorical Fiction*, pp. 101–135. Chicago: University of Chicago Press, 1975.

THE CRYING OF LOT 49
Abernethy, Peter L. "Entropy in Pynchon's *The Crying of Lot 49.*" *Critique* 14, No. 2 (1972), 18–33.
Davis, Robert M. "Parody, Paranoia, and the Dead End of Language in *The Crying of Lot 49.*" *Genre* 5 (1972): 367–377.
Kirby, David K. "Two Modern Versions of the Quest." *Southern Humanities Review* 5 (1971): 387–395.
Kolodny, Annette, and Peters, Daniel J. "Pynchon's *The Crying of Lot 49*: The Novel as Subversive Experience." *Modern Fiction Studies* 19 (Spring 1973): 79–87.
Leland, John P. "Pynchon's Linguistic Demon: *The Crying of Lot 49.*" *Critique* 16, No. 2 (1974), 45–53.
Lyons, Thomas R., and Franklin, Allan D. "Thomas Pynchon's 'Classic' Presentation of the Second Law of Thermodynamics." *Bulletin of the Rocky Mountain Modern Language Association* 27 (1972): 195–204.
Mendelson, Edward. "The Sacred, the Profane, and *The Crying of Lot 49.*" In *Individual and Community: Variations on a Theme in American Fiction*, edited by Kenneth H. Baldwin and David K. Kirby, pp. 182–222. Durham, N.C.: Duke University Press, 1975.
Trachtenberg, Stanley. "Counterhumor: Comedy in Contemporary American Fiction." *Georgia Review* 27, No. 1 (Spring 1973), 33–48.
Wagner, Linda W. "A Note on Oedipa the Roadrunner." *The Journal of Narrative Technique* 4, No. 2 (May 1974), 155–161.

GRAVITY'S RAINBOW
Friedman, Alan J., and Puetz, Manfred. "Science and Metaphor: Thomas Pynchon and *Gravity's Rainbow.*" *Contemporary Literature* 15 (Summer 1974): 345–359.
Levine, George. "V-2." *Partisan Review* 40 (Fall 1973): 517–529.
Lhamon, W. T., Jr. "The Most Irresponsible Bastard." *The New Republic*, March 11, 1973, pp. 12, 14.
Locke, Richard. "*Gravity's Rainbow.*" *New York Times Book Review*, March 11, 1973, pp. 1–3, 12, 14.
Mendelson, Edward. "Pynchon's Gravity." *Yale Review* 62 (Summer 1973): 624–631.

Ozier, Lance W. "Antipointsman/Antimexico: Some Mathematical Imagery in *Gravity's Rainbow*." *Critique* 16, No. 2 (1974), 73–90.

———. "The Calculus of Transformation: More Mathematical Imagery in *Gravity's Rainbow*." *Twentieth Century Literature* 21, No. 2 (May 1975), 193–210.

Poirier, Richard. "Rocket Power." *Saturday Review of the Arts*, March 1973, pp. 59–64.

Rosenbaum, Jonathan. "One Man's Meat Is Another Man's Poisson." *The Village Voice*, March 29, 1973, pp. 24, 26.

Sanders, Scott. "Pynchon's Paranoid History." *Twentieth Century Literature* 21, No. 2 (May 1975), 177–192.

Simmon, Scott. "*Gravity's Rainbow* Described." *Critique* 16, No. 2 (1974), 54–67.

———. "A Character Index: *Gravity's Rainbow*." *Critique* 16, No. 2 (1974), 68–72.

Thorburn, David. "A Dissent on Pynchon." *Commentary* 56 (September 1973), 68–70.

Wood, Michael. "Rocketing to Apocalypse." *New York Review of Books*, March 22, 1973, p. 22.

General

Fussell, Paul. *The Great War and Modern Memory*, pp. 328–334. New York and London: Oxford University Press, 1975.

Harris, Charles B. "Thomas Pynchon and the Entropic Vision." In *Contemporary American Novelists of the Absurd*, pp. 79–99. New Haven: College & University Press, 1971.

Henderson, Harry B., III. "Liberal Conscience and Apocalyptic Parody." In *Versions of the Past: The Historical Imagination in American Fiction*, pp. 177–285. New York: Oxford, 1974.

Hendin, Josephine. "What Is Thomas Pynchon Telling Us?" *Harper's* 250 (March 1975), 82–92.

Kazin, Alfred. *Bright Book of Life*, pp. 275–280. Boston: Little, Brown, 1973.

Lehan, Richard. *A Dangerous Crossing*, pp. 157–162. Carbondale, Ill.: Southern Illinois University Press, 1973.

May, John R. "Loss of World in Barth, Pynchon, and Vonnegut: The Varieties of Humorous Apocalypse." In *Toward a New Earth: Apocalypse in the American Novel*, pp. 172–200. Notre Dame: University of Notre Dame Press, 1972.

Poirier, Richard. "The Importance of Thomas Pynchon." *Twentieth Century Literature* 21, No. 2 (May 1975), 151–162.

Schmitz, Neil. "Describing the Demon: The Appeal of Thomas Pynchon." *Partisan Review* 42, No. 3 (1975), 112–125, and subsequent exchange with David Leverenz in *Partisan Review* 42, No. 4 (1975), 643–644.

Schulz, Max F. *Black Humor Fiction of the Sixties*, pp. 61–64, 77–82. Athens, Ohio: Ohio University Press, 1973.

Slade, Joseph W. *Thomas Pynchon*. New York: Warner paperbacks, 1974.

Sperry, Joseph P. "Henry Adams and Thomas Pynchon: The Entropic Movements of Self, Society and Truth." *Dissertation Abstracts International* 35 (February 1975), 5428A. (Ohio State University.)

Vesterman, William. "Pynchon's Poetry." *Twentieth Century Literature* 21, No. 2 (May 1975), 211–220.

Winston, Mathew. "The Quest for Pynchon." *Twentieth Century Literature* 21, No. 3 (October 1975), 278–287.

Bibliography

Herzberg, Bruce. "Selected Articles on Thomas Pynchon: An Annotated Bibliography." *Twentieth Century Literature* 21, No. 2 (May 1975), 221–225.

Weixlmann, Joseph. "Thomas Pynchon: A Bibliography." *Critique* 14, No. 2 (1972), 34–43.

Notes on Contributors

MARJORIE KAUFMAN is Emma Kennedy Professor of English at Mount Holyoke College. She has published on Henry and William James, Ellen Glasgow, and Willa Cather, and she has lectured on the personae of Yankee Doodle and the readability of Gertrude Stein. She is always at work on a book on Henry James's middle novels.

W. T. LHAMON, JR., is Assistant Professor of English at Florida State University. He has written widely on postmodern literature and on rock music, and he is writing a book on contemporary style, to be called *Surviving Doom*.

ANNE MANGEL wrote her essay on *The Crying of Lot 49* when she was a graduate student at the University of Illinois. She moved with her husband, a molecular biologist, to Berkeley and then to London, apparently following the movements of Pynchon's novels. She is currently resisting the temptation to see if the explosion of IRA bombs follows a pattern predicted by the Poisson equation.

EDWARD MENDELSON is Associate Professor of English at Yale. He is finishing a critical study of W. H. Auden and, as Auden's literary executor, is preparing collected editions of Auden's work. With Michael Seidel he has edited a collection of essays on the European epic and dramatic traditions.

RICHARD POIRIER is Director of the Graduate Program of English at Rutgers University. His books include *The Comic Sense of Henry James*, *A World Elsewhere*, *The Performing Self*, and *Mailer*. He is now writing a book on Robert Frost.

SCOTT SANDERS is Associate Professor of English at Indiana University. He is the author of *D. H. Lawrence: The World of the Five Major Novels*, various articles on modern fiction and the sociology of literature, and two unpublished novels.

CATHARINE R. STIMPSON is Associate Professor of English at Barnard College. She also edits *Signs: Journal of Women in Culture and Society* and writes on modern literature, education, and the women's movement.

TONY TANNER is a fellow of Kings College, Cambridge. His books include *The Reign of Wonder* and *City of Words*, from which this essay is excerpted. He is currently finishing a book on adultery and the novel.

WILLIAM VESTERMAN is Associate Professor of English at Livingston College, Rutgers University. He has a book forthcoming, *The Stylistic Life of Samuel Johnson*.

MATHEW WINSTON is Assistant Professor English and Comparative Literature at Columbia University. He is writing a book about contemporary black humor.

BRUCE HERZBERG is a graduate student at Rutgers University. He is writing his dissertation on Pynchon and critical theory.

DAVID LEVERENZ is Associate Professor of English and Chairman at Livingston College, Rutgers University. He has written on various aspects of American literature, and is completing a psychoanalytic study of Puritanism.

GEORGE LEVINE is Professor of English at Livingston College, Rutgers University. He is the author of *The Boundaries of Fiction* and many essays and reviews on modern literature. He is currently editing an anthology of essays on *Frankenstein*.